FRANÇOIS MAURIAC

FRANÇOIS MAURIAC

A Study of the Writer and the Man

By

ROBERT SPEAIGHT

1976

CHATTO & WINDUS

LONDON

Published by
Chatto & Windus Ltd
42 William IV Street
London WC2N 4DF

*

Clarke, Irwin & Co. Ltd
Toronto

PQ2625. A932
742136

cc

ISBN 0 7011 2145 9

© Robert Speaight 1976

Printed and bound in Great Britain by
REDWOOD BURN LIMITED
Trowbridge & Esher

For DENISE and LOUISE TOUTON
with whom we followed
the *itinéraire mauriacien*–
–In affection and gratitude

CONTENTS

ILLUSTRATIONS

The photographs are reproduced by courtesy of Madame François
Mauriac, excepting that of Mauriac with his granddaughter, for
which grateful acknowledgement is made to Madame Ivan
Wiazemski.

J'appartiens à la race impudique, celle qui ne peut pas ne pas parler de Dieu.

J'aime les coeurs qui battent et, à certaines heures, furieusement.

Ma place est parmi les Gentils, et ma mission de dire ce que je crois vrai sans demander aucun mot d'ordre, sans engager personne que moi-même, en demeurant partout et toujours un témoin.

François Mauriac

INTRODUCTION

I first met François Mauriac in September 1944, three weeks after the Liberation of Paris. Having translated his *Cahier Noir* – passages from a Journal kept under the Occupation and published under a pseudonym – and introduced them to the English reader, I was emboldened to call upon him without formality. In the heady euphoria of the moment, convention was freely dispensed with. I climbed the five storeys to his apartment in the avenue Théophile Gautier, and was about to press the bell when I heard slow steps on the stairs behind me. Then a tall, thin figure came into view, and I had no difficulty in recognizing the features that Georges Duhamel imagined as a subject for El Greco in some studio of the Elysian Fields. It reminded an American visitor of a 'straight vertical line made with the point of a pencil'.[1] Moreover the startled expression on his face gave me a clue which I have tried to follow throughout these pages. It was the expression of a man who responded with a quivering intensity to everything he saw and heard; the same expression that an English friend noted on his features, a few years later, when a butcher's cart was about to run over a dog in a Wiltshire village. 'You must forgive my apprehension' he said 'but in these days one never knows whom one is going to find at the door.' It was not so long since the Gestapo had stood where I was standing, and Mauriac was now being threatened by those who thought he indulged his charity too freely to those who were accused of helping them.

I introduced myself, and he welcomed me inside, leading me down into his study which was on a slightly lower level than the rest of the apartment. 'Take care of those steps' he said with a flash of mischief, 'many a candidate has narrowly escaped slipping on them when they have come in quest of my vote for the Académie française.' We sat and talked, and on the wall behind his desk hung Jean Colin's poster of resurgent France. It was the first of several visits in those years of the *après-guerre* for, as I soon discovered, we had friends in common. He invited me to the reception of the Prince de Broglie at the Institut de France, where I found the ceremony more easily comprehensible than the speeches; and to his daughter's wedding, at which we drank

[1] A.J. Liebling: *The New Yorker*, May 1958.

the wine from his vineyard at Malagar.

In the summer of 1946 I came over with Ronald Duncan's play, *This Way to the Tomb*, for a short season at the Studio des Champs-Elysées, and Mauriac applauded loudly at what he could not possibly have understood. He boosted us in a generous postscript to his regular article in *Le Figaro*. He knew no English and had, I think, been only once to England, but he was well acquainted with English novels in translation. Hearing that I was at work on a small book about George Eliot, he hoped that I admired her. We spoke of Graham Greene – a writer after his own heart – and of Maurice Baring who was then lying mortally ill in Scotland. He was struck by the 'penetration of grace' which ran through Baring's novels without the reader being made too consciously aware of it – thinking, no doubt, of *Cat's Cradle*, which was then popular in France under the title of *La Princesse Blanche*. Baring was deeply moved by this judgment, when I passed it on to him very shortly before his death.

Mauriac's conversation, in that hoarse but strangely haunting voice, had the intensity of his temperament and the sharp edge of his critical *esprit*. He was brilliant except when he was bored. On one occasion I happened to mention that the *bonne à tout faire* of some mutual friends had her illegitimate daughter living with them in their apartment, and that her father was reputed to be a scoutmaster. This launched Mauriac into an hilarious improvisation on the mortal sins of scoutmasters, for which he held their hirsute limbs to be responsible. Such effervescence is impossible to reproduce in cold print, but anything was liable to set it boiling; and it should be borne in mind by those who cannot understand why he wrote 'all those morbid novels'.

Of the political drama where he exercised his daily polemic I knew little at the time, but of his influence there was no doubt. With the British Embassy, where before the war he had been a close friend of Sir Eric and Lady Phipps, he now had little contact – though his political options should have made him welcome there. He wrote to me, more in sorrow than in anger, over Anglo-French differences in Syria. His most recent novel, *La Pharisienne*, had only confirmed his place among contemporary writers. Nevertheless the war had shaken the foundations of that narrow provincial world which had furnished the raw material of his fiction, and the criticism of Jean-Paul Sartre had, for the time being at least, undermined his self-confidence. It was a crucial turning point in his career. He had his public, but for what public should he write? For Mauriac, as for Malraux, literature was no longer enough; each was forced by the tremendous pressure of events into the arena of public debate. More novels were to come, though at longer intervals, and they showed no falling off in power, and no difference in style. The *nouveau roman* held no attractions for Mauriac; he had never regarded himself, or wished others to regard him, as a writer of the *avant-garde*. But few people could have then foreseen that, for many readers, the five volumes of *Bloc-Notes* would come to appear more 'relevant' — if the horrible catchword must be used — than the novels which had earned him the Nobel Prize; and that the author of *Thérèse Desqueyroux* would take his place, whether one agreed with him or not, as the most important political journalist of his time.

After the premature death, in 1955, of the friend — a Bordelais like himself — who had kept us intermittently in touch, I did not see him again for many years; though we corresponded on one or two occasions. If his name came up in conversation with a member of the French Establishment, more often than not it was accompanied by an exasperated 'ce fou de Mauriac.' Yet there are few of his *partis pris*, passionately and lucidly argued, that time has not vindicated to the letter. In the autumn of 1965 my wife and I were the guests of Sir Patrick and Lady Reilly at the Embassy, and it was there that I met him for the last time — on the eve of his 80th birthday. The intervening years had changed him very little. He was shortly leaving for Bordeaux to drink from 'the chalice' reserved for a favourite son, and he had no doubt that it would be 'filled with honey'. I had written a good deal, here and there, about Mauriac as a writer; it did not occur to me that I should ever be writing about him as a man. I have no wish to be compared to the Frenchman of whom it was said that he had 'known Marcel Proust very well, *after his death*'; but I am glad to have known François Mauriac a little while he was still alive.

In the summer of 1974 I went down to the Gironde to follow his footsteps in the city and the landscape which had made him and which his imagination had caught and, in a measure, transformed. There were exhibitions in his honour at Bordeaux and Bazas; the technicians of the French television were looking for a site on which to film *Le Mystère Frontenac*; university professors from many countries had recently met to analyse his fiction. A group of sixty English visitors were expected at Malagar; and when a cupboard of the old house was opened for me, and I saw the array of panama hats inside, it seemed as if I had only to step out on to the terrace, and there I should find Mauriac himself on the stone bench under the fig-tree, gazing out over the valley and the vines to the level horizon of the *Landes*. For in all that I had seen and heard there was little sign of that purgatory which is said to await the greatest writers, once they have laid down their pen. Perhaps, after all, fiction would prove stronger than politics; and if so, Mauriac would have defined the reason for it:

You can read the whole of humanity in some peasant of our country, and all the landscapes of the world in the horizons we have known as a child. The gift of the novelist consists in the power to show the universality of that narrow world where we were born, and where we have learnt to love and to suffer.[1]

When Julien Green was elected to Mauriac's place among the 'Immortals' of the Académie française, he may not have been far wrong in suggesting that of all Mauriac's novels his own life was the best. Nevertheless this book is primarily a study of the writer: it should not be read as in any way a definitive biography. It treats of his life mainly as his writing was affected by it, for the two cannot easily be separated. If, and when, his correspondence is published, a fuller picture of the man himself may be possible. Among his close contemporaries only his relations with Gide – and these were of great importance – have been fully documented, and I have freely drawn upon them.

To all those who have helped me I extend my warmest thanks. To Madame François Mauriac, in particular, to M. Claude Mauriac, and M. Jean Mauriac, who have all given me every encouragement; to Madame Guy Cazenave who kindly received me at Saint-Symphorien; to M. and Madame Louis Touton who gave me – and not for the first time – their hospitality at Bordeaux; to Lady Phipps; to M. Jean Blanzat; to Mrs St George Saunders of Writers & Speakers Research; and to M. and Madame Jean Chauveau of the French Radio and Television who arranged for me to see and hear everything necessary for my purposes.

I am grateful, once again, to Mrs Pat Brayne for typing my MS with exemplary precision and speed.

Benenden: 1975

---

[1] *Discours de Stockholm,* 10 December 1962.

THE PROVINCIAL

1

The family were of peasant stock and had lived in the Gironde for 300 years — nourished on the game and preserved goose flesh from their farms among the interminable pine forests of the *Landes*. François Mauriac was to write of 'the bitter honey of Guyenne stored up inside me'; but by the middle of the nineteenth century they were established in Bordeaux, solidly *embourgeoisés*. They did not belong to what is called 'the aristocracy of the grape', although they possessed vineyards at Malagar and Sainte-Croix-du-Mont; and François' great-grandfather would always send the first asparagus from his garden to the Marquis de Lur-Saluces — a tribute to Château-Yquem as well as to its chatelain. His mother's family had owned an important refinery in Bordeaux, burnt down before the end of the century, and her father had made a small fortune out of sheets and Indian shawls. They did not, however, on either side, confine themselves to business, producing their fair quota of doctors, lawyers, magistrates, and priests. François Mauriac always felt a stranger to the oligarchy of commerce whose private houses lined the Pavé des Chartrons, and whose *jeunesse dorée* disported themselves on the fashionable tennis courts and competed at the Arcachon regattas.

In 1860 Jacques Mauriac was able to build the château at Langon, 47 kilometres south-east of Bordeaux, on the banks of the Garonne and overlooking the railway line to Cette. With its white camellias, mimosa bushes, and pines, and the main building flanked by two pavilions, this furnished a sombre setting for *Génitrix*, the first novel to bring his grandson celebrity. It was known as the 'Château Mauriac', and the family vault stood up against the wall of the cemetery near by. Through his marriage with Mathilde Lapeyre — or, as the saying went, with 'tout ce qu'il y a de mieux dans la lande' — Jacques Mauriac acquired 1,000 acres of pines between Villandraut and Saint-Symphorien, and the resin extracted from these enabled him to wind up his business in Bordeaux. He had two sons, of whom the elder, Jean-Paul, had marked literary tastes; but in spite of winning all the prizes at school he was withdrawn from the lycée at Langon before taking his bacca-lauréat, and sent first into his father's business and, when this was closed down, into banking. He married Claire Marguerite Coiffard, and they had five children, four sons and a daughter, of whom François Mauriac was the youngest.

He was born on October 11, 1885, in the rue du Pas-Saint-George, a narrow street in the old quarter of Bordeaux. He was christened after St François-de-Sales. Less than two years later, on June 11, 1887, his father died from an abscess on the brain after a short illness. He was only 35 years old. Never a professed believer, he had left among his papers — discovered many years later by his grandson, Claude Mauriac — the account of an argument in the train about the respective claims of science and religion. A young man had told him that he ought to believe in religion unless he could prove it to be untrue. Jean-Paul Mauriac replied: 'If I said that on the moon the mountains are made of diamonds, the rivers of cream slice, and the fruit of sugar candy, I could put you in the position of having to believe me or demonstrate the contrary.'[1] But now, as he lay dying, he tried to hold a crucifix to his lips — a gesture which his brother, who shared his scepticism, was ingenious to misinterpret. The little François cried when he was taken into the room for a last look at the father whose face he was only to remember from a photograph, and whose memory was honoured by the huge black hat enshrined in his mother's wardrobe. His grandfather noted that there was 'still a deficit' on the income from his son's properties, and that it might be better to leave them to someone who would develop them to more advantage.

Madame Mauriac, never content to stay for long at the same address, now moved to the rue Duffour-Dubergier close by, where she occupied the third floor of a house belonging to her mother. Two cousins were also living there, Louise with her pretty curls and Jeanne with her nose in the air. These were cramped quarters for a widow and five children, and the room adjoining that of Madame Coiffard was never entered except on Christmas Eve when the candles were lit around the crib. Madame Mauriac was a woman of profound and scrupulous piety. Every evening the brood would gather round her for family prayers, as she sat beside the lamp, with a black shawl about her shoulders. There was much argument as to who should kneel between the bed and the prie-dieu — for it would not be noticed if one nodded off to sleep with one's head buried in the curtains that fell from the four-poster. Only the final petition was liable to wake one up. 'Uncertain as I am whether death will not surprise me during the night, I commend my soul to you, O God! Do not judge me in your wrath.' Death had already taken their father, and it had other surprises in store.

[1] *Le Temps Immobile,* Claude Mauriac, 1974, p. 336.

Their grandmother, Madame Jacques Mauriac, died the next year. On his last visit to Bordeaux Jacques Mauriac was looking at a group of family photographs, and pointing to his own likeness, he exclaimed: 'What a cemetery! Now I am the only one left.'[1] Three days later, as he was returning from a game of whist with a lady of his acquaintance, he consented to enter the church where he had not set foot for years. He collapsed in the street on his way home, and his last words – 'We are saved by faith' – seemed like an answer to the prayer which perhaps he had never uttered, but which others had uttered on his behalf. The bed to which he was brought never had another occupant. Now and again, however, François would push open the door of the room and, peeping inside, experience a *frisson* of fear. He remembered how his grandfather used to whistle from the steps of the porch when it was time for luncheon; 'his short bust, his neck disappearing into his shoulders, his bristly white beard; and the way he would rinse his mouth with curaçao after the dessert.'[2] Every year, on the anniversary of their grandfather's death, the children, excused from school for the day, would stand with their mother before the family vault, too reminiscent of a pagan temple for her taste, while she recited in French the *De Profundis*. Nothing was so important as a 'good death'. They told François how the coffin of a great-aunt had been opened because they had forgotten to bury her with a missal. The gloomy château, with its wide hall that no fire could warm, miserably furnished with chairs of rattan cane, remained empty except for the mentally deficient sister of Jacques Mauriac who lived in one of the wings with her three servants.

Sudden death was always a possibility. The jolt of the victoria as it crossed the suspension bridge would awaken memories of a hasty act of contrition; and a funeral, in that acquisitive society, was almost as festive as a wedding. Death was emphasised in order that life should presently contradict it. The corpse, if it were a woman, was arrayed in its best clothes; black gloves were provided for the mourners; every mirror in the house was covered with a sheet; and the luncheon that followed the interment, muted when it began, ended in 'Bacchic gaiety'. The sincerity of grief was measured by the length of crêpe; and if this were not long enough, or if the dress underneath it were too well cut, the comment went round: 'There is someone who has lost no time in finding her consolation.'[3] The social round was the more exciting because a death-bed was always liable to interrupt it.

François was a sensitive child, suffering terribly from chilblains, and

[1] *Le Temps Immobile*, 47.

[2] *Les Maisons fugitives* (1939): *Oeuvres Complètes*, 337. IV.

[3] *La Province: O.C. IV*, 472.

fleeing in tears from a juggler met on the road to Malagar – the Mauriac property above the right bank of the river at Langon. More serious was an accident to his eye while he was playing with one of his brothers. A piece of iron from the end of a whip had lodged in the eyelid, which had to be sewn up without an anaesthetic after the nursemaid had too forcefully extracted it. This left one lid lower than the other, and earned for the boy the embarrassing nickname of 'Coco-bel-oeil'. He was already inclined to feel different from other children, and this emphasised the difference.

Louis Mauriac, the irreligious uncle and magistrate, whose portrait François was to draw in *Le Mystère Frontenac*, acted as guardian to the children. A sharp ear was kept on his conversation, and indeed he kept a fairly sharp ear on it himself. 'Be careful what you say, the child may be listening' was a frequent warning; and then – 'but it doesn't matter, he can't understand.' The child was certainly listening, and just as certainly understood. He was now sent to a nursery school in the rue de Mirail, under the charge of two Sisters, one as sympathetic as the other was severe. He remembered how roughly Sister Ascension would rub out the ink-stains on his hands with a pumice-stone, and the smell of chlorine in the lavatories. In October 1892 he entered the Institut de Mirail run by the Marianist Fathers in the same street, opposite the lycée Michel Montaigne. It was an imposing building with its courtyard entered between two pillars, and the caryatids over the windows. Here, for the first time, he knew the meaning of unhappiness, furiously erasing with his handkerchief the marks that placed him at the bottom of the class. He stayed for two years at the school, and described them as his 'années noires'. It was a daily consolation to return home to the rue Duffour-Dubergier, where 'the smell of gas and linoleum on the staircase delighted me more than any perfume . . . step by step brought me closer to my happiness, my love, my mother, to the book I was reading, and the long supper under the lamp.'

In 1894 the family moved again to 1 rue Vital-Carles, at the corner of the Cours de l'Intendance. This was in the 18th-century heart of Bordeaux, and from here the child could watch the carnival, held in defiance of custom on Good Friday, and the military parades. It was here, from an upper window, that in 1895 he called out 'Vive Félisque!', when President Félix Faure drove by and, looking up, rewarded him with a smile. A year later, on May 12th, 1896, he made his first Communion in the chapel of the Institut de Mirail. A first Communion is a kind of spiritual vaccination; sometimes it takes, more often it does not. There was no doubt that it took with François Mauriac, and nothing was spared to emphasise the solemnity of the occasion. The children entered singing the Magnificat, and before going up to

18

Communion they were made to kneel before their parents and ask forgiveness for any faults they had committed. Madame Mauriac, who had left off her widow's weeds for the occasion, traced the sign of the Cross on the forehead of her son, and then the whole congregation sang 'Le ciel a visité la terre' in voices blurred with emotion.

A rigorous Jansenism then reigned among the *bourgeoisie* of the Gironde. Either one was anti-clerical, or pious to the point of absurdity. Frequent Communion was not yet encouraged, and many *dévots* would approach the altar only on the greater feasts after an agonised confession of peccadilloes. Those who were not *dévots* would make their genu-flections, as they might have made their curtseys at Versailles. The refinements of casuistry were grotesque. Mauriac was to write of 'the lie wrapped up in the truth' which deformed the conscience of a child in that narrow provincial world. Teal might be eaten on a Friday because it was considered first cousin to the fish; and although wild duck could plausibly claim a similar relationship, a certain curé was much exercised as to whether he might eat it in Lent since its eggs were hatched in his own hen-roost. On Good Friday even eggs were prohibited. At Candle-mas, however, on Shrove Tuesday, and in the middle of Lent, pancakes were compulsory. If one swallowed a few drops of water while one was cleaning one's teeth, one could not afterwards go to Holy Communion. Whatever Jeremiads might be launched from the pulpits of Bordeaux against the pharisaism of the Catholic *bourgeoisie*, the *bourgeoisie* complacently went its way, giving and taking in marriage, and confronting death not only with prayer but with property. Capital in any form 'appeared to us holy and venerable, useful to the State, and agreeable to God.'[1]

Piety and prudery went hand in hand. It was explained to François that Daphnis and Chloe embracing in a piece of statuary were brother and sister; and that 'gynaecologist' was another name for a throat specialist. A treatise on obstetrics found among a boy's text books incurred the gravest censure. Sin was at once omnipresent and un-mentionable. If a person of doubtful character came up in conversation, it was said that he or she 'had had a very full life'. François Mauriac, when he looked back upon his childhood — and he never ceased to look back upon it — recognized the stupidity of these taboos. If he kept his faith, it was in spite of his upbringing, not because of it. Of no important writer is it more true to say that the child was father to the man; and at quite an early age he was asking four things of people: 'that they be good, that they be just, that they be intelligent, that they be

[1] *Les Maisons fugitives. O.C.IV*, 323.

19

pure.'[1] This was asking a good deal; nevertheless it was asking for the right things.

2

By the autumn of 1898 Madame Mauriac had moved yet again. She occupied a wing of a rather stately old house at the corner of the rue Margaux and the rue Chéverus. It was spacious and chilly, and plagued by the huge mosquitoes that came up from an underground river. Apart from the salamander always kept burning in the dining-room, only the salon and Madame Mauriac's bedroom saw a fire. François was now enrolled at the Ecole Grand-Lebrun, also run by the Marianists; a large, modern building on the outskirts of the city, adjoining an elegant private house, built under Louis XVI and incor-porated in the school. They were the first houses in Bordeaux to be equipped with central heating, standing in their own grounds, with an indoor playground and swimming pool, and shaded by immense plane trees. Chestnuts, magnolias, and a large acacia separated the two buildings. François was roused at 5.30 a.m. and waited for the *parcours* − or horse-omnibus − which collected the pupils from various parts of the city. On a rainy morning its arrival was announced by the loud crack of the coachman's whip, and then it was a thirty-minute jog-trot to the school. Half-an-hour of lessons; a short recreation; two more hours of study; a quarter-of-an-hour's break; more study till noon; an interval for luncheon; and from 1.30 study again till 6.30 − such was the gruelling routine.

There were thirty pupils to a class. For much of the teaching the Marianists relied on laymen; and through this breach in the wall of celibacy speculation was free to roam. François remembered how one boy had filled a page of his note-book with the plan of a bedroom, supposedly belonging to the young man who taught them Greek − in the case of François with no success whatever − and in the middle of it a rectangle to indicate the double bed. The brothers in their silk hats and absurd frock-coats walked the corridor in felt slippers − which gave them the advantage both of silence and surprise. Above them were the priests, excellent men for the most part, and generally of high intelli-gence. The Superior had few illusions about the parents of his pupils, and took no trouble to conceal what he thought of them. The school owed much of its academic prestige to the abbé Péquignot, myopic and emaciated, with a passion for ideas. Equally exacting for the substance and the style of a composition, it was he who gave François a taste for

[1] *Nouveaux Mémoires Intérieurs*, p. 45.

Montaigne and, more importantly, for Pascal. The Brunschvicg edition, which kept him company through life, was the same that he used at school when he was sixteen.

Every Saturday he would wait his turn outside the abbé's room to make his confession. Sin, though it could not be mentioned at home, could be mentioned here – and not only in confession. There were boys who could not remember a time when they had been chaste; others would produce a picture of Aphrodite, hidden between the pages of a text-book, or a photograph of Jeanne Fabri, a popular dancer in the circus; others again would snigger about the Meriadek quarter of Bordeaux where a prostitute stood in every doorway, and one caught sight, through the open window, of the broad red eider-down within. 'We were no better than the children of today' Mauriac wrote as he looked back 'our upbringing was perfectly designed to arouse the monster which in every human being seeks a way of escape.'[1] When he got home he was aware of his mother's anxious scrutiny. He had been initiated into the love of God, and to a mother's love he knew there were no limits. But love had now become a word of many meanings.

It was the secret of his power as a writer that he was equally interested in other people and in himself. His novels are a temperament viewed through a fiction, and his polemic is history viewed through a temperament. From the age of seven his observation had been acute and now, in the first years of adolescence, introspection came to meet it. He filled his notebooks with a diary, and kept up a close correspondence with his friends. 'Don't let us forget to write each other some beautiful letters' was a common resolution on the eve of the *grandes vacances*; and he came to discern in this the sign of his vocation as a writer. He had one particular friend, André Lacaze, who was exceptionally intelligent, and knew it. 'You are not as intelligent as I am' he would say to François 'but very nearly.' François was not, however, a favourite pupil. One of the masters, red-haired and lantern-jawed, took a dislike to his close cropped head and drooping eyelid; and another, who taught him German, found his way, many years later, into the pages of *La Pharisienne*. If he liked a pupil – and he liked very few of them – he would empty his pocket of a snuff-box and dirty handkerchief and hand the boy a biscuit. During the hours of recreation François preferred the seclusion of the lavatory to the noise and rough and tumble of the playground.

History and politics – and in France they mean the same thing – provided a counterweight to introspection. In Bordeaux the names of

---

[1] *Bloc-Notes III*, 415.

the streets — rue Saint-*James*, where his mother had been born; rue Pas-Saint-*George* — recalled a time when the city was an English possession. A number of the vineyards in the Médoc were still in English hands. François' maternal grandfather had made his fortune in the shadow of the Grosse Cloche, a belfry which the English had built, surmounted by a lion rampant. After the Revolution a great-uncle had marched with the Girondins; *Le Monde Illustré* of 1870 showed the Prussian shells bursting round Strasbourg cathedral: Alphonse Daudet's *La Dernière Classe* revived all the regret for the lost provinces; and the boy would sing, with Paul Deroulède, 'Sentinelle, ne tirez pas; c'est un oiseau qui vient de France.' This nostalgic patriotism was seasoned with a strong dose of anglophobia. Jeanne d'Arc, whose statue had a place of honour in his mother's room, was not forgotten; neither were dum-dum bullets against the Boers, nor Bonaparte on St Helena.

> *Combien, au jour de la curée,*
> *Etiez-vous de corbeaux contre l'aigle expirant?*

Alfred de Musset's rhetorical question echoed indignantly in the heart of any French schoolboy; and before long another popular appeal was not to go unanswered.

> *Jeunes hommes des temps qui ne sont pas encore*
> *O bataillons sacrés!*

But France was at war with itself while part of it was itching for war with Germany. When Mauriac looked back on the bright spring day of his first Communion, he could not forget that Alfred Dreyfus was then on Devil's Island. The *affaire* had tormented him from the moment he took note of it, and the more so because there was little sympathy for the victim in his own milieu. The boys, as they crossed the Jewish market, would twist the corner of their capes into the shape of a pig's ear, and call out 'Oreille de cochon'; they gave their chamber-pots the name of 'Zola', whose famous 'J'accuse' had reverberated from the other side of the barricades; and one of them was found tearing off the wings of a fly in mockery of Dreyfus' degradation. These sentiments were fed by *La Nouvelliste*, the royalist newspaper of Bordeaux, and by the *Action Française* which then came out only once a week. 'Sem' could be watched at work on his first caricatures in the Cours de l'Intendance.

The rehabilitation of Dreyfus brought its revenge with the anti-clerical legislation of President Combes, and the *bien-pensante* press hit back. Combes was caricatured in *Le Pèlerin* with the horns and hooves of the Devil, and a tail frisking between the skirts of his frock-coat. Maurras' *camelots du roi* replied with incitement to violence, and

François remembered a cousin of his shouting for a sabre. The belli-
cose songs of the *bourgeoisie* might call for 'Dieu dans nos écoles', but
that did not prevent His expulsion; and the Jesuits who lived next door
to the Mauriacs in the rue Chéverus, and appeared never to quit their
confessionals, were now busy packing their bags. This was the price the
Catholics of France were obliged to pay for sacrificing an innocent Jew
for political or military reasons. Yet, as time would show, the price was
not to prove too heavy; and Mauriac was not alone in thinking that
Emile Combes, a former seminarist, had done more good to the Church
than if he had never left it.

3

François was seven years old when he began to read for pleasure; and
on the title page of a touching story, *Sans Famille*, he had pencilled:
'This is a beautiful book because it has made me cry.' The sentimental
novels of Zénaïde Fleuriot also made him cry. One of her heroines with
the romantic name of Armelle Trahec had freckles which found their
way on to the face of more than one young woman among the characters
of his fiction. He had no taste for dwarfs and fairies; le Père Noël played
no part in the ritual of the family Christmas; but he delighted in the
ordeal of 'le Petit Poucet' lost with his brothers in the depths of a dark
wood. Anglophobia was counteracted by *David Copperfield*, *Oliver
Twist* and *Nicholas Nickleby*. *Wuthering Heights*, with the face of Emily
Brontë, hinting so much and telling so little, haunted him all his life.
He felt, as he brooded over the novel, that he was in communication
with the author rather than the book. His mother, on edge as to what
he might get his hands on, would ask if this or that were 'suitable', and
he went into hiding to read the early novels of Colette. Others he would
throw on to the fire in fear of discovery. The books in his mothers'
salon were mostly poetry, and therefore considered less dangerous.
Among them was the edition of *Les Fleurs du Mal*, which Jean-Paul
Mauriac had bound up for his young wife, and which François hit upon
when he was fifteen. Two lines, in particular, stuck in his memory:

> *Et l'ange qui le suit dans son pèlerinage*
> *Pleure de le voir gai comme un oiseau de bois.*

He never doubted that an angel, good or bad, was at his heels, but
the dreamy boy who discovered Baudelaire was anything but gay.
'Mystique et raisonnable' was how he summed up his character; and to
the end of his days he walked a tightrope between the dual tendencies.

Tolstoy and Balzac were early favourites, and he would read the
Mercure de France from cover to cover. But his natural bent was for

poetry. Lamartine was 'the god of my adolescence' — and, as the poet himself had written in verses set to music by Gounod, 'the winged bard of my solitude'. Musset ran him close, although here Baudelaire threw out a formidable challenge. He towered above his century because, alone among the romantics, he faced the fact of original sin. The complete works of Musset were in a pair of volumes inherited from a great-uncle whose general taste in literature was as doubtful as his conduct in life, and most of whose library had been burnt. Musset, like Lamartine, invited you to feel, not to think. Rostand was held in contempt by the masters at Grand-Lebrun, but for the young Mauriac he survived their disapproval. The boy knew *Cyrano* and *L'Aiglon* by heart, and the 'Hymn to the Sun' from *Chantecler*:

> *Soleil qui fais des ronds par terre*
> *Si beaux qu'on n'ose pas marcher.*

Hardly sublime — but 'that' he was to write in old age 'was what we meant by poetry when we were little.' These and other poems — Maurice de Guérin and Hugo's 'Ode à la colonne' — were all in an anthology much in use at Grand-Lebrun. François' attachment to Maurice de Guérin grew fervent as the years went by, and not for literary reasons alone. 'When I was an adolescent a few lines from Maurice de Guérin's *Journal* were enough to bring me closer to him than his Cayla is to my own Malagar.'[1]

Most influential of all, however, though hardly suspected at the time, was Racine. The initiation was gradual as he moved up in the school; *Esther*, *Athalie*, and the others came afterwards. Racine was seminal for the development of his own writing. Mauriac is the most Racinian of novelists, for it was Racine who showed him the strength of passion 'dans un éternel éclairage'.[2] This composes the theme of one book after another, where there is not a screw loose, nor an unnecessary ornament, on the structure. Mauriac was right to emphasise the poetic strain that suffused his realism; but, as with Racine, the poetry is in the whole rather than in the parts. When he is writing at his best, the integration is flawless.

He was ten years old when he began to write poems — pastiches of what he had read or heard read aloud. At sixteen he was exchanging verses with a friend, Charles Caillard, met on the *plage* at Saint-Palais; and he had already, the year before, written a letter to Anatole France — without receiving an answer. France was among the triumphant Dreyfusards in the world of letters, and he appealed to that side of

[1] *Journal, Vol. I, O.C.XI*, 89.

[2] *Nouveaux Mémoires Intérieurs*, 144.

Mauriac which, in defiance of his milieu and upbringing, was always to be critical, and even *contestataire*. Behind the well-trimmed beard of Anatole France, and the elegance of his prose, the Voltairean sneer was generally apparent, and the nascent irony in Mauriac responded to it. The wide sale of his books — and his undisputed reign in Madame Caillavet's salon — suggested that success was not incompatible with *contestation*. Mauriac's own career, particularly in its later stages, demonstrated the same thing.

Madame Mauriac used to complain that François was the only unmusical member of her family. This was not quite fair. He had little voice, so to speak, even before he lost it in early middle age; but his appreciation of music was intense. His mother was a pure mezzo-soprano with a particular fondness for Gounod's 'Le soir ramène le silence' and 'Le rossignol'; 'Nuit resplendissante et silencieuse' from his *Cinq-Mars*; and Elisabeth's 'O vierge sainte' from *Tannhäuser*, which she sang in church — while at home François and his brothers sang the Pilgrim's Chorus. He remembered Schumann's 'Les Amours du poète' almost murmured in his mother's rendering 'as the night breeze shook the flames of the candles and the moths, with their singed wings, fluttered on the rosewood piano.'[1] His sister played a little Beethoven and Mendelssohn, and he was introduced to César Franck by the organist of St André Cathedral. But when his mother told him that he had no ear for music, he believed her because he considered her infallible. She seemed to him, when she sang, to be the messenger of 'all the love and all the sadness in the world'.

Octavie, the maid who served the family for years, sang for him too, and he liked her to tell him stories. When she came to the end of one she would lapse into her native patois, and exclaim: 'Cric, crac, mon counte es acabat'. She was at his side as he composed a juvenile tragedy, *La Fille de Jephté*, but this should not be taken as evidence of a close acquaintance with the Old Testament. The Bible was virtually a closed book in the Mauriac household, although François discovered it for himself as time went on. He was rarely taken to the theatre and his first, clandestine, visit was a sore disappointment. Plays were regarded as less respectable than music, and a local priest had been severely sanctioned for attending a performance of Gounod's *Faust*. But François enjoyed the plays of Henri Bernstein, with Lucien Guitry; and Régina Badet in *Carmen* dancing on the table in the posada. A touring company brought Corneille to the Grand-Lebrun, and François himself was chosen for the role of 'Piety' in the Prologue to a college performance of *Esther*.

[1] *Bloc-Notes I*, 353.

The family travelled very little, although they had the means and the opportunity to do so. Jacques Mauriac had rarely ventured further than Saint-Symphorien or Bordeaux. François was taken, as a boy, to stay with a certain Comtesse de Penautier at Bagnères-de-Bigorre in the Pyrenees; and great was the scandal when it was discovered later that she was not the wife, but the mistress, of the Comte. At the age of ten he spent a short holiday at Saint-Sebastian with an abbé whose formidable ugliness in a bathing costume provoked the quotation: 'Le flot qui l'apporta recule épouvanté.' But for sea air the family would generally go to Taussat on the *bassin* at Arcachon. This had been much frequented by Toulouse-Lautrec; people spoke with contempt of his drunkenness and of the little flask of cognac which he kept in the knob of his cane. He was buried quite close to the Mauriac property at Malagar.

The young François was content with these limited horizons, for they gave him everything he wanted as a boy and, in later years, all that he needed as a writer. Time did not turn him into a traveller. With regard to Bordeaux itself, however, his feelings were ambivalent. It was his cradle and his nursery, but something less than his home. A home is primarily a house, and since he had spent his childhood and early youth in no less than five different houses in Bordeaux — Madame Mauriac having now moved to the rue Rolland where she lived with her married daughter — his deeper attachments, as we shall see, lay elsewhere. Yet, in another sense, Bordeaux was too much a part of himself to be viewed without prejudice. If he was happy he liked it; if he was miserable he detested it. It reflected his moods, and his moods were many. For Stendhal it stood unrivalled among the cities of France; a miracle of proportion and style. But the romantic adolescent was insensitive to its rational charms; he lamented the absence of trees; and the estuary with its traffic of merchandise excited no spark of *Wanderlust*. 'Tu ramènes tout à toi' was a constant reproach of his mother's, and what he met with his eyes was registered, and generally transformed, in his memory.

On a close evening in July he might linger in the public garden and muse in front of the marble adolescent embracing its chimera; inhale the moisture of the pavement after rain; creep into Saint-André and kneel under the cool, incense-laden vaulting of the nave, even if he were in no state of grace to approach the altar; catch the wailing of fog-horns in the mist; jolt along the familiar streets in a tram which reminded him of a 'yellow caterpillar';[1] loiter beside the docks with their smell of brine and their dead waters, stained with petrol, observing with a mixture of

---

[1] *Le Désert de l'Amour.*

curiosity and compassion the scrofulous figures who lurked there. So many roads led to the port, or converged upon the Grand Théâtre, and more often than not a stroll through the city would end up at the foot-bridge that ran alongside the railway where it crossed the Garonne. In March and October the fair in the Place des Quinconces drew its crowds, and in the Théâtre de l'Aérogyne the lady who danced in her tinselled tights gave promise of 'pneumatic bliss'.[1] On New Year's Day a beggar would be found at the corner of the street, and even at the door of the kitchen, with a bag of crusts on his back – while at the same time the family were enjoying their chocolates and marrons-glacés, to the rustling of silver paper and the exchange of insincere embraces. That too was not forgotten by the boy who was later to stand before his native city as the uneasy conscience of the bourgeoisie. 'My books' he wrote 'bear witness that, although I live in Paris, I have never left Bordeaux. It would be truer to say that Bordeaux has never left me.'[2]

4

No boy ever looked forward to the holidays with more passionate longing than François Mauriac; no writer has recalled them in more affectionate detail. His maternal grandmother had a house, Château Lange, at Gradignan, 7 kilometres south east of Bordeaux. The acacias climbed up to his bedroom window; there was a fishpond in the grounds; and behind the privet hedge an old dovecote had been turned into a chapel. By an exceptional privilege the Blessed Sacrament was reserved there. Here Mme Coiffard moved about in a 'pious eddy of soutanes', the holy medals jangling from her rosary, during the summer months, and when a weak heart prevented her from moving about any longer François remembered her seated in an armchair with a hand-bell, a box of pills, and a bag of sweets beside her. If he took one of these without being offered it, she threatened him with her stick. She was a formidable woman with what Mauriac described as 'the remains of ugliness'; and was liable to cut short an argument with an imperious 'Who is mistress here?' – and then 'every nose would incline towards its plate'.[3]

As she lay dying a priest saw fit to pronounce a kind of premature funeral oration to the family and dependents gathered round her bed. 'She was a great soul...' – for, after all, she had spoken to St Bernadette – but François could not help wondering whether she really *was* a great

---

[1] T.S. Eliot.

[2] *D'autres et moi*, 25.

[3] *Nouveaux Mémoires Intérieurs*, 130.

soul? The rents from her properties in Bordeaux had assured her a very comfortable passage from this life to the next. But perhaps she had suffered more than he suspected, particularly from the secret scandal attaching to the life of her only son, now dead, and from the fear of death which no precaution of piety could exorcize. Her faith was Spanish in its fierce intransigence, and much of it she had handed on to her daughter. The formula – 'outside the Church there is no salvation' – was literally understood, and François was shocked by this as soon as he was of an age to be shocked by such matters at all. Judgement came easily to these *dévots*. 'There were the good books and the bad books, the good press and the bad press, the Catholic workers and the other workers.'[1] As he listened to the unctuous words pronounced over his dying grandmother, the boy was struck by the discrepancy between appearance and reality, between behaviour and belief; and the novelist was to remember it later on.

After her death Madame Mauriac sold the château, and built a chalet with the name of Johanet in the forest just outside Saint-Symphorien, the last *bourg* in the department of Gironde, and François helped to trace the paths that led to it. It was here, among the pines bent by the Atlantic winds – 'the secret forests of my childhood', many of them to be 'effaced like a schoolboy's drawing on a blackboard'[2] – that Mauriac's imagination was quickened and his personality matured. 'Blessed by my native soil' he wrote 'for without it I should not have been the child whom Cybele intoxicated, and whom the trees protected from men.'[3] Here, on the feast of the Assumption, he would decorate with flowers the Virgin's statue, and gather with his brothers on the steps of the chalet to sing 'Dieu de paix et d'amour, lumière de lumière'. Here was the little stream of La Hure, where he would sail his miniature boats, made out of the stripped bark of the pines, and whose clear waters came to symbolise the spring of all his writing. The summers at Saint-Symphorien, with the equinoxial gales which kept him awake at night, and the flies buzzing in the salon during the siesta, and the smell of fresh manure, and the blue-striped wallpaper in his bedroom, and the moon that he would watch from his window as it rose above the pines, and the Druidic oak-tree which he used ritually to kiss, summed up the whole atmosphere of the *grandes vacances*.

He cultivated his own garden behind a kiosk, carting the gravel for it in a small wheelbarrow. But in the great heat of August, when the

---

[1] Ibid., 137.

[2] *Bloc-Notes II*, 83.

[3] Ibid., 54.

house was shuttered from 10 a.m. until six in the evening, he was glued to his text-books. For a couple of years, before he moved to Grand-Lebrun, a tutor from Bordeaux came to supervise his studies. 'The abbé Carreyre will open your mind' his mother would say; and there was no need, in that 'secret forest' of the *Landes*, for anyone to open his eyes. With the hot sand under his bare feet, the prick of the pine needles and the dead bracken, the moss for a pillow, the gentians in the marsh, and in his ears the mingling of the sheep-bells and the Angelus and the chirping of the grasshoppers, he was storing up the images and sensations which he was afterwards to reproduce in one book after another.

There was a constant coming and going of family and friends; sometimes as many as forty sat down to table. With its gaudy patterning of bricks – red, green, black and yellow – and the ceiling of the salon the colour of pink whipped cream, the chalet was a place where the children loved to play, Pierre Mauriac pretending to be a priest and his elder brother the director of a turpentine factory. François' ambitions, in so far as he had any, did not lend themselves to impersonation. More distant, and rarely visited, were the giant oaks and chestnuts at Pieuchon – a kind of sacred wood where it was forbidden to cut the smallest branch. Shooting was popular – and indeed canonical – with the menfolk and the older boys; larks when the rye had been harvested, and wood-pigeons after October 18th. 'A la Saint-Luc, le grand truc' – the cry went up, but François had by then returned to school. He was fifteen when he shot his first squirrel, and in later years he hardly shot at all. A photograph shows him deep in a book and crouched on the damp soil of the *palombière*, a pigeon-shooters' 'hide', while the others were sitting alert for the first sign of the wood-pigeons. On the other hand he was an ardent, if slightly ashamed, *aficionado* of the bull-fights in Bordeaux, or at Saint-Vincent-de-Tyrose. What he relished was the same atmosphere that enchanted him in the last act of *Carmen*:

> the red and yellow posters, and the young men in their straw boaters with coloured ribbons or grey felt hats which they took to be Spanish . . . the cafés exuding their fresh smell of absinthe on to the roadway . . . the hard, emaciated faces of the matadors in their old victorias . . . a strange variety of clergy, in their robes of red and gold, violet and silver.[1]

But he left the arena with a vague feeling of distress at the suffering of beasts who had done no harm and were doomed to certain death.

The bull-ring displayed the ritual of death, and its reality was not far

[1] *Le Désert de l'Amour.*

away. Tuberculosis was rampant among the young of his age, and several of his cousins had died of it. He was haunted by the last words of a lad of twenty, warned that he would not last the night: 'At least I shall have seen the day'; and of another who merely said: 'How dark it is!' Many girls of his acquaintance, who had barely learnt to dance, died before their first ball. If Easter fell in March the boys were kept back for the ceremonies of Holy Week. On Maundy Thursday they went the round of the churches, visiting the altars of Repose; and on Good Friday the chanting of the Gospel at the Mass of the Pre-Sanctified left an ineffaceable impression. 'The kiss of treason in the garden at night, where the torches lit up the bearded faces convulsed with fear or hatred – here, as it has always seemed to me, was one of the sources – perhaps the only source – of everything I was to write, even of what apparently has least to do with it.'[1] Yet at Langon the biggest trade fair of the year was held on Good Friday; and even in Bordeaux the thoughts appropriate to the day were tempered with a pagan exultation as François looked forward to Easter Monday morning when the coachman of the station omnibus would bring down the trunks, and they would soon be listening to the first woodpecker at Saint-Symphorien. If Easter fell in April Madame Mauriac would give a modest *déjeuner* to the local farmers who had fulfilled their religious duties.

The holidays, nevertheless, were not a time of unclouded happiness. 'Why don't you cry?' his mother would say 'that will make you feel better.' The hot summers were a stimulus to adolescent day-dreams, and the expectation of a rosy future to which François could not as yet give a name. The shadow of the *rentrée* overhung the last days of September; the ring-doves flew in from the north; and an odour of decay was distilled from the wet leaves and the stream where he had sailed his boats. An early poem contained the line: 'C'est en moi qu'est l'orage', and his memory of Saint-Symphorien was less of sunshine than of storm. 'What I owe to our Guyenne is an atmosphere which has enveloped me ever since I was a child – the storm which composes the unchanging climate of my books, and a glimmer of fire on the horizon – all this is the legacy of my native land.'[2]

5

Jules Laforgue wrote of the 'cough in the dormitory' when the boys came back after the *grandes vacances*; and although François Mauriac

[1] *Bloc-Notes III*, 129.
[2] *Bloc-Notes IV*, 114.

had spent only a miserable fortnight as a boarder at Grand-Lebrun, the contrast was depressing between the sunlight falling on the leaves and the gaslight falling on the linoleum. In 1902 he passed his first baccalauréat, and described himself standing on the steps of the Faculty after the beadle had handed him his certificate 'motionless and fascinated on the threshold of life'.[1] In the following year, however, his philosophy let him down. So for the last time he heard the orchestra in the balcony above the playground start up with the overture to *Si j'étais roi* or *Voyage en Chine*; listened to the choruses from *William Tell* or *Athalie*; and watched the prize-giving. He retained many affectionate memories of Grand-Lebrun, and left his initial carved on one of the desks.

He now moved, of his own choice, to the *lycée* and spent a year there with the brother-in-law of André Gide as his professor. But Gide, in spite of his growing reputation, was not yet a name to conjure with in Bordeaux. François' studies were interrupted by a severe attack of pleurisy, which left him extremely weak, and any unusual physical exertion was henceforth forbidden him. In October 1904 he started to prepare his *licence ès lettres* at the University of Bordeaux. Fortunat Strowsky, an eminent authority on Pascal, was his teacher; and when he was successful his examiner remarked: 'And to think that you will now have the right to teach geography!' – for a *licence ès lettres* evidently opened the door to many classrooms. In 1905 François studied under André Lebreton for a dissertation on the following theme: 'Meditation on death is a snare because it makes us forget to live.' François had thought a good deal about death, and even come near to it himself; and he obtained 18 marks out of 20 for his treatment of the subject. Pascal had here been useful to him, but could not save him from a 'zero' for Greek at his *viva voce*. He returned to the University in 1906, and began to work for a thesis on the origins of the Franciscan movement in France. With this, however, he did not persevere: he was now twenty-one, and had other matters on his mind.

Before we follow him where he had determined to go, we must retrace his steps over three important, though indecisive, years. He was growing up, and the *esprit critique* was asserting itself in opposition to his milieu. This should not be exaggerated, however; it was, as he put it, a 'revolution à ma manière'. Mauriac was not a natural revolutionary; temperamentally, he was – and remained – a conservative, but the stupidities of French conservatism, both in politics and religion, were so flagrant that he was forced to the left of centre. This was particularly true at the outset of his career when he might have been expected to

[1] *Block-Notes I,* 337.

rebel, and at the end of it when he might have been expected to conform.

Religion and politics are never easily separated in France, and the aftermath of the Dreyfus *affaire* found them deeply involved. The *Action Française*, now published daily, was read even by those who abhorred its opinions. It espoused the cause of the Catholics who had lost their schools, and of the army that had lost its scapegoat. Pierre Mauriac, in contrast to his brother, adhered to the movement all his life; and this led to discussion, though never to hostility. François was drawn to the only opposition in sight – the Sillon, a Christian democratic movement founded by Marc Sangnier. He had heard Sangnier lecture in Bordeaux, and met him the next day at Langon, where he had gathered a few of his followers – mostly students, workers, and employees – at midnight after a stormy meeting with the local anti-clericals. Any concession to royalism was strictly non-political, and it was perhaps on this occasion that a school teacher, describing Anatole France as 'the prince of French literature', added that in literature princes were admissible. Sangnier read aloud to them a play – hardly a tactful initiative at so late an hour – and when Mauriac observed that there were no women in the cast an awkward silence reigned in the rosewood salon. Sangnier was essentially a mystic, and although Mauriac frequented his meetings for a time, where everyone rather self-consciously addressed each other as 'camarades', he presently ceased to do so. His friend, the abbé Desgranges, who had done much to convert him to the Sillon, founded a similar movement of his own, and Mauriac adhered to it. The Sillon lacked the intellectual rigour and political effectiveness of the Action Française, and it was later condemned by Rome during the reactionary pontificate of Pius X. Its democratic ideals, however, had taken root in the minds of many French Catholics; and when they enjoyed a brief honeymoon in the wake of the Liberation, Mauriac could echo the words of Maurras under Vichy: 'Mes idées sont au pouvoir.'

The movement at least offered a reply, however tentative, to what Mauriac already saw as a scandal – the defensive alliance of the Church and the *bourgeoisie*. He was to write in *Le Désert de l'Amour* of the 'desert that separates the classes as it separates the individuals'. He remembered the docility of the servants who had taken him on their knees; how his grandfather, when he saw them sitting down, would tell them to stand up; and how his grandmother would suggest to the postman that he go round to the kitchen for a nice glass of water! Some of the young women had lost their teeth by the time they were twenty-five; but if a servant girl were pretty the lads of the village would gather, 'like tom cats', in the garden when it was dark.[1] The farm labourers shared the innocence of the animal creation, and the priests who were the victims of their indifference enjoyed a hardly better standard of living. Rigidity in private morals found its compensation in the passion for property. Greed wore the halo of virtue, and a good deal was the equivalent of a good deed. Marriages were made, if possible, between persons not only of the same town but of the same parish; and what counted was not only the dowry but the 'espérances'. The girls who were not likely to marry – who had neither 'espoir' nor 'espérances' – went about in pairs, advertising their hapless virginity. If a girl showed any reluctance before the choice which had been made for her, the reply was categorical: 'The family insists upon it.' When he came to the end of his life Mauriac could reply to André Gide's 'Familles je vous hais' with 'Familles je vous bénis', but he had seen enough of other people's families in his youth to understand what Gide had meant. How well – how implacably – he understood, his novels were to make plain.

These were years of acute religious crisis. Modernism had come to challenge a petrified theology. Loisy, under the spell of German exegesis, had followed where Renan had led the way. For some years Mauriac refused to read the Fourth Gospel, because he supposed it to be apocryphal; it was not till later that the great scholarship of Père Lagrange confirmed its authenticity. He was attracted to the ideas of Maurice Blondel, Jules Leroy – the friend of Teilhard de Chardin – and particularly Père Laberthonnière. All these writers suffered from the most ruthless inquisition the Church had known in modern times; and the same instinct for justice which had turned Mauriac into a Dreyfusard placed him at their side – little qualified as he was to separate the grain from the chaff in their teaching. His school friend, André Lacaze, who was afterwards to become a priest, was himself sympathetic to modernism, and influenced Mauriac in the same direction. Now, if François were offered a *nougat* in the shape of the Sacred Heart, he was no longer edified; and he exasperated the curé of Saint-Symphorien by arguing that if President Combes was acting in good faith, he would earn his reward in the life to come. On these occasions Madame Mauriac was ready with her familiar rebuke: 'You're talking nonsense' or 'You think everyone else is so stupid'. Nevertheless, those early modernists were very different from the secularising clergy of today; they were preoccupied with the interior life. Mauriac had little mind for theological niceties, but once he had lighted upon Newman's *Apologia*, the book rarely left his side. 'Two luminous and self-evident beings – myself and my Creator' remained the text of a dialogue which

[1] *La Province. O.C. IV*, 463.

not even sin could interrupt. When he described himself as a 'child of Port-Royal and La Chesnaie' it meant that Pascal and Lamennais were his masters and, through Lamennais, Lacordaire. With both of these men political reform and spiritual renewal had gone hand in hand, and in the case of François Mauriac they were not to be separated.

He was now reading Huysmans and, on the rather surprising advice of a local wine merchant, Léon Bloy. Alexis Léger – to be known to literature as Saint-John Perse – came to Bordeaux from his native Guadeloupe, and dined with Madame Mauriac. Afterwards he read aloud from Claudel and Francis Jammes. Jules Lemaitre, whose elegant style was held up as a model of good writing, lectured at the Alhambra; no critic of the time was more highly esteemed. But for Mauriac the reigning prince of literature was Maurice Barrès. *Sous l'oeil des barbares* held him firmly under its spell, for what Barrès meant by the 'barbares' were all those insensitive people who did not understand him – a category of mankind that Mauriac discovered, easily enough, in his own family and milieu. The Barrésien 'culte du moi' appealed to his own ambitions; he felt the need to pull up his roots before he pushed them down again. They went deeper, however, than he then realised.

It was now Malagar that he came increasingly to think of as his home. The property, with its vines, had been bought in 1843. Modest in size, it stood above the Garonne, and no one doubted that on a clear day you could see the Pyrenees from its upper windows – although no one had ever actually done so. It was shaded by elms of great antiquity, and François' great-grandfather had planted four rows of hornbeam. These were not yet clipped as you see them today, and they grew untidily. 'The wild serpents of an ancient ivy-bush strangled the invisible pillars of the porch'; 'a plot of grass encircled the old courtyard';[1] a fig-tree stood at one corner of the terrace; and there was a stable for four oxen. The country was quite wild on the opposite bank of the river; no road as yet ran direct to Arcachon, and the wheels of the trap were obliged to follow the tracks which the farm carts had already made. In the forests of the *Landes* there were shepherds who had never seen a train and still insisted on being paid in *écus*; but here the railway passed close by. Hardly a mile away was the Calvary and church of Verdelais where Jean-Paul Mauriac had served Mass as a boy. With its statue of the Virgin found buried and disinterred by a mule, and the wax effigy of Saint-Exupérance resting her head on a silk cushion, it was a popular centre of pilgrimage. You walked to it from Malagar across the vineyard. But the peasantry were not particularly devout; keeping their oxen in the stable on a Sunday was the extent of their observance.

[1] *Les Maisons fugitives. O.C. IV*, 318.

When François was eighteen he had inscribed the following quotation from Barrès in his notebook: 'The vast libraries where these lovely objects are set out on their shelves . . . and make you tremble with joy – 500,000 volumes well catalogued.' Like so many other young provincials, he dreamt of the literary salons, perhaps of the Académie française. At eighteen one does not read Balzac for nothing. Visits to Paris were very rare. Once he had been to the Variétés with an uncle, who recalled his previous visit in 1869 and a glimpse of Napoleon III standing between two pillars. But to Paris François was now determined to go, little guessing maybe how passionately in the future he would always long to get back to Malagar. It was therefore agreed that he should study history at the Ecole des Chartes. He had never been given more pocket money than was strictly necessary, but he now had adequate private means; and in October 1907 he set out on the great adventure. Among the immaterial contents of his luggage were 'an honourable family, a province, memories of childhood, a religious sensibility fortified by an inhuman inhibition, the favour of the Muses, and the gift of writing.'[1] No doubt Eugène de Rastignac's[2] challenge to the city from the cemetery of Père Lachaise was echoing in his mind: 'à nous deux, maintenant!' It would not have echoed there in vain.

[1] *Les Maisons fugitives. O.C. IV*, 321.

[2] A principal character in Balzac's *Le Père Goriot*.

THE PARISIAN

1

The intellectual and artistic life of Paris between 1880 and 1914 has been well described as 'The Banquet Years',[1] but François Mauriac arrived there towards the end of the feast, and he was not in all respects tempted by the menu. Surrealism attracted him not at all; he had known two of its pontiffs, and they had both committed suicide. But he was introduced to the music of Ravel, and an exhibition of Cézanne opened his eyes to Post-Impressionism – the last school of painting in which he was ever to feel really at home. A friend lent him *The Brothers Karamazoff*, and Dostoievsky now competed with Balzac for his enthusiasm. For the rest, he was content to admire the reigning planets, Maurice Barrès, Paul Bourget, and Jules Lemaitre, comforted to know that they acknowledged the talent of Anatole France, Dreyfusard though he might have been. They admired him because he both thought and wrote like Voltaire. This did not mean that they agreed with Voltaire, any more than the young Mauriac agreed with him; but Voltaire had clear ideas and expressed them clearly. Mauriac held that the first duty of the writer was to give pleasure, and then to be easily understood. He was not possessed by the 'demon of the avant-garde', and very soon became aware of 'a strange little world known to me alone and which I had to bring to life with the most ordinary words.'[2] But his reading of Dostoievsky and Claudel was beginning to teach him that the daylight also has its mystery and that too bright a sunshine may destroy it. In the case of Claudel the most ordinary words became 'like gold coins which had not yet entered into currency.'[3]

With these views and ambitions, Mauriac took up his residence at 104 rue de Vaugirard, the Paris house of the Marianist Fathers. The superior was Père Plazenet. Mauriac now set about preparing his entry to the Ecole des Chartes, the school of historical studies which was part of the Sorbonne, and he was admitted on a second application.

[1] Roger Shattuck, 1958.

[2] *Bloc-Notes V*, 13.

[3] *Block-Notes II*, 223.

But he remained there for only six months, and wrote to his mother from a marble-topped table in the bar of the Palais des Champs-Elysées that he had decided to devote his life to literature. She took the information on the chin. He was moved to this decision by a chance meeting on the boulevards with his old friend, Charles-Francis Caillard, with whom he had exchanged verses while he was still at Grand-Lebrun. Caillard wanted to know if he still wrote verses, and, hearing that he did so, offered to publish them, if Mauriac would bear the cost. In the event, 500 francs was to prove a cheap investment. Caillard also edited a review to which Mauriac agreed to contribute, and introduced him to the 'dames poètes' of his acquaintance; the duchesse de Rohan and her 'thés poétiques' in a salon which was described as a 'street with a roof on top of it'; and Madame Guillaume Beer who had been loved by Leconte de Lisle and wrote hymns to the sun.

Mauriac had already shown a spirit of independence not altogether to the liking of Père Plazenet, and he presently moved to the Hôtel de l'Espérance, also in the rue de Vaugirard, where the son of the house was ubiquitous in the beds of the maids. With Plazenet's permission, however, Mauriac was elected as president of the student circle which met at the Marianist house – a choice which was hailed as a victory for the Sillonists over the members of the Action Française. Well-known writers were invited to attend the meetings, and on one of these occasions it was Mauriac's duty to welcome René Bazin, himself an adherent of the Action Française, on whom a talk was to be given. Mauriac had decided to improvise his introduction but, having drunk too much champagne beforehand, found himself incapable of speech. Humiliated and ashamed, he fled the next morning to Brussels, where he discovered Colette dancing, half naked, in a music hall. It was a long time before he risked another improvisation. Meanwhile he had left the Hôtel de l'Espérance for a four-room apartment at 45 rue Vaneau, for which his mother sent the furniture from Bordeaux, including an iron bedstead impossible to take to pieces. This remained his address for the next five years.

Les Mains jointes – his collection of verse – was published by Les Editions des Temps Présents in November 1909. Mauriac always maintained that the springs of his poetry were to be found in Racine, but the springs were both hidden and relaxed in *Les Mains jointes*. He was to criticise these verses for their want of backbone, and to admit his indifference to the technique which would have supplied it. They revealed, he thought, a cowardly and introspective adolescence, nourished on religiosity rather than belief, and an idleness which sought to justify itself by the first edifying excuse. He even wondered whether this were not the 'sin against the Holy Ghost'. Others, however, were more indulgent. Maurice Barrès had noticed a copy of the book on the table of Paul Bourget, and on New Year's Day (1910) Mauriac learnt in Bordeaux that he had ordered a copy for him on *papier de luxe*. Shortly afterwards the housekeeper at the rue Rolland, where Mauriac was staying with his mother, brought him a black-bordered envelope — a sign of mourning, maybe, for the lost provinces. Inside was a letter from Barrès:

> Monsieur.
>
> You are a great poet whom I admire; a true poet, controlled, tender and profound, who does not try to force his voice in order to move us with memories of our childhood. I should like to say this in public: and that is why I have delayed in thanking you for this precious little book, read and re-read every day for the past two weeks. I am deeply grateful to think that we have a poet.[1]

On the 21 March 1910 Barrès wrote that he had written an article on the poems for the *Echo de Paris*. It appeared on the 21st March when Mauriac was again in the Gironde for the Easter vacation. Barrès wrote of

> great control, no cheating, the gentlest and truest chamber music, gathering all its emotions around a centre of Catholic thought. It is the poetry of a child from a happy family, of a little boy, sensible, delicate, and well brought up, for whom nothing has clouded the sunshine, over-sensitive, and striking a wild note of sensuality. This is the moment when the colours change and are difficult to capture, the age of ambiguity when the boy is a child no longer, when he develops and is transformed into an adolescent. Which road will he choose to take? Will he follow in the steps of a Sainte-Beuve or a Renan — those rather too fleshy prophets who often seemed to think that the delightful relaxation of the soul in the midst of pleasure — what the Greeks called *anesis* — fluidity, reverie, and dispersion, were the higher forms of life? Or will he rally to the band of those great minds who have always sung the praises of *tonos* — by which I mean the tension and vibration of a soul mistress of itself, insensitive to any other pleasure but that of mastering itself and mastering its fate? We like to think that a book so fragile as this should have fixed the ephemeral moment of an eternal disquiet.[2]

[1] *O.C. IV*, 181.

[2] Ibid., 203-7.

Inquiétude éternelle sums up the whole psychology of François Mauriac, in his maturity even more forcibly than in his youth, and Barrès was quick to detect it. His eye was on the future of his *protégé,* and he goes on to note

> Reluctance to quit the shore, the vague regret for so gentle a childhood, so mild and tender a tranquility, an infinite sensibility which is pulling itself together and no longer hankers for the wastefulness of youth or the sober reveries of the sunset. Everything here is tender, dreamy, and indecisive, still warm from the west. It is a twilight moment, and quickly passes. But the author must put the tenderness of this troubled April behind him, and become a man; he must choose his path and his point of view; he must cease to stagnate. What will be the future of this charming stream? . . . . Everything is pure in its first bubblings, but when it flows far from the shade that protects it, it will reflect many faces, and receive many tributaries. The adolescent will no longer be of an age when he is lovable and certain to please. Will he know how to grow up? That is the great problem.
>
> It does not require much cleverness to be a wonder at twenty. The difficult thing is set oneself to the perfecting of life, and its enrichment in proportion as it snatches from us its earlier gifts. The young François Mauriac, in this volume where I cannot detect a single stupidity — and for a poet that is really prodigious — finds an excellent word to describe himself; he speaks of his past as that of a child 'mystic and reasonable'. I can confirm his diagnosis; he is possessed of reason, and even of good sense, so that his poetic genius, whose April I am happy to salute, may yield for us its four seasons of flowers and fruit.[1]

This article has been quoted at length not only because Mauriac never ceased to refer to it with a touching and almost naive gratitude, but because it revealed, beneath the artifice of its style and what seems the excess of its compliment, an exact understanding of where Mauriac stood at the outset of his career. He naturally wrote to Barrès who replied as follows:

> One is afraid to do you harm by admiring you at close quarters, and to influence you in any way . . . You must write without forcing your will; all the care of a good workman, of course, but let the springs of your thought spurt up naturally. Put aside all systems, and listen to your own secrets and what comes to you

[1] Ibid.

from the depths of your own experience.[1]

It is not easy for the English reader – or the French for the matter of that – to conceive the effect of Barrès' commendation. Barrès is little read today, and princes no longer reign in literature. But in 1910 he was in his heyday as a *cher maître*, even though Francis Jammes, from his rural retreat in the *Pays Basque,* described him as a 'merchant of artificial ice-cream', and Claudel could not do with him at all. Elected as the nationalist deputy for Nancy at the age of 25, he was not a royalist and therefore escaped the opprobrium that fell upon the Action Française. By now his *anti-Dreyfusisme* was forgiven him and Mauriac, who had always sat at his feet, would of course have forgiven him anything. He had already, under the spell of *Sous l'oeil des barbares,* imitated the Barrésien style in his own note-book:

> Live on the summit of a tower of indifference, dominating the vast plain where the barbarians have pitched their tents. On this peaceful night, when the lamp whistles ever so slightly, or when the dinner still troubles your digestion, give a thought to your physical and intellectual health. Fortify yourself to justify, day by day, your contempt and your disgust.[2]

He describes how the frantic preparation for his entrance examination at the Ecole des Chartes had been interrupted 'by smoking, the reading of Barrès, and drinking at the bars.' There were bars in Bordeaux, but there is no record of Mauriac frequenting them.

Barrès had said all that needs to be said about *Les Mains jointes.* In a preface to the new edition of the poems in 1927 Mauriac wrote as follows:

> I disavow this cowardly and timorous adolescence, so turned inward upon itself. I do not go back upon my faith at that time, any more than I renounce my poetry; but my way of belief was worth no more than my way of rhyming: how facile!

It is not upon his verse – though he was to write better verse than this – that Mauriac's reputation depends. Nevertheless, the secret of his art was poetic, and Barrès, not suspecting the novelist shortly to be born, had perceived it. Mauriac recognized it too.

> The die was cast from the beginning. I could not be other than this child of the bourgeoisie who, thanks to poetry, would transfigure an inheritance of business men and landed proprietors.

[1] Ibid., 207.
[2] *O.C. IV*, 183.

But the matter of this transfiguration were farms and vineyards, with their population of farmers, servants, and overseers.[1]

On the 23 February 1910 Barrès was giving a lecture on his own book *Voyage de Sparte*. Mauriac, wearing a carnation in his button-hole and a tie where a red mask stood out flamboyantly against the black silk, went up to the platform afterwards and introduced himself. 'So you are not a little seminarian!' said Barrès. Mauriac walked with him across the Place de la Concorde to the Chambre des Députés, and they spoke of literature – and of *Les Mains jointes*. Barrès admired Anna de Noailles and detested Francis Jammes and Paul Claudel, who were Mauriac's favourites among contemporary poets. But it was enough to be walking with Barrès down the Champs Elysées beflagged for some national occasion, and to receive the compliment: 'This is in honour of *Les Mains jointes*'. Barrès later observed to a third party: 'I must give this young Mauriac a picture of myself that suits his temperament.' But Mauriac, in his brief euphoria, wore a mask on his temperament as well as on his tie.

2

In 1926, his celebrity as a novelist now assured, Mauriac published a long essay entitled *Le Jeune Homme*.[2] In the same series Colette had written on *La Femme*, and Giraudoux on *La Jeune fille*. Mauriac's essay was a polished exercise in a genre where the French excel, and behind the *idées générales* a retrospective self-portrait of Mauriac could be discerned by anyone who knew him. He quotes as an epigraph Shelley's comparison of youth to a 'wild swan', and then speaks of it as the 'time of disorder and sanctity, the time of sadness and joy, of mockery and admiration, of ambition and sacrifice, of greed and renunciation.' It was all very well to look down, with Barrès, on the 'barbarians encamped on the plain', but there was 'nothing so dangerous as noble sentiments in a young man who has given himself up to pleasure; if a "beautiful soul" has not discovered God, his disgust for life and his contempt for the world often land him in the abyss.' Despair was 'also a career. Certain candidates for suicide are people incapable of living orderly lives, who turn their disorder to advantage.' Remembering, perhaps, the Barrésien advice he had once given himself, Mauriac now writes:

> The young man knows how precious he is. He takes care of his body, lovingly exercises his muscles, cuts himself off from

[1] *Nouveaux Mémoires Intérieurs*, 198.
[2] *O.C.IV*.

pleasure, agrees to sacrifice too keen a sensuality for the sake of
his sovereign strength. The narcissism of young people often
saves them from dangerous excess. Narcissus is enchanted with
these appearances, and in order that nothing shall change them,
he wills to remain chaste.[1]

Mauriac was lunching one day with Forain, who had shared a room
with Rimbaud. 'What was he like?' asked Mauriac. 'Like a big dog,' came
the reply. The example of Rimbaud illustrated the stark alternatives
between which it was so difficult to choose. On the one hand, the
desire for the absolute; on the other, the appetite for risk – the
association of excitement and death. 'Even the most balanced and the
most sensible . . . ardently seek the possibility of death; for them, there
is no real pleasure without this vertigo, like the frenzy of a speeding
motor-car.' Or an aeroplane, he might have added, for it was not so
long, in that first decade of the century, since Blériot had crossed the
channel.

Mauriac was writing from hindsight, at a period of professional
success and personal crisis, and it is interesting to enquire how far the
young man he then described corresponded with the young man he once
had been. For just as he looked back with nostalgia on his childhood
when he was an adolescent, and on his adolescence when he was a
man, so, from the threshold of middle age, he looked back upon his
youth. He remains a fascinating character because he was always a
divided character; single-minded in his beliefs and his industry; paradoxical and sometimes perverse in his behaviour; running after false
gods, yet never losing his faith in the true one; passionately interested
both in himself and in other people. Given his talent, it was the right
equipment for a novelist, but it did not make the 'spiritual exercises'
any easier. And there was never a moment in his life when Mauriac did
not bow before the superiority of the saint, although his 'regard
perforant et catholique' detected sanctity where others would have
passed it by, and was reluctant to recognize it where others would
have discovered it too easily. The same 'regard' taught him his own
weakness when he was priding himself on his strength, and his Barrésien
disdain.

He was the first to admit, perhaps too readily, that the Devil lay
in wait for him. Indeed one sometimes wonders what Mauriac would
have done without the Devil; he was a kind of therapeutic necessity
which kept him young and kept him gay. Of Mauriac's gaiety there is,
of course, no trace in his writing, but like 'poor Yorick' he could

---

[1] *O.C. IV*, 422-3.

always 'set the table on a roar'. If it is true that the Devil collaborates in any important work of literature, he was conspicuous in the Paris of 1910. Mauriac had already fallen under the spell of André Gide, and was never, for all his lucidity, to escape from it altogether.

> Many young people, who hardly read at all, nevertheless profess today that their first duty is to give a free rein to all their instincts. They excuse their disorder by the obligation of sincerity, and to deny themselves nothing, even the worst.[1]

This was as true in 1910 as in 1926, and although Gide is not named the reference is clear. He had published *La Porte étroite* in 1909, and it was in that year that Mauriac met him. Each was in the throes of emancipation, the one from a Catholic, the other from a Protestant, milieu. They both came from prosperous bourgeois families. And with Gide the spiritual anxiety, which kept Mauriac on tenterhooks, had not yet been soothed – or apparently soothed – into a pagan serenity. By the time Mauriac came to write the passage quoted above, the two men were reasonably well acquainted.

Paris went to Mauriac's head – not surprisingly – and the head, as we have seen, was not always as strong as it might have been. There were the restaurants and the bars; the 'Taverne du Panthéon', 'Fouquet's' with its benches of worn leather, and gregarious dinners at 'Le Boeuf sur le Toit' with Cocteau, Radiguet, and Drieu la Rochelle, where 'a very little alcohol was enough to make me lose my head, and where I felt wounded by every face around me.' There were the nocturnal wanderings in dancing slippers, and the occasional visits to a *mauvais lieu*. On one of these, in company with a friend, Jean de la Ville de Mirmont, he found himself in a narrow and putrid cellar, where wretched prostitutes and men 'with the faces of assassins' were lounging around. Suddenly a voice was heard, live or recorded, and Gounod's 'Ave Maria' transformed the atmosphere. 'It's the Virgin who has got us out of there' observed Mauriac to his friend, as they made their escape. But Jean de la Ville de Mirmont was a Protestant, and would not perhaps so readily have taken the point.

Mauriac was never at his ease in such places. In a 'special' – a very 'special' – bar in the Place Pigalle, the entertainer was well into his stride of obscene stories when a companion called Mauriac by his name. The entertainer stopped in his tracks and asked him, 'You are . . .?' Mauriac bowed his head, and the man apologised; even on Montmartre the author of *Les Mains jointes* was not unknown. Mauriac was at once haunted, and excited, by his scruples; he found 'a sombre enjoyment

[1] *Le Jeune Homme. O.C. IV*, 444.

in the knowledge that one can lose one's soul on account of a single thought'. He might be savouring, with alternations of pleasure and disgust, the Paris of 'la belle époque', but he was still kneeling in a confessional of Bordeaux. Gide was to reproach him, as he reproached so many others, for his need of spiritual 'crutches'; but Mauriac also felt the need of the 'thicket' where the game, pursued by the Hound of Heaven, could hide and recover its breath. Sin would lose half its savour if the tang of remorse were not there to flavour it.

The modernist crisis still preoccupied him, and there were lively debates in the rue de Vaugirard where the Thomists and the Immanentists – in effect the *camelots du roi* and the Sillonistes – went at it hammer and tongs. Here again Mauriac was divided. He refused to enlist among the 'gendarmerie of tradition', but he was equally opposed to those who denounced 'as a mirage the enchanted country of the faith'. He was equally repelled by the Thomist theologians. The latter were as delighted by Pius X's condemnation of modernism as the more mystically inclined were disconcerted by it. Mauriac came to admit that the condemnation was necessary, even if it was clumsy and cruel, because 'God must be associated in the flesh with the adventure of humanity'. He sympathised, however, with Laberthonnière and Maurice Blondel, whose review *Annales de Philosophie Chrétienne* had been suppressed at the instigation of the Action Française; and with a man like Georges Goyau who was generally taken for a liberal, but held that the Redemption had actually 'happened'. This was in contrast to the 'imperceptible wink of certain intrepid defenders of the faith'.[1]

The controversy was brought closer when he met Monseigneur (later Cardinal) Baudrillart on the day that Baudrillart had lost his election to the Académie française. Mgr Duchesne, a great liberal scholar and theologian, had been elected in his place; 'an opponent' observed Baudrillart 'too clever, if not perfidious'. He need not have despaired. The time would come when he sat among the Immortals defending the invasion of Ethiopia in the name of Western solidarity. Another visitor to the rue Vaugirard was the future Cardinal Gerlier, then a brilliant young advocate. He took Mauriac by the arm and gave him lengthy advice from one who was also trying to keep his attachment to this world without losing it with the next. But Mauriac was not impressed. 'This fellow can talk' was his silent comment. Quiet reassurance came from the Sunday visits of his brother Jean, who was in many respects closer to him than the other members of his family, and was now studying for the priesthood near by.

Friendship counted a great deal for one whose life had hitherto

[1] *Ecrits Intimes.*

been dominated by women – a grandmother he feared, and a mother he adored. Jean de la Ville de Mirmont was a Bordelais and had sat on the same bench as Mauriac in the Faculté des Lettres. His father was an eminent Latin scholar, who enjoyed teasing the pupils of the Jesuits when they came up for examination, and Jean had been educated at the lycée. He and François were only casual acquaintances in Bordeaux, but they met again on the 'Boul' Mich' ' and were for a time inseparable. When they were not walking the streets till 3 a.m. they were chatting round the fire in Jean de la Ville's apartment in the rue du Bac, exchanging their 'senseless ambitions and absurd enthusiasms'.[1] Mauriac remembered his friend's 'strange and gently nasal voice', and the smoke from endless cigarettes curling round his face. It was weather to keep one indoors:

> Paris has been cold these last days with its sky of unpolished glass, the clear *grisaille* of the great boulevards and the sharp clip-clop of the horses' hooves on the wooden paving. It has been humid, as it is today; the night falls early, and the gas jets have a transparent halo.[1]

Other friends would join them for the reading aloud of poetry – a pastime of which the French never seem to tire. Jean de la Ville was himself a poet, and a line of his, not included in *l'Horizon chimérique*:

> *La mer des soirs d'été s'effeuille sur le sable*

haunted Mauriac, like the physical presence of its author. It was he who found the title for *Les Mains jointes*, and wrote to Mauriac after reading Barrès' avuncular encomium:

> Barrès counts on your reason and your good sense but I count even more on something else. Whatever he hopes from your 'four seasons', whatever we all of us hope for, I think I shall never like anything you write more than these *Mains jointes* that I have seen clasped in our obscure friendship – these verses that you read to me in a hotel bedroom.[3]

In 1911 they spent the Easter holidays together in the *Landes*, where Jean de la Ville amused Mauriac's young nephews and nieces by pretending to be a savage, and building huts among the pines. The children accepted him as one of themselves because he understood their secrets, and because the poetry which was his native element 'had

---

[1] *D'autres et moi*, 51.

[2] Letter from Jean de la Ville de Mirmont to Louis Piéchaud. Ibid.

[3] *D'autres et moi*, 53.

preserved in him intact the grace of childhood'.[1]

Mauriac's other intimate, André Lafon − perhaps the closest he ever had − was also a poet. Never a year went by that Mauriac did not read *La Maison pauvre* with its line 'la route allonge un geste pâle' evoking any landscape in France that came to mind. Lafon's novel, *l'Enfant Gilles*, awarded the first 'Grand Prix du Roman' by the Académie française in 1912, told something of his story and much of his character. He was of humble parentage in the Gironde, where his father was secretary to the mayor of Blaye. He had the same attachment to his native soil as François Mauriac, and could not understand how François could burn the midnight oil in Paris when he might have been sitting on the terrace at Malagar. As an usher at the college of Sainte-Croix-de-Neuilly he felt an exile. Like Mauriac himself, he could not escape the deeper memories of childhood, and did not wish to do so. Their friendship was unclouded for five precious years, and Mauriac treasured it, as he treasured few others, until the end of his life. It echoes, memorably, in *La Vie et la Mort d'un Poète*, and in *Galigaï*, one of the last novels he was to write. He described Lafon as 'une âme franciscaine à l 'état pur', and Lafon compared their friendship to 'a clear window in the long corridor of my solitude.'

Lafon was acquainted with Mauriac's verse. Calling on him one afternoor, he found Jean de la Ville leaning up against the mantelpiece and reciting Baudelaire. With Robert Vallery-Radot − who was later to become the intimate of Georges Bernanos − and others of a similar way of thinking, he and François collaborated in a Catholic literary review, *Les Cahiers de l'Amitié de France*. This was edited by a professor at Grenoble, Georges Dumesnil, who also had a house at Lassagne in Gascony. Here they would all meet in the *grandes vacances*. Dunesnil did not moderate either his language or his laughter, to which the rafters echoed in that wide salon with its two Cézannes, and the poultry pecking at the crumbs below the table. Mauriac and Lafon were lodged in a peasant's house at the bottom of the garden, 'full of old furniture, warming pans emblazoned with the family arms, and rustic lamps'[2] which reminded Mauriac of the seven Wise Virgins.

The *Cahiers* were treated with indifference or disdain by certain pontiffs − Léon Daudet and Paul Claudel − who might have been expected to sympathise with its aims. Only Francis Jammes recognized the group as disciples worthy of his patronage. Jammes was a rather ostentatious convert to Catholicism, who had shared the admiration of Barrès for *Les Mains jointes*. Mauriac preferred his earlier poems which

---

[1] Ibid.

[2] *La Vie et la Mort d'un Poète. O.C. IV*, 381.

were more vaguely religious, and in the following year he paid him a visit at Orthez with André Lafon. It was late in the evening when they arrived. The house appeared to be asleep in the moonlight, and Jammes, patriarchal with his flowing white beard, read aloud to them from his *Georgiques chrétiennes*. They found it hard to imagine a poet more greedy for admiration or more famished for want of an audience. His vanity was fed by his solitude. 'I am perfectly aware of my place in French literature; it is the first.'

Lafon twice visited Malagar after the meetings at Lassagne; he and Mauriac also made two retreats at the Saulchoir, the French Dominican novitiate then exiled to Belgium by the anti-clerical laws. Like so many young men at that time, he had lost his religious faith through a reading of Renan's *Vie de Jésus*, and then recovered it – to the disadvantage of his second novel which was spoilt by the wish to edify. A natural contemplative, he became increasingly withdrawn, even from his closest friends, giving an impression of controlled force and of a calm not easily achieved. 'People like us' he had written to Mauriac 'ought to get over our youth' – and in the case of André Lafon circumstances were tragically to complete the cure.

The *grandes vacances* of 1910 were spent with the Vallery-Radots at Avallon, and then in Italy. They took the opportunity, on the way, to call on Anna de Noailles, who was eager – or at least ready – to receive a young poet who had been praised to the skies by Barrès. But Mauriac appeared too submissive to Barrès' sensible advice for a woman whose romanticism knew no bounds. Anna de Noailles, considerable poet though she was, knew only one prayer: 'Levez-vous, orages désirés!' For Mauriac the 'orages' might, or might not, be 'désirés', and they would rise without solicitation. This was the world of the *salons littéraires*, particularly that of Mme Alphonse Daudet in the rue Bellechasse, where Mauriac was now received. Here the *chers maîtres* would regularly gather – Maurice Barrès, Jules Lemaitre and Léon Daudet. They were anti-Dreyfusards to a man, but this had not prevented a quarrel between Daudet and Lemaitre, now reconciled under those flattering chandeliers. Daudet was a voracious *bon vivant*, as well as an intransigent royalist, and Mauriac remembered how Anna de Noailles 'showed the white of her eyes' as she looked up at the broad landscape of his face and exclaimed 'Ah! Léon!' It was here too that he met Jean Cocteau, with his 'slender hands and his slight squint'; the frivolous darling of the *avant-garde* with one foot on the parquet floor of the Establishment, and reciting

> *Mes frères de Paris, notre divin royaume*
> *Rayonne autour de la place Vendôme...*

47

They took to each other at first sight. 'Mauriac' wrote Cocteau 'had the eye of a young colt below his temple. Gay, naive, petulant, sly, adorable Mauriac.' Mauriac was not quite sure about the 'sly', but that people either liked him very much or disliked him just as strongly was a fact of life to which he was reconciled.

But how did he appear to others outside the magic circle of friendship and precocious celebrity? There was the abbé Desgranges, with whom he had made a retreat at the Trappist monastery of Notre-Dame-de-Sept-Fonds. When Desgranges met Mauriac again, he seemed to think that his life, too, could do with a change.

> I had a talk this morning with François Mauriac, all radiant with his fresh glory; a little in thrall to the capricious advances of M. Barrès and the Countess Mathieu de Noailles, thinking how he can justify his premature reputation, produce something rare from his pen, and one day enter the Académie. Here is a rich young man on the road to fame, and I don't envy him in the least.'[1]

Mauriac admitted the heavy price he had to pay for concealing his true nature 'by nonchalance, unconscious calculation, surrender to easy pleasures, and above all by the lack of intellectual rigour.'[2] He was certainly thinking of something new to justify a slender reputation, and was at work on a second volume of verse, *Adieu à l'adolescence*, and his first novel, *L'Enfant chargé de chaînes*. The early chapters of this were written in 1909, but the book did not appear in the *Mercure de France* until 1912. It was published by Grasset in 1913. The 'chains' in question were the temperament, heredity, and milieu of the hero, and, needless to add, the author. Since Mauriac, in prefacing an illustrated edition of the novel in 1929, described the hero as 'ridiculous', it may be deduced that he was looking back on his *début* with derision. But even when he regarded it at close quarters there was no lack of self-criticism. Jean-Paul, oscillating between the Sillon and Montmartre, and at one point tempted to suicide, is a spineless and introspective character. His life is polarised between Paris and Guyenne, good books and good intentions, liturgical piety and the spasmodic zeal for a social apostolate. The novel explains, as Mauriac does not explain elsewhere, why his attachment to the Sillon was so fickle. The young bourgeois with literary aspirations was ill at ease in that classless clientele, just as they were uncomfortable with him. There is no reason to take as autobiographical the scene in which Jean-Paul rebuffs the artisan who seeks his friendship, and the later scene where the rebuff is not forgiven.

---

[1] *Carnets Intimes.*

[2] *Ecrits Intimes.*

Nor need one conclude that Marc Sangnier – the Jérôme Servet of the novel – regarded Mauriac as an insidious element in his movement. But the impression is clear that as the movement grew, its spontaneity became stifled by its machinery. Mauriac was never a man for movements. His destiny was to walk alone, although the prospect of a happy marriage adumbrates the last pages of the book. For the rest, it shows no sign whatever of the novelist he was later to become.

He did not, it seems, disown the poems of *Adieu à l'adolescence*[1] since they were republished in the year of his death. The mood is similar to that of *Les Mains jointes*, and the hands are still intermittently joined in a prayer which is half an introspection. Regret and reverie and reminiscence are carried on the smooth Alexandrine prosody. The poems have much accomplishment, although their languorous romanticism enervates after a little. The head has not yet come to the rescue of a heart sensitive and unsatisfied. For all the poet's eagerness to escape the 'bitter-sweet honey of Guyenne', he knows that he is the 'prisonnier d'une enfance trop douce', and he returns with an invincible nostalgia to the

> *après-midis lourds et grinçants de cigales,*
> *Quand mon front, caressé de paix familiale,*
> *Penchait sur les cahiers des devoirs de vacances . . .*

He evokes

> *les soirs de ma douzième année*

and his mother saying the family prayers in the victoria so that the children shall be sooner in bed; and how, when they were finished, he would exclaim

> *Voici le jour des prix et la fin de l'année.*

Here is the badly tuned piano in the chalet, and the chequered sunshine of the *grandes vacances*, when the sand dunes were wreathed in mist, and the pines loomed out of it

> *fantômes blessés*
> *Comme des amitiés et des amours passés.*

There is tender memory for the young lives cut short by tuberculosis; and once again he walks with his school-fellows along the quays in a crocodile:

> *Collégiens pensifs, aux songes imprécis.*

[1] *O.C. VI.*

The dreams are still imprecise, in spite of Maurice Barrès to whom he dedicates this *Adieu* to his 'grave adolescence', and the delights of friendship, and the promise of fulfilled ambition. Reality has not yet broken in to give them substance, and he knows it.

> *Ah! le coeur n'est pas mort de ton adolescence.*
> *Veux-tu donc le traîner toujours, comme une croix?*

His forehead still feels the imprint of

> *anciens baisers –*
> *Et voici que reflue, en ton coeur apaisé,*
> *La pieuse et souffrante humilité des choses.*

But when he returns to Bordeaux he is conscious that the room he slept in as a child knows him no longer. Only the pervasive, and perhaps reproachful, influence of his mother, and echoes of the 'Moonlight Sonata' which she had played for him, reach him beyond the clatter of *fiacres* in the rue Vaneau.

> *Que la simple grandeur de cette âme chrétienne*
> *Fasse dans notre coeur l'amour silencieux.*

Anyone comparing *l'Adieu à l'adolescence* with *l'Enfant chargé de chaînes* might well have prophesied that Mauriac's future lay with poetry rather than fiction. The title of the verses was premature, to say the least; he never said good-bye to his adolescence, and his last completed novel, *Un Adolescent d'autrefois*, proved that time had deepened, but in no way distorted, his vision.

Meanwhile, however, a mentor was at hand to stiffen his intellectual backbone. Jacques Rivière was born in Bordeaux, where his father was a doctor and a professor at the Faculty of Medicine. He was a year younger than Mauriac, and in their student days they hardly knew each other. But he became a close friend of André Lacaze, who wrote of his gift for friendship, an appetite for sensation which he owed to Gide – the 'fruit plein de saveur sur des lèvres pleines de desirs' – and also his dogmatism and intolerance. His masters were Descartes, Racine, Marivaux and Ingres – 'that is to say, those who refuse the shadows'. He reminded Lacaze of an 'inquisitor who exercised a fine choice in his victims', and Mauriac was understandably nervous of being introduced to him.

They met, however, though no more than casually, when Rivière was studying at the Sorbonne, and when he afterwards became secretary of the newly launched *Nouvelle Revue Française*. This was a capital date in the history of French literature, and Mauriac was quick to realise its importance. Here was a movement of minds, fastidious, critical, and sincere, altogether more serious than the academicism of the

Revue des Deux Mondes and the eclecticism of the *Mercure de France*.
The minds – Jacques Copeau, Jean Schlumberger, André Gide, and
Rivière himself – did not all think alike, but they thought, so to speak,
on the same level. A comparison with T.S. Eliot's *Criterion* immediately
springs to mind, and indeed criteria were what they were after. Their
admirations included Maurras and Péguy, Claudel and Romain Rolland,
Rimbaud and Mallarmé. For the moment they took little notice of
Mauriac, but this was the company he longed to keep, and he was eager
to be judged by them. The ambition did not, however, prevent him
teasing Rivière by praising Massenet's *Werther* at the expense of
Debussy's *Pelléas and Mélisande* – for Rivière's criticism was directed
to music and painting as well as to literature. A mutual acquaintance
of theirs did much to estrange them, and Rivière, on Mauriac's own
admission, regarded him as 'a young bourgeois poseur, worldly, and
without any real talent.'[1] But Rivière's development and deviations
were to bring them together before many years had passed.

His closest friend was his brother-in-law, Alain-Fournier, author of a
single masterpiece, *Le Grand Meaulnes*. Mauriac, in reply to a questionnaire about what the young were then reading, had permitted himself
some hasty words about Renan whom he admitted never to have read.
'We find this bogus fellow Renan a bore!' Fournier published a sharp
note in *Paris-Journal*:

> The poetry of M. François Mauriac is feverish, but sensitive. . .
> the work of a rich and highly intelligent child who never gets
> dirty when he is playing . . . and goes to Mass every Sunday. The
> young people of today do not read only the good authors quoted
> by M. François Mauriac. . . . They have spent an anxious, an
> unhappy, and often a poverty-stricken adolescence, for they are
> not all of them rich, and not all of them believers. 'The artist'
> says M. Mauriac 'should amass in the shade of his adolescence a
> treasury of ineffable memories.' What answer has M. François
> Mauriac for the young people who will say to him: 'Our memo-
> ries are not ineffable'?

Rivière admired the same authors as Mauriac – Barrès, Jammes, and
Claudel; nevertheless he confessed himself irritated by Maurras' call to
'order and discipline', and Mauriac admitted that he accepted too
readily certain formulas with which Barrès and Maurras were challenging
the 'romantic agony'. His attachment to these was not, however, as
unquestioning as it once had been. In opposition to the 'gendarmes of
tradition' there lurked an adversary too evasive for their frontal tactics.

[1] *Le Figaro*, 16 March 1940.

The relation of André Gide to the Catholics who deemed him ripe for
conversion because they had been converted themselves is matter for a
study in itself. Mauriac was not a convert, and his relations with Gide
were correspondingly easier. 'Ever since my adolescence' he was to
write to him in 1917 'you were the secret master whose prestige I tried
to resist up to a certain point, because I was subject to another discipline.'[1] In *La Revue Hebdomadaire* (April 1912) he published a
favourable criticism of Gide's *Le Retour de l'Enfant Prodigue*, but put
his finger on an evident deformation of the parable. 'I cannot believe
that God looked with favour on this tired prodigal who himself leads
his young brother out on to the steps of the house, and incites him to
every forbidden pleasure.'[2] Gide had politely refuted the criticism,
but the equivocation was characteristic, not only of Gide himself but of
'the fiend that lies like truth'. Equivocal in another sense, and also
characteristic, was Mauriac's attachment to Gide. In the same letter
he writes: 'You have often troubled me, but I have received from you
nothing but good, if it is a good thing to love life better than I loved
it before I knew you.'[3]

3

To a young Englishman, many years later, Mauriac exclaimed – almost,
it seemed, with envy: 'Pour un jeune homme de votre âge la femme
doit être quelque chose de *merveilleux!*' It is easy to recapture the
emphasis in that broken voice of his, so much more memorable than
voices which are still intact. He had a sentimental misadventure in 1911,
and this was no doubt the reason why he did little work. Then in 1912,
at la Tresne, near Bordeaux, he met Jeanne Lafont in the house of a
friend. Her father was a figure of some importance in the financial
world; polytechnician, treasurer-general of the Gironde, formerly a
director of the Banque d'Algérie, and Regent of the Banque de France.
No one was better qualified to excite Mauriac's contempt, and the distrust was mutual. Hearing that a young poet, far from penniless, to be
sure, but sublimely indifferent to the vacillations of the Bourse, wished
to marry his daughter, he summoned Mauriac before him. Already
warned of a refusal, Mauriac appeared for a painful interview. M. Lafont
asked him if he expected to become a member of the Académie
française, and Mauriac, with irony on the tip of his tongue, replied that
since the Académie had to find forty members out of each generation

[1] *Cahiers André Gide II*, 62.

[2] Ibid.

[3] Ibid.

of writers, it was impossible that such an honour should escape him.
M. Lafont returned the irony with a smile. A long battle of wills and
wits ensued, of which echoes may be caught in *Génitrix* and *Le Noeud
de Vipères*. At last, on the 3rd June 1913, the marriage took place at
Talence, the Lafont property outside Bordeaux: and the honeymoon
was spent at Bellagio.

An early portrait by Jacques-Emile Blanche shows Jeanne Mauriac
as a young woman of considerable beauty; and many years later an
observer was to write of her 'Leonardesque smile'.[1] She was also
possessed of sharp intelligence and decisive character. For nearly sixty
years her dignity was the admiration of all who knew her. She with-
stood, and to some degree, no doubt, assuaged, the anxieties of her
husband. She is said to have declared that, when François was with
her, she never knew a moment of boredom. The tribute implied its
corollary, that neither did he. She was the strong centre of an
exceptionally happy family which finds no reflection whatever in the
novels she so industriously typed from François' manuscripts or dictation.
André Lafon was among those who knew her at the time of her
marriage; he divined what François was to confirm later to his son: 'A
heart so absolutely tender and faithful, one of the very best that I
have known.'[2]

They set up house, modestly enough, at 89 rue de la Pompe in the
16th arrondissement. The apartment later accommodated a small
'cagibi' — or 'den' — where François could work. In April 1914 Claude
Mauriac was born; and in June of that year *La Robe prétexte* was
published by Grasset. Mauriac hesitated to include this among his
Collected Works, and only did so to show its inferiority to what he was
presently to achieve. It is easy to understand his reluctance and the
distaste with which he looked back upon the book. *La Robe prétexte*
takes its title from the white, purple-edged tunic which the Roman
boys discarded when they emerged from adolescence. Its narrative
structure is very slight; the author launches himself upon a stream of
reminiscence, interesting for what it tells us about Mauriac at the age of
transition, but giving little indication of the novelist who had not yet
discovered his power. The setting is Bordeaux, the Château Lange, and
the college of Grand-Lebrun. Certain family relationships are changed.
The narrator's father, a painter, had died in Tahiti, and his mother has
also died from tuberculosis. He is brought up by his grandmother, a
portrait drawn from life down to the last detail, not without a controlled ferocity. Here is the matriarch of a provincial bourgeoisie — 'the

---

[1] Robert de Saint-Jean: *Journal d'un Journaliste* (1973).

[2] *Le Temps Immobile*, 540.

stiffest and most self-satisfied in France' — with a Sister always in attendance whose 'eyelids, habitually lowered, gave one half a glimpse of an eye round and inexpressive, like that of a cautious hen.' In the chapel they knelt on padded *prie-dieux*, while the boy had to be content with the straw-bottomed variety which left unsightly marks on his bare knees. Here, too, is the uncle — a brasher version of 'Oncle Louis', drifting in from the casinos of Aix-les-Bains; and Octavie, the faithful servant, is given her real name, like the rue Vital-Carles, which is the family's address in Bordeaux.

Grand-Lebrun is easily recognizable, with the Corpus Christi processions, and the invocations to 'Notre-Dame du Bachot' before the examinations, and the crown of gold paper on the head of the successful candidates, and the mutually hostile flags of the Pope and the Republic, and the repellent Alsatian professor. As for marriage, we learn from 'grand' mère' that 'one marries one's girls how one wants to and when one wants to'. Surrounded though she is by deferential clergy, her greed is equal to her devotion; and we learn, too, that the wine trade is the only respectable commerce, and that families are to be ranked according to the quality of their vineyards. The caricatures in *Le Pèlerin* show the 'masonic aprons wrapped around the ridiculous bellies' of obese anti-clericals. There are glimpses of the port where the huge cranes remind the narrator of 'Indian elephants'; and the narrator himself is simply a self-portrait drawn without indulgence. We see him as a child sleeping with his hands modestly folded on his chest; as a boy starting to read a book, like one 'setting out on a long voyage', and falling in calf-love with his cousin; as an adolescent fleeing the advances of a dancer from the Paris opera, and then, having second thoughts on the subject, recalled to Bordeaux by the death of his grandmother. The 'robe prétexte' has fallen from his shoulders; his cousin no longer responds to his doggerel verse and moonlight raptures; the château is put up for sale; he is alone with his fastidious and troubled purity and his vague ambitions. The book is not unreadable because its style is so graceful and fluent — despite Mauriac's disclaimer — and its memories so vivid and precise; but they have not been transformed into what can properly be described as fiction. It is fair to recall, however, that Mauriac's former professor, Fortunat Strowski, who was nothing if not an *esprit critique*, professed and published a warm admiration for the novel.[1] He knew, better than most reviewers, the world about which Mauriac was writing.

Europe was now dancing to its near destruction, with Yvette Guilbert miming the passion of Christ with her belly, and the Ballets Russes

---

[1] *La Liberté du Sud-Ouest*, 18 June 1914.

casting their spell over *tout Paris*. But in 1914 Nijinsky was no longer there to leap through the window into the shadows, and for many who had waited for that yearly miracle his absence came to seem like a foreshadowing of the 'great eclipse'. Mauriac's ear was not attuned to the adventurous discords of 'Les Six'; he preferred to recognize in Schumann and Beethoven — Mozart was a later discovery — 'saints and martyrs who had not found their God'.[1] When the concert or the play was over, and the last café had let down its shutters, he could watch the dawn come up over Les Halles with its 'mountains of pink carrots and fresh lettuces';[2] or, by day, observe the faces in the métro, and contrast the wretched lodgings of the poor with the luxury of the famous restaurants and the 'fauna' who frequented them. A blistering phrase of Léon Bloy put the Barrésien 'culte du moi' and the Maurrasian call to order in a sober perspective. 'I am aware of all the reasonable arguments that virtuous people employ to console themselves for the temporal reprobation of three quarters of mankind.'[3] Then it was that Mauriac remembered his peasant forbears, and felt that, in him, something of their character lived on. His great-grandmother had read the novels of Dumas by the light of a resin candle stuck into the hearth, and his great-grandfather who bought Malagar reminded him of a moralising peasant out of Walter Scott. Charles Caillard dined with Mauriac in Bordeaux on his way to Spain where he was to enter a Trappist monastery, and to die so soon afterwards, remote from the distant rumours of war. Mauriac still believed, however, with Michelet, and others of his own generation, that 'France would declare peace to the world'. Few suspected, in that hectic and halcyon summer, that a different declaration was at hand.

---

[1] *Journal d'un Homme de 30 ans. O.C. IV*, 222.

[2] Ibid.

[3] *Le Désespéré.*

HORS DE COMBAT

1

On the 2 August 1914 Mauriac saw a young peasant in tears on top of the slopes above Malagar. He might have stood for all the 'bataillons sacrés' which Mauriac himself was unable to join. Barrès used to say that 'servir' was the most beautiful word in the French language. François Mauriac would have been glad to serve as so many of his friends were doing, but the effects of the pleurisy which had brought him near to death made him unfit for military service. Meanwhile Paul Claudel, passing through Bordeaux, assured him that the war would be over by November; and when November came and went, Mauriac enlisted, with Jean Cocteau and others, in the Red Cross, under the direction of Etienne de Beaumont. France was mobilising not only for war, but for suffering. An unaccustomed murmur of prayer went up from the churches, as the women trooped to the early masses and lit their votive candles. It was the 'finest hour' for the militants of the Action Française, and Mauriac felt closer to Maurras than he had felt before. The assassination of Jaurès, the socialist tribune, and the scandalous acquittal of Madame Caillaux on the charge of murdering her husband, showed the parliamentary republic in a squalid light. As Mauriac followed, day by day, the pitiless analyses of Maurras, the seeds of his future adhesion to de Gaulle were falling on fruitful soil. Awaiting further instructions, he plunged into Dostoievsky's *The Possessed* and Tolstoy's *War and Peace*. Nietzsche's prophecy was being fulfilled to the letter; 'the intellectual youth of France, now dying so bravely, has been melted up between those strong arms',[1] and God had given way to 'a delirious polytechnician, hidden behind his spectacles, whose problem is to kill the greatest number of people in the shortest possible time.'[2]

André Lafon, waiting to be called up, was looking after wounded German prisoners at Blaye. In November he was mobilised, and in March (1915) he snatched an hour of leave to visit Mauriac at Malagar. It was a Sunday, and there were clouds scudding over the low hills.

[1] *Journal d'un homme de trente ans. O.C. IV, 226.*
[2] Ibid.

Lafon wanted – perhaps for the last time – to breathe the odour of the salon where he and François had so often talked. They talked again – of that afternoon, perhaps, in the gardens of Versailles when Lafon had pressed a tuft of lilac blossom to his two cheeks, and of their long walks in the *pays Basque* during the torrid summer of 1911. André had given François a little gold cross bought in Saumur, observing that it had 'perhaps belonged to Eugénie Grandet' – although Rousseau and Dostoievsky had now become his favourite reading. Two months later he lay dead of scarlatina in a military hospital in Bordeaux, and Mauriac, now enrolled in the Red Cross, was not there to stand beside his grave.

In 1913 Jean de la Ville de Mirmont had moved to an apartment on the Ile Saint-Louis where, incidentally, he threw his mistress out of the window. Mauriac was engaged to be married, and accused him of changing his friends at the same time as he changed his address. Their intimacy cooled until, just before the outbreak of war, he visited Mauriac in the rue de la Pompe. They promised to see each other in the autumn, and it was the fault of neither that the promise was not kept. Jean de la Ville was killed on the Chemin des Dames, leaving his verse to be immortalised by Fauré's settings. Death had surprised him in the same attitude as Péguy: 'with his head raised and his rifle to the front, ready to leap forward.' With the death of Jean de la Ville and André Lafon a certain quality of friendship evaporated from Mauriac's life, and nothing ever quite replaced it.

> I have no visual memory and retain practically nothing of my travels, but I remember voices so clearly that I seem to hear them. I only need to read a verse of André Lafon or Jean de la Ville de Mirmont, both of them returned to dust now so many years ago, to recover their slightest inflexions, and even their silences when they were getting back their breath. They will be alive for so long as I am there to listen to them.[1]

Of André Lafon he wrote in a preface to a new edition of *La Vie et la Mort d'un Poète:*[2]

> Of the friends that I have lost, André Lafon is the one that I have lost the least: this absent one is always there. Perhaps he glides in the wake of my guardian angel. 'I know him' he says to the angel 'the two of us will not be too many'.[3]

---

[1] *Le Figaro,* 4 July 1949.

[2] *O.C. IV,* 354.

[3] *Le Quotidien,* 6 June 1933.

They would certainly not have been. In the difficult years that lay ahead, the memory of Lafon may well have counteracted other influences, as dubious as they seemed to be delightful. When Mauriac had been elected to the Académie française and after the publication of *La Vie et la Mort d'un Poète,* Fortunat Strowski published an article on the two friends. 'I have seen them both once again; the one alive, and now immortal; the other dead and now brought back to life.'

Stationed at Châlons-sur-Marne in July 1915, Mauriac had seen – if not at the closest quarters – what Nietzsche was talking about. The credulous anti-clericalism of his medical superiors was a further cause of depression. What could a young writer who claimed Barrès as his master say to a surgeon whose master was the chief specialist of 'the *rectum* and the *anus*'? Where Mauriac saw everything in the light of his religion, there was another man from a similar background and suffering from the same Jansenist *régime,* who could only vomit what Mauriac was able to digest. The guns were silent during this Holy Week making 'less noise than the larks over the fields'.[1] Mauriac gave much thought to his family; would he see an image of himself in his son, as he selfishly hoped and unselfishly feared?

By the summer of 1916 he was inhabiting a dug-out at Ravin de Placy, cheek by jowl with a repellent middle-aged man 'for whom Greece and Rome, the Middle Ages and the Renaissance, and all the books that had ever been written amounted to nothing more than a series of obscene vignettes.'[2] Later he had the dug-out to himself and admitted that all his misery came from the 'obligation to leave his room'. The mosquitoes swarmed in what was little more than a box where he had not the space to stretch his legs, and the rain fell on the sheet-iron roof. The daily traipse of the infantry up to the front line was like 'the continual carting of the condemned to execution.'[3] Robert Vallery-Radot, slightly wounded, was recovered by Mauriac's brother-in-law, and the presence of a Dominican among the Red Cross personnel helped to restore the security of belief, if not the peace of mind. For here, all around him, was matter for sombre introspection. 'We carry within ourselves a maniac and a madman, several maniacs and several madmen, that we let loose in the playground of our imagination.'[4]

Jeanne Mauriac's family had a country house at Vémars, near Paris, in the valley of the Oise. Here François spent a short leave and then, on the 3rd December (1916) sailed on the *Bretagne* for Salonika.

[1] *Journal d'un homme de trente ans. O.C. IV,* 229.

[2] Ibid., 229.

[3] Ibid., 230.

[4] Ibid., 231.

Before embarking at Marseilles he climbed the hill to the shrine of Notre-Dame-de-la-Garde, its walls plastered with votive tablets, and returned with a manual of prayers which was rarely far from his side. The tedium of the voyage was alleviated by discussions on Pascal with the ship's doctor, and by exercises in case of a torpedo attack. These were quite useless since the passengers were warned by the captain that the ship would sink in two minutes. At Salonika Mauriac was lodged in the Villa Alatini, which had been given over to the Red Cross, and found himself fairly comfortable in a room embellished with Macedonian pottery and coloured hangings. There was a chapel in the house, and a Sister of St Vincent-de-Paul who seemed to think Mauriac in danger of losing his soul. It was a danger to which he was never insensible, but he wished she would not knock at his door so persistently to remind him of it. The Germans had now captured Bucharest, and were ready to talk peace. It was a critical moment, and Mauriac noted: 'If we lose the war, it will be because we have not produced a man. A hundred years of democracy have destroyed all the *élites*. We are obliged to crown Briand as a genius.'[1] The individualist in Mauriac was attracted by Maurras, but Maurras had tied the Church to a party, and the Sillonistes, with whom his heart still beat, albeit faintly, were naturally exasperated when an atheist and positivist took them to task. Mauriac was too much of a child of his milieu to pay the price of equality, for it was the cult of equality — as he saw it — which had deprived France of effective leadership. Fortunately Clemenceau was in the wings, still waiting for his cue.

Mauriac remained in Salonika, gripped by fever, till March 1917, when he was invalided home on the *André-Lebon*. His last memory of the place was of the queues waiting outside the closed brothels on a Sunday, and the poor singing and perfunctory sermon he had listened to in the morning.

2

On reaching France he went straight to Bordeaux; spent a fortnight in convalescence at Arcachon; and by the end of May was alone with his mother at Malagar. The white carnations and syringa were in flower, and cockchafers falling from the leaves on to the mown grass. The crickets were chirping and the butterflies fluttering around. Over the vines one saw the back of a patient ox and the white shirt of the drover. At Saint-Symphorien the long bamboos and the premature mushrooms sprang up overnight from the damp moss. But where

[1] Ibid., 234.

another writer, returning to his roots, would have planted them even deeper, for Mauriac Paris was inevitable – and alluring. He went back there in June, physically restored but spiritually sick. His diary for the next year is a chronicle of profound malaise, perplexing and even perverse in one who had every reason to be satisfied with the way his life was going – marriage, fatherhood, and *Les Mains jointes.* There is more than a hint here of the crisis which was to gather and come to a head ten years later:

> *9 June*: Paris. Temptations. Passions go on velvet feet in the jungle. Huge beasts. Perfume of sensuality.
> *18 July*: Must free our body of desire.
> *28 Jan* (1917): My son Claude to keep me pure.
> *2 March*: Paris is disgusting. 'Great ladies', pederasts, lesbians, everyone is procuring for somebody else.[1]

Behind these jaundiced jottings social and literary contacts were renewed, and a pattern of life established which was not to vary for some time to come. He lunched with Barrès who told him that German gold in France was a greater menace to the country than German guns. They walked from Barrès' house in Neuilly to the Porte Maillot and back again. But Mauriac was now sensitive to Barrès' limitations. His nationalism was his strength and also his weakness. He showed Mauriac a lithograph of himself as an adolescent:

> the fine hair of Bonaparte, long and rather untidy, reveals a child, equally foreign to the most trifling and the most important worldly disciplines – the social and moral laws. . .Sensuality in the mouth, and asceticism on all the rest of the face. . .For the young Barrès Catholicism was an instrument of personal culture; for the Barrès of today it has become an instrument of French culture.[2]

For François Mauriac it was never anything but an instrument of personal salvation – and it generally hurt.

He now sat for his portrait to Jacques-Emile Blanche; visited Maurice Denis in his studio at St Germain, where the painter was at work on an 'Annunciation'; and listened to Cocteau reading *Le Cap de Bonne Espérance.* Cocteau was 'reduced to playing the genius in front of society, or in front of Picasso who doesn't care a damn for it.'[3] Mauriac was now swimming in fresh salons, although they did not contain particularly

[1] Ibid. (original edition).
[2] Ibid., *O.C. IV*, 244-5.
[3] Ibid., 244.

fresh water. He was constantly at Madame Mühlfeld's, where André Gide seemed like 'an anxious priest who would rather go to confession himself than hear the confessions of other people';[1] and at Madame Alphonse Daudet's where, in February 1918, he met Proust for the first time: 'with his very high collar, and the pupils of his eyes dilated, as it seemed, by drugs.'[2] In the previous September he and his wife had been staying with Blanche at Offranville in Normandy. Blanche had made a simple farmhouse out of the brick and flint of a Louis XIV building, and he and Mauriac set about writing a play together, which came to nothing. At other times, they would listen to Gaby Deslys at the Casino de Paris, and watch the allied flags painted on the buttocks of the chorus.

On the 31st January 1918 bombs fell on Paris, the overture to Ludendorff's last offensive. The children – for Jeanne Mauriac had given birth to a daughter, Claire – were sent down to the basement – and François, with many others, rather shamefully besieged the confessionals. He was remembering, no doubt, a sermon by the Dominican preacher, Père Sertillanges, at Saint-Etienne-du-Mont. Sertillanges had recognized him among the congregation, and what he said seemed to be directed at him. Mauriac wondered whether the head of the Venus of Milo would, even now, have joined her arms in the dust; and wondered, too, now that Georges Mandel was private secretary to Clemenceau, whether 'France would once again become the great conservative and reactionary force in the world'.[3] With the 'tiger' at large this was highly improbable. The nocturnal bombardments continued through March; and the nerves of Paris, where life – and what passed for love – had gone on much as usual, were so upset that Madame Mühlfeld was obliged to cancel a luncheon party. Mauriac spent Easter at Bordeaux:

> Silent prayers in the churches. . . Walked alone by the quays. . Shreds of the past; like rotting pontoons. Ships wrecked in the basin of the river.[4]

At Malagar the poplars, just putting forth their leaves, reminded him of 'adolescent knights in their new armour'.[5] He was thinking of his next novel. The first volume of *Du côté de chez Swann* must not be taken as a model, but as a stimulant for everything he had to say.

By the end of May Rheims and Soissons fell to the German advance,

[1] Ibid., 248.
[2] Ibid.
[3] Ibid.
[4] Ibid., 250.
[5] Ibid.

and the railway line between Paris and Châlons was threatened. Clemenceau might be an 'old pimp', but he was indomitable. On the 1st June the march on Paris had begun, and a dangerous offensive was developing between Noyon and Montidier. Then the tide turned, and the certain presentiment of victory sweetened the summer at Malagar. In September Mauriac received a letter from the young Henri de Montherlant, whom he had never met: 'You are building an arch so that certain ways of feeling may be sure of survival in the land that lies ahead.'[1] Later in the month the Mauriacs were at Salies-de-Béarn with Claude who was unwell. In Bordeaux they saw a good deal of Claudel; and Mauriac was introduced to Count Albert de Mun, who wanted to engage him as his secretary. Every afternoon, from the church of Notre-Dame, the cry went up: 'Sauvez la France, sauvez la France'; and when the Armistice came in November, Claudel was unabashed by his former prophecy: 'Well, you see, the war was over in November, as I said it would be.' François wrote in his diary:

> The war is ending on a picture postcard where we see the French re-entering Metz and Strasbourg. . .Frightening absence of God in the triumphal cries of Clemenceau.[2]

It was through no fault of his own that Mauriac ended the war as he had begun it — as an *homme de lettres*.

[1] Ibid., 255.
[2] Ibid.

CELEBRITY

1

The provincial had by now seen enough to appreciate the difference between Paris and the provinces, and he summarised it in a pithy essay.[1] Paris was a thickly populated solitude; a provincial city was a desert where a man could not be alone. The provinces were certainly pharisaical, but they still believed in good and evil, and the obstacles they set up against your passions created the situations which might be useful to the novelist. Paris, on the contrary, was a place where Phaedra seduces Hippolytus every day, and Theseus himself doesn't care a damn about it.' Paris creamed off the talents of the provinces, but not their virtues. It was a city of individuals — of individuals who met in bed — while in a provincial city the family grew where it stood, pushing out its branches like a great tree. But the façade which presented no cracks to the eye concealed ferocious rivalries. Decrepit relatives appeared on the more solemn gastronomic occasions, their presence excused on the grounds that they were members of the family. In Paris the world was watching you — more often than not with a hostile gaze — but in the country you were only looking at yourself. Nevertheless the whole of romantic literature was the work of embittered provincials, and the ambitions stifled in the provinces were fulfilled on the metropolitan stage of politics and commerce. Of love, also, for Paris was an 'indefatigable accomplice', where no subject of conversation was prohibited, and where 'a woman who got talked about' was not regarded as beyond the pale. Every moment of recollection was the result of a crucial choice, for the opportunity was always at hand to do something else. Nothing even obliged you to go to bed. But although life in the provinces was cemented by a network of lies, which death itself could not disentangle, Mauriac could never wholly detach himself from its rather plodding good sense, its unchanging rhythm, and the occasional revelations of sanctity which its obscurantism and hypocrisy could not conceal.

In describing his life as 'sedentary', Mauriac was stating what is true of any writer unless, like Malraux or Graham Greene, he requires the

[1] *La Province*, 1926. *O.C. IV*, 455-77.

spur of action. In the case of Mauriac it was particularly true because he preferred to write, at least in later years, seated on a divan with a pad upon his knees. But if his life was uniform in its routine and regular in its habits, rarely chequered with public or private events, it reflected the ideas and manners of a crucial period, so that the private drama of André Gide or Jacques Rivière, and the public drama of Charles de Gaulle, can be read in the way that Mauriac responded to them. His own drama, to which his talent gave discreet publicity, is no less legible than theirs, even if one has to read between the lines.

The mornings were industrious in the 'cagibi', but in the evenings the Mauriacs went out a great deal. Their children carried into middle age the memory of their mother's perfume and *tenue de soirée*, when she came into their room to kiss them goodnight. Jacques-Emile Blanche lived in a charming house near by, standing in its own garden, where Manet's 'La femme au gant' and Renoir's 'Les baigneuses' adorned the walls. Here, in the Japanese salon, the Mauriacs were frequent visitors. Réjane had asked to read the play that Blanche and François had written in collaboration, although her interest in it went no further. François, for all the difficulty he confessed of living in a crowd, could not resist the literary salons. He knew that he could shine, whatever other planets were in competition. Here were Cocteau, compared by Abel Bonnard to 'a butterfly burnt by the lamp and dying on the tablecloth, while the company go on eating their dinner unawares'; Claudel – 'under the arcade of his eyebrows magnificent as a cathedral vault' – as he passed through Paris on his return from Rio; Anna de Noailles, killing all conversation with her monologue, and declaring that only her sex prevented her election to the Académie. For Mauriac her poetry had been the nectar of his adolescence. He now compared her to a young Minerva 'revenue de toute sagesse et docile au seul vertige', 'alone possessed of a beauty transfigured by genius.' Her unpunctuality was proverbial; if she came to dinner you were lucky if you sat down to table before 9.30. Her star was declining while that of Paul Valéry was in the ascendant, but she was still to be met with at Madame Mühlfeld's. 'Are you leaving us already?' the insatiable hostess enquired; and Anna de Noailles, not feeling in the best of health, had replied: 'I am the last intelligible poet in France, and I must look after myself.' But when another guest declared that 'no one is writing poetry any longer today', she might have taken it either as a compliment or a criticism. Madame Mühlfeld was known as 'la Sorcière', and although she received Mauriac, she did not take to him, nor he to her. He described her as 'Madame Verdurin transformed into a mermaid'. She later married a strange adventurer and died in a villa at Grasse.

In April 1919 M. Lafont died, and his widow continued to live at

Vémars until she had celebrated her 100th birthday. The tall, square house stood at the top of a steep, circular drive at the entrance to the village, shaded by huge pines and cedars. A line of poplars were ranged behind the wall separating the road from the fairly extensive grounds. This now became a second home for the Mauriacs, and they generally went there in July. But in the summer of 1919 François was laid low by the scourge of influenza, which had carried off in three days the young woman living below them in the rue de la Pompe. He was therefore sent by his brother Pierre — already rising high in the medical profession — to spend four months at Argelès in the Pyrenees. His wife joined him there with the three children, for Jeanne had now given birth to a second daughter, Luce. In the autumn he returned to Paris where his new novel, *La Chair et le Sang*, already begun before the war, was appearing serially in *Ecrits Nouveaux*. It was published by Emile-Paul in October 1920.

Among the first things to greet him in the months following the Armistice were Valéry's *La Jeune Parque* and the second volume of *Du côté de chez Swann*, each caught sight of in a bookseller's window. He was able, however, to resist what he so ardently admired. The fashion was now opposed to the 'roman fleuve' — by which the French understand a novel that goes on and on, like *Bleak House* or *War and Peace*. *La recherche du temps perdu* was nothing if not a 'roman fleuve' and Mauriac, though he enjoyed reading such books, realised that his own talent pointed in a different direction. It was now expected of a writer — unless he were Marcel Proust — that his novels should be 'written quickly and served hot'. Mauriac's novels were invariably 'served hot', although they were sometimes written too quickly. The best of them, however, obey the recipe, and already, in *La Chair et le Sang*, he was beginning to follow it.

The narrative is clear and concise, and the poetic dimension, though it over-decorates the story now and then, does not obscure it. The central character, Claude Favereau, is the son of a rough vigneron who manages the vineyard once belonging to the Marquis de Lur — not to be confused with the Marquis de Lur-Saluces — and now passed into the hands of a rich and repellent business man, Dupont-Gunther. The latter is widowed with two children — a son, Edward, who tries to paint like the Cubists; and a daughter, May, who is musical, capricious, and not yet come of age. The house is run by a Spanish woman of dubious antecedents, Madame Gonzalès, a former mistress of Dupont-Gunther, at once Machiavellian and grotesque. Claude Favereau has just left the seminary, though for reasons inadequately explained, and returns home to classify the books in Dupont-Gunther's library. He thus meets the family, and makes friends with Edward, while relations between himself and May ripen into a tentative love affair. Madame Gonzalès, surprising them in the exchange of a single and almost accidental kiss, forces May into marriage with the son of a neighbouring proprietor, Marcel Castagnède, in whom she has shown no interest whatever — an alliance on which her father, from motives of economic greed, has set such heart as he possessed. The Castagnèdes are Catholic and the Dupont-Gunthers are Huguenot, but May is persuaded to change her religion. The conversion is no formality. Distrusting the dictates of her 'inner voice', she feels the need of that spiritual direction of whose advantages Claude had tried to persuade her. It is to satisfy her conscience that she flees from the man she loves — and with whom marriage would of course have been unthinkable — to marry the man whom she does not. But there is no conversion of the heart. Her love for Claude is transformed rather than consumed by its sacrifice. The married couple return to Lur for the first night of their honeymoon, and Claude, esconced behind the hornbeam avenue — recognizably the *charmilles* of Malagar — is surprised to see them walking hand in hand, and on the features of May no trace whatever of the horrors he imagines her to have just endured. For to one still haunted by the scruples of the seminary the marriage bed, though it might sanctify passion, could not exorcise disgust. In Claude Favereau 'the most animal sensuality was mingled with a crucifying desire for purity'. Expressed a little less crudely, this was true of the novelist.

Madame Gonzalès has a daughter, Edith, whom Dupont-Gunther, deserted by his latest mistress, now wishes to marry. The mother enters into the scheme, and Edith is invited to Lur where she falls in love with Edward instead; follows him to Paris; and, like any other literary hostess, yearns for the day when she too will have 'table ouverte'. The two live together, and then in separate establishments.

> In women who live alone in society the instinct of self-defence and self-preservation develops a political ferocity, and a subtle spite which begins by merely belabouring its victim and ends with moral assassination. Edith recognized no one in her entourage but allies, benevolent neutrals, suspect neutrals, and enemies.

When the liaison becomes too well known for Edith's comfort, she proposes a *mariage de convenance*. Edward refuses and the separation is complete. Having failed as a painter, and now succumbing to a mortal *ennui*, he addresses two letters — one to Claude Favereau, on whose gauche piety and simple faith he relies, and the other to Edith Gonzalès, informing them that unless they come to him at a certain hotel at Châlons-sur-Marne by a certain time, he will commit suicide. Claude obtains the money for the journey from his parish priest, but a three hours' delay at Orléans prevents him from reaching Châlons before Edward has put a bullet through his head. He is still alive, however, and is able to repeat the last words of Jacques Mauriac: 'We are saved by faith'. By the time Edith reaches his bedside, it is too late; various receptions in honour of a Dalmatian poet had agreeably delayed her departure. She is easily consoled, however, by her mother's assurance that 'If a man has died for you, my pet, your fortune is made.'

The suicide of Edward was inspired by that of Charles Demange, the nephew of Maurice Barrès, and its treatment, though a little summary, shows that Mauriac could take a hint from Dostoievsky when it suited him. Otherwise none of his portraits is drawn from life. One or two of them — Madame Gonzalès and Dupont-Gunther — come close to caricature, and their scheming conveys a whiff of melodrama. Mauriac is here tempted by the satiric impulse to which in his next novel, *Préséances,* he was to give fuller rein. He does not spare the literary salons and the pretentions of the avant-garde. Only recently he had attended a Cubist Festival at Isaac Rosenberg's and noted the 'machines, rails, and ferry-boats; an attempt at cosmic synthesis, absence of thought and absence of soul.'[1] In the novel a painter is explaining Cubism to the Dalmatian poet:

> First of all, you understand, I see the tones; then I illustrate them by certain shapes — a pipe or a tube. I build up my painting in a scheme which expresses my interior life. The wall-paper you see in the lavatories of country houses is of an adorable blue.

There is an echo of Jean Cocteau in the dislike of music that 'one listens to with one's head in one's hands'; and an echo of many a soirée at Madame Mühlfeld's or Madame Alphonse Daudet's in the Dalmatian murmuring his poem in an undertone while 'the guests attentively lean towards him, like the heads of the Apostles in the Last Supper of da Vinci.' Mauriac had not lost his lucidity among the fauna and flora of the salons, much as he enjoyed frequenting them.

There are echoes, too, of theological perplexity in the problems which had beset Claude Favereau's professors in the seminary — the exegesis of Loisy and the mysticism of Tyrrell;[2] of the 'tyranny of the flesh' that a young man finds hard to resist 'in the heat of the afternoon'; of the literary conversions then *à la mode* in the milieu of the *Nouvelle Revue Française;* of *Carmen* at the Grand Théâtre in Bordeaux; and of other evenings at the theatre when Madame Gonzalès speaks with 'that accent of irritated tenderness, and of pride which fears to be importunate,

---

[1] *Journal d'un homme de trente ans. O.C. IV,* 257.

[2] George Tyrrell, S.J. : 1861-1909.

so well known at the Conservatoire'. But most interesting of all is the novelist's perception of class distinctions. May wonders whether she would have felt so ashamed after her single kiss with Claude if it had been exchanged with someone of her own milieu? Mauriac understands his peasantry, and does not romanticise them.

> Favereau smiled with a paternal hypocrisy, pickled in his infused science, having reduced mankind and the universe to his own scale, passing judgment on everything in heaven and earth with the intrepidity of his own nothingness.

A curious comparison will puzzle the English reader. Edward is described as exhibiting 'that mixture of delicacy and good health that one sees in the students of Magdalen College'. Mauriac had never been to England; what did he know of Magdalen? Was this a reminiscence of young Raymond Mortimer whom he had recently met? But Mortimer had been to Balliol. The book also opens the question that Jean-Paul Sartre was later to put in a challenge that troubled Mauriac a good deal. How far does he manipulate his characters in order that they shall behave as he would like them to behave, rather than as they would naturally have behaved, being the people that they are? In a word, is he too anxious to save their souls? The question has, of course, no meaning for the reader who doubts whether people have souls and is well assured that, if they do, they are in no need of salvation. He will see in the climax of *La Chair et le Sang* an arbitrary extrapolation of theology into fiction. But the belief that the virtues of one person can atone for the vices of another is not in itself unreasonable. This reversal of merits must, however, carry conviction in its particular context. In *La Chair et le Sang* both the suicide and the salvation of Edward have been carefully prepared for; Mauriac shows considerable invention in securing that Claude arrives too late to save his body but in time to save his soul. The problem will recur, more acutely, in *Les Anges Noirs* – a work of far greater significance. It is the problem of the Catholic novelist.

This was examined in a short essay[1] by Charles Du Bos, who became an intimate friend of Mauriac and was arguably the most penetrating critic of his time. He shared Mauriac's religious beliefs, but he had been converted to them, whereas in the case of Mauriac they were something the novelist could not get rid of, although at times he would have liked to. 'Far from casting a shadow over my childhood, religion enriched it with a pathetic joy.' But emotion and liturgy had contributed the larger part of this enrichment; doctrinal instruction was almost entirely

[1] *François Mauriac et le problème du romancier catholique*, 1933.

lacking. And, as Jacques Maritain had emphasised, 'the piety of the child cannot last unless the man feeds it with knowledge and with prayer.' Mauriac's faith had never wavered, but his piety was at the mercy of his temperament. As a novelist he was torn between his vision of things as they were and his vision of them as they ought to be.

It was a false dilemma because the business of the novelist is to recognize what St Paul had defined as 'the sanctity of truth', and what Hardy described as 'the coil of things'. The desire to edify is literally mistaken for it is not for the novelist either to 'construct' life according to his own specifications, or 'to preach about it; nor under the pretext of serving God, to turn oneself into a *deus ex machina*.'[1] Life must be regarded in its height and in its depths, and its transmission must regis-ter both its deeper and its sharper resonance. The sonority of a Catholic novel, suggested Du Bos, should be 'the sonority of a *mezzo*'; the Catholic novelist 'could and should *use* the privileges' of his faith — and for Mauriac its truth was evident in its correspondence with reality — 'but he should beware of *abusing* them'. It is for the reader to decide whether he does abuse them in *La Chair et le Sang,* or in *Le Fleuve de Feu* which was the next but one of his novels. In the best of his work, however, the question does not arise. Either he does not raise it at all; or the 'sanctity of truth' persuades us.

2

The relations between Mauriac and Gide during these years of the early nineteen twenties throw a valuable light upon two itineraries which sometimes ran parallel, sometimes diverged, and on occasion almost coincided. Of Mauriac's admiration for Gide as a writer there was never the slightest doubt; moreover their formations, respectively Jansenist and puritan, provoked similar reactions. *Les Nourritures terrestres,* read in his last years at Grand-Lebrun, had awoken Mauriac to the possibilities of sensual enjoyment. Later he came to realise that there were many people whom these 'nourritures' no longer satisfied; and that the style of Gide, distilled every day into a greater simplicity, revealed 'a soul singularly apt to refuse its choice, and to serve not only two masters, but several'. Nevertheless on the 25th December 1931 he sprang courageously to Gide's defence.

Henri Massis, a brilliant polemicist of the extreme right, an ardent Catholic and Maurrasian, had delivered a mordant attack upon Gide in *La Revue Universelle,* accusing him of a 'demoniac' influence on the young. Mauriac, in *L'Université de Paris,* questioned whether this was

[1] Ibid.

an epithet that one Christian had the right to use about another – even if he were André Gide. Conversion was in the air, and Paul Claudel was only one of those who were running after Gide, like sheep dogs after a straying member of their flock. Gide was in fact so ripe for conversion that he was being converted daily to a different truth; nevertheless this desperate search for sincerity compelled respect. Massis had written of the 'opposition between morality and aesthetics' in his work; Mauriac replied that this guaranteed its humanity. Gide did not ask to be judged as a Catholic, and his attitude was therefore not unreasonable. 'No doubt the disorder of his soul becomes the matter of his art, but that is the noblest use to which a man without God can put his unhappiness.' Massis later included his attack in a collection of essays entitled *Jugements,* and Mauriac wondered whether certain of these 'judgements' would not leave many people with a permanent distaste for the Catholicism by which they were inspired. He recalled how passionately Gide had defended Christ in Madame Muhlfeld's salon against the other *gens de lettres.* Was Gide any more 'demoniac' than Socrates, accused of corrupting the youth because he had taught them to know themselves a little better?

Gide was greatly touched by this article. Mauriac was the first to come to his aid, although he was followed by Jean Schlumberger, Malraux, and Rivière. Gide reminded Mauriac of that 'fire in the sky trembling on the horizon between two worlds' – to which Maurice de Guérin had compared his own temperament; in the case of Gide it flickered between the Kingdom of God and the *nourritures terrestres.* Mauriac admitted that his own darkness had been lightened by it. 'Nevertheless' he continued in the same letter 'I think that one must choose to be a saint. You have taught us a sincerity which forbids the least complacency towards what seems to us the only logical attitude, *apart from the Faith.* The stupidity of Massis is in claiming to apply the Catholic law to an unbeliever, and he is lying when he pretends to be indignant because the unbeliever does not write as if he believed. The "religious politics" of a Barrès or a Maurras do not shock me – far from it; but I cannot help preferring a soul incapable of pragmatism. The "utilisation" of the unimaginable Trinity for social or moral ends shocks me more than the drama of a torn and divided heart – no doubt because this drama is my own.'[1]

On the 24th January 1922 Mauriac was working in his salon when Gide was unexpectedly announced. He came to read his extracts from a note-book relating to a period of his life when he had been touched by mysticism. They revealed a great tenderness for the person of Christ,

[1] *Cahiers André Gide 2.,* 66.

but the moment had passed. Gide was incapable of automatic belief, and Mauriac reminded him of Pascal's 'He blasphemes the thing that he knows', adding that if he had had access to the sacraments at that moment of fervour, perhaps it would not have passed so soon. Gide did not disagree, and went on to define sin as 'that which we cannot help doing'. Mauriac led him up into the 'cagibi', and showed him the place of honour occupied by his books. 'Two years ago' he noted in his diary 'this visit would have overwhelmed me with joy, but I am past the age when one is impressed by the prestige of famous writers. One is too close to them oneself . . . young people are beginning to address me with deference, hostility, or envy.'[1]

Mauriac was now writing dramatic criticism for the *Revue Hebdomadaire*, and six months after this rare visit to the rue de la Pompe he reviewed Gide's *Saül*, produced by Jacques Copeau at the Vieux Colombier. He noted how much of the text could easily have been written in verse, and contrasted the purity of style with the trivialities that Rostand had put into the mouth of Christ in *La Samaritaine*. Nevertheless there was danger in adding anything to a biblical subject, and here, as in *Le Retour de l'Enfant Prodigue,* Gide had not always avoided it. He had made the original author say what perhaps he had not intended to say. Gide had the skill to infuse with poison the most musical phrase; and when Saul, disgusted with his sins, twice exclaims: 'How shall a man console himself for his fall except with that which has caused it?', Mauriac protested that what a man requires is not to be consoled but absolved. 'How shall a man console himself for his fall except with Him who assumed it?'[2]

The press was, in general, very severe on the play, and Gide regarded Mauriac's review as the most intelligent he had read. He had intended *Saül* to convey a moral warning, and wished he had made his meaning even clearer. In *Les Nourritures Terrestres* he had preached a gospel of the senses; now he was anxious to show the decadence to which the cult of sensuality could lead. Gide's 'disponibilité' stopped short of nothing – not even the teaching of scripture. Mauriac, whatever his private deviations, never attempted to reconcile in his writing what was radically opposed; there was no doubt as to where he stood – or wavered – between God and Mammon. 'Our work' he wrote to Gide later in the same year 'can only be the image of that inconclusive struggle, of that trial in our heart, between God and the passion to which He subjects us, and which is nevertheless willed by Him.'[3] François

[1] Ibid., 219.
[2] Ibid., 70.
[3] Ibid.

Mauriac and André Gide were predestined to appreciate, understand, and in the last analysis to disagree with one another. Where Mauriac stumbled with his eyes fixed on a goal almost inaccessible, Gide could always turn round in his tracks and walk away in quite the opposite direction. Mauriac, as we shall see, could never be sure whether he would find him at his side, or scarcely within his sight.

Whatever credit his next novel, *Préséances,* published by Flammarion in 1921, may have gained for him in Paris, it can have earned him nothing but disfavour in Bordeaux. The target of his satire was the rich *'fils'* of the commercial aristocracy 'all of them correct (and dressed by the same tailor), all of them sporting and free to leave their offices at five o'clock, all of them exempt from the common laws of civility, choosing whom they would greet and whom they would not, incorruptible in their dispensation of contempt.' This was not the society in which the Mauriacs normally moved, but it sent its sons to Grand-Lebrun, and although there is nothing autobiographical in the story of *Préséances,* Mauriac knew what he was writing about. A woman who had read the novel observed to him 'There is no need to ask you if you come from Marseilles', but she must have been alone in suffering from this illusion.

The principal character in the book, Augustin, is a second-hand amalgam of Rimbaud and Augustin Meaulnes. His story is told through a narrator, whose sister, Florence, falls in love with him but uses him to achieve marriage with a typical member of the *'fils'.* She then passes from one *'fils'* to another until she gives her favours to a ludicrous *parvenu* from outside the magic circle. Augustin had at last revealed the secret of his birth; that he was the illegitimate son of an apostate priest who, repenting of his errors, had eventually found refuge in a Trappist monastery. He was admitted there as a lay assistant on the penitential condition that he had no communication with his son. Augustin, having told his story, disappears to Africa, but Florence remains haunted by his memory.

She has engaged as governess to her daughter a woman, Mme Etinger, who had acted as housekeeper to Augustin's father when he was contributing to rationalist periodicals, and had known Augustin as a boy. The narrator of the book, aware of his sister's neurasthenia, engages Mme Etinger to find Augustin, of whom for some years there has been no trace. Convinced, however, that her search will be in vain, he persuades a friend — also from the outside magic circle — who bears a close resemblance to Augustin to present himself at the hour fixed for Augustin's re-appearance. The trick works for a moment, and Florence is taken in. But then Mme Etinger arrives in triumph with the real Augustin whom she has tracked down through the Ministry of War.

Florence survives her disappointment, if indeed she has been disappointed at all. She enjoys a passionate liaison with the false Augustin until, aware that her previous association with the *parvenu* had resulted in her ostracism from the magic circle, he leaves her in the lurch. After confinement for some time in an asylum, she returns to discover in spiritualism some of the consolations of a love-affair. The real Augustin — very much a Rimbaud *redivivus* — follows his obscure destiny after a last stroll with the narrator along the quays.

All this is improbable in the last degree, and Mauriac looked back on the book with no satisfaction whatever. He was slightly ashamed of the venom expended on 'the aristocracy of the grape' — affirming — heavens knows, with reason — that 'our royal wine has the right to ennoble the families which serve it.' Some wished that he had pursued a promising vein of satire, but he concluded that this was less suited to fiction than to journalism, where in good time he would have every opportunity to indulge it. He had this, at least, in common with the narrator of *Préséances* — 'I am one of those addicted to the sombre mania of adoring what in itself is dead. They are burdened with images, memories, and sensations like embalmed corpses.'

Nevertheless the uneasy alliance of sensibility and satire in the novel attracted the attention of Marcel Proust. He thought it 'the most remarkable, the most original, book that I have read for a very, very long time, and the most different from what I could ever have imagined.' He caught the echo of 'an interior life that I am not sure that I understand, and that I wish nevertheless, more than anything else, that I could come to love.'[1] Mauriac had been some way ahead of Gide in recognizing the genius of Proust, and if Proust had lived a warm acquaintance might have ripened into a close friendship. Mauriac was easy and uninhibited with people he did not particularly admire, but he confessed to Proust that admiration made him unsociable. He was afraid of giving an impression of 'mediocrity' — a 'mediocrity' not of the mind but of the heart. Inscribing a copy of *Sodome et Gomorrhe* with 'affectionate admiration', Proust described himself as 'swaddled in a winding sheet like Lazarus', for the end was now not far off. Mauriac, sensing this, had quoted to him the words of Chateaubriand shortly before he died. 'It is nothing to break with real things, but it is much to break with memories. The heart breaks to separate from its dreams, for there is so little of reality in man.' Supping at his bedside with Henri de Régnier, he was long to remember the 'fine wasted features, the beard, and the olive complexion':

The world of the senses, against which he had no defence, has

[1] *Du côté de chez Proust: O.C. IV,* 281.

permeated this invalid, year after year, to the very depths of his being, at the meeting point of flesh and spirit. He was engulfed by it, and his memory brought it to the surface. All his characters have been soaked in it, and the changes they have undergone are the result of this physiological immersion.[1]

Proust, for his part, recalled the same occasion. He now recognized in Mauriac's way of writing, 'the particular, charming, and energetic manner' of the way he spoke. Would he have liked to hear a Quartet? But no; all that Mauriac wanted was to talk to the man whose work he admired beyond that of any other living writer. Proust died on the 18th November 1922. For some days he had refused to eat or to see anyone. 'When my work is finished' he had said to Céleste 'I shall take care of myself'; and he had dictated his 'sensations de mort', which would come in useful for the death of Bergotte. Paul Morand's comment was to the point: 'a man doesn't create so many human beings without giving his life to them.' Mauriac paid his last respects to the 'beau visage endormi'; attended the Requiem Mass at Saint-Pierre-de-Chaillot; and followed the cortège to the burial on the summit of Père Lachaise. Barrès was there with his umbrella and his bowler hat, and in saying farewell to Proust Mauriac was also saying farewell to Barrès, for he never saw him again. 'Ah well' observed Barrès of Proust 'he was our young man'. He could with a more delicate modesty have said it of Mauriac, although Mauriac was by now nobody's young man. Nevertheless, as he stood by the graveside, it might have occurred to him, that born *entre deux mers,* he was now standing for a brief moment *entre deux maîtres.*

In his last letter Proust had written of their 'equal and reciprocal admiration'. Yet Mauriac noted what others have noted, that 'the lack of moral perspective impoverishes humanity in Proust and narrows his universe . . . those who follow him, and for whom his desperate audacity has opened the way to territories unknown, bringing submerged continents to life under the dead seas, still need the restoration of Grace to this new world of theirs.'[2] The world of Mauriac was very different but its need was just as great, and he did his best to supply it.

With his next novel, *Le Fleuve de Feu,* he forced the gates of the *Nouvelle Revue Française,* where it appeared in three instalments (December 1922, February and March 1923). It was afterwards published by Grasset. Mauriac owed much to the influence of Rivière, of whom he was now seeing a good deal. Rivière had been converted to Catholicism by Claudel during his captivity as a prisoner of war, but Gide had delivered him both from Claudel and from Péguy. His was a

[1] Ibid., 284.
[2] Ibid., 292-3.

career open to temptation as well as to talent. Mauriac, on his side, had come a long way from *La Robe prétexte*; and what Rivière admired in *Le Fleuve de Feu* was 'a drama strictly religious' to which the novelist had given a persuasive reality. On a first reading he had wished to understand it, largely, no doubt, because it pricked his 'better conscience'. The question remained, however, whether those with less vulnerable consciences would be so easily persuaded.

A young man, Daniel Trasis, finds himself alone in a hotel at Argelès — the same, no doubt, as that in which Mauriac had spent the summer of 1920, recuperating from influenza. He dreams of sexual conquest, and decides that if no one arrives to interest him within three days, he will leave. At last a young girl, Giselle de Plailly, takes up her reservation, and is followed a day or two later by a middle-aged woman and a child, for whom she has been waiting. Daniel has his eyes on Giselle, whose apparent virginity excites him, and an intimacy grows up between them. It is a little time, however, before he detects from the identical laughter of Giselle and the child, Marie, that Giselle is really its mother. He confronts the elder woman, Madame de Villeron, with this discovery; and on the night before she has decided to leave with Giselle and Marie, Giselle passes a letter under the door of his room. He opens the door; Giselle needs no persuasion to come inside; and when she leaves a few hours later Madame de Villeron is waiting in the corridor. Such is the first half of the novel, and the only part on which Mauriac looked back with satisfaction. He had reason to do so, for the character of Giselle is haunting in its ambiguity, and the claustrophobia of a small hotel in a Pyrenean valley is admirably conveyed. As always, Mauriac shows himself a master of atmosphere.

Nevertheless much had still to be explained. Madame de Villeron, reluctantly married and early widowed, has devoted herself to good works. Giselle, *enceinte* as the result of a brief love affair with a soldier, met in a cinema and subsequently killed during the war, turns to her for help. She adopts the child, for whom its mother is 'Tante Giselle'. On leaving Argelès, Madame de Villeron takes Marie to Versailles, while Giselle returns to her father in the country. She daily expects a letter from Daniel, but expects in vain. At last she seeks out Madame de Villeron, and admits that what threw her into the arms of Daniel was the intolerable supervision of the woman who had taken care of her child. Delivered of her resentment, she is now delivered of her desire. Meanwhile Daniel, for whom a 'vierge mère' is better than no 'vierge' at all, feels the stirrings of lust during the dog-days of a Paris August. He takes the train to the village in the Valois where Giselle is living, and finds her at the organ in the church presiding over the Children of Mary at the Mass of the Assumption. When everyone has left she remains kneeling there alone, and Daniel waits for her at the back of the church. 'If she does not rise from her knees in three minutes, I shall give her up.' She does not stir, and Daniel, dipping his finger in the holy water stoup, makes the sign of the Cross and goes out.

The ending shows Mauriac at his weakest; Rivière's conscience must have been very vulnerable indeed to be pricked by it. For so ferocious a *coureur* as Daniel Trasis, frustrated of his prey, to make such an edifying exit was implausible in the last degree. Mauriac's merciless understanding of the type only made it more so. We are no better prepared for Giselle's access of piety; it smacks too much of Oscar Wilde's observation about women who find in religion all the consolation of a love affair. Mauriac admitted these inconsistencies. Where his psychological realism shows at its best is in the portrait of Lucile de Villeron, a first sketch for Brigitte Pian in *La Pharisienne*. Here is a woman dedicated to good works, who is responsible for a great deal of harm in doing them.

> 'Woe to those who pride themselves on not giving way to the temptation they will never feel!' She was fond of repeating that, with a reference to herself, because she hated the flesh, and she was fearful of experiencing its pride. . . . God alone knew whether Lucile de Villeron, delving into her heart and turning it over like arid soil, could not have discovered, all of a sudden, a seed which she had not suspected, buried there from all eternity. If God alone knew it, at least He willed that she should never find it, and that a heart delivered from evil should never be troubled in its depths.

Yet the moment came when Lucile, too, felt the need of human consolation, although she did not recognize in these tender longings the unaccustomed warmth of the 'fleuve de feu'. Why otherwise did she sit with her hands upon her 'open knees'? What alms was she begging? Mauriac answers the question all the more convincingly by leaving it in suspense.

3

Le Fleuve de Feu was a considerable *succès d'estime; Le Baiser au Lépreux* which followed in the same year was the first of Mauriac's novels to enjoy a wide popularity. He had previously been content with a sale of 3,000 copies, but this ran into several editions. The book is indeed a minor masterpiece, restricted in scope but flawless in execution, and in length hardly exceeding a long short story. The characters are few and drawn with an unfailing certainty of touch; and there is no attempt to edify. This, one says to oneself, was the way things happened in the *Landes.* It is a curious fact that in Mauriac's *Mémoires Intérieurs* there is no mention of Turgeniev; yet it is with Turgeniev that *Le Baiser au Lépreux* invites comparison. It leaves a similar bitter-sweetness in the memory. Charles Du Bos was not exaggerating when he wrote that 'from the very first page (Mauriac) reveals a mastery that would never leave him' and that the book virtually abolished everything he had written before. It was the first of a series of novels, appearing in quick succession, upon which alone his reputation might well have rested.

Jean Péloueyre is the physically repulsive, but not unintelligent son of a widowed landowner. The reading of Nietzsche — and Mauriac himself had passed through a Nietzschean phase — has persuaded him that if mankind is divided between masters and slaves, he belongs, irredeemably, to the second category. He has only to look into the mirror to read the confirmation of his servitude. Mauriac had often seen his prototype in the square at Villandraut, although here he was not so ugly that a woman might not have come to love him, and what happens to him in the novel was invented from first to last. Jérôme Péloueyre, his father, and the parish priest, shepherd him into marriage with Noémi d'Artiailh, a Raphaelesque, though slightly dumpy, virgin of the same village, who submits to the alliance with a mixture of docility and disgust. She comes from one of those 'pious homes where the children of the *Landes* dream of the next shoot as they sit over their lexicons', and 'her newly ironed frock cleaves the air' when she goes to mass on Sunday. She is faithful to her marriage vows, giving to her husband 'the kisses that in other times the lips of saints would give to lepers', although the sight of a young doctor passing her window on his rounds troubles her a little. 'She was a very young girl, ignorant and carnally minded, without understanding of her own heart.' Prompted by the priest, Jean goes to Paris on a mission of historical research, and it is noticed how Noémi blooms in his absence. On his return he succumbs to the prevalent tuberculosis, and dies. Noémi is condemned to permanent widowhood by a clause in her marriage contract which she has not the will to break, although the young doctor is clearly attracted to her, and she to him. She looks after her property with competence, and dispenses charity to those around her. For all her limitations, 'she was under sentence of greatness; a slave, it was decreed that she should rule. This slightly plump *bourgeoise* could not help surpassing herself; every path was closed to her, but renunciation.'

Mauriac wrote a final chapter to the novel, which was published separately in his Collected Works.[1] Now grown excessively corpulent,

---

[1] *O.C. VI.*

Noémi is chained to the bedside of her father-in-law. 'I don't desire his death' she says to herself 'but I like to imagine how my life will change when he is no longer there. No more reading aloud, no more basins and spitting bowls to empty. And the warm flannels, and the frictions...' When she hears a groaning and a gasping from the sick room, 'she trembles with joy, filled with a horrible, irresistible hope.' The angel of resignation has lost a few inches of sublimity, but Mauriac evidently shied away from so cynical a full stop.

As a study in sexual assassination *Le Baiser au Lépreux* invites even more sympathy for the executioner than the victim. It was the first of Mauriac's works to be translated into English, and Jacques-Emile Blanche wrote from London that 'all Chelsea' was reading it. All Paris was reading it too. The sales — 18,000 copies — enabled the family to take a holiday at Beaulieu on the Côte d'Azur, where they lived comfortably in a modest hotel for 100 frs. a day. They took with them a young Alsatian girl, Catherine Bechler, whom François had engaged as a servant soon after his marriage, and in the absence of his wife. He usually judged people by their faces, and in this case appearances were not deceptive. She remained with the family for more than fifty years.

When a novelist sets about creating a world as well as telling a story, it often happens that the same characters recur, albeit incidentally, in one book after another. Thus we learn, not without surprise, that Daniel Trasis has taken up a literary career, and is in correspondence with Jean Péloueyre. More significantly, Jérôme Péloueyre has a widowed sister, Félicité Cazenave, who will be the dominating figure in the following novel, *Génitrix.* Deprived of a husband, she totally possesses her son, Fernand, who lives with her in Jacques Mauriac's gloomy château at Langon. He is a 'timid fifty-year old with his eyes, at once ingenuous and obscene, enlarged by the pockets underneath them, the result of agreeable exhaustion, his dirty hands, his open shirt, and on his girlish neck the contusion of the latest kiss.' Félicité, with her 'spherical bust, and the head of an aged Juno attached to her bosom' is no less repellent, and her visits to the Péloueyres are a 'weekly scourge'. Riding down all opposition, she declares: 'If Fernand should marry, my daughter-in-law will die.' *Génitrix* is the story of how she keeps her word, and the price she pays for it.

The château is described as it stands today, secretive behind its screen of trees. The trains grinding over the viaduct compose a kind of *musique concrète* to accompany the drama played out inside. Fernand is no longer the docile bachelor, who pays occasional visits to his 'habitudes' — in other words, his mistresses in Bordeaux. The Cazenaves are bitterly anti-clerical, and Félicité raises no moral objections to these sombre indulgences. For her there are only two kinds of women: 'those

78

who want to get you into their clutches, and those from whom you will catch a disease.' An 'habitude' was one thing; a wedded wife was quite another. Eventually, however, Fernand is ensnared by a calculating school-teacher, and is not prevented from marrying her since 'the eternal family' was all the Cazenaves could 'oppose to the inevitability of death'. The victory is short-lived, however. Before long Fernand is sleeping once more in the night nursery which adjoins his mother's bedroom; and his wife, Mathilde, is left to herself in an isolated wing of the house, where, as the book opens, she is seriously ill from a miscarriage. Deliberately neglected by Félicité, she presently dies, and Fernand, victim of an obscure remorse, leaves his little bed for the nuptial couch where the body of Mathilde had lain. Félicité is crushed by this desertion, and there ensues between mother and son a war of love and hate, waged not with open recrimination but with veiled or averted looks, and the barbed small talk of two people who dare not confess their feelings. Only when Félicité herself has died is her ultimate victory secure. Fernand lives on, enchained to her memory, and looked after by the old servant who has taken her place.

The book reflects the matriarchy under which Mauriac passed the early years of his life. In Félicité Cazenave there is perhaps a reminiscence, many times exaggerated, of his maternal grandmother — and of other grandmothers as well. A photo still exists showing the son of Madame Lafont drawing near to his mother and away from his wife. A boy sent Mauriac a photograph inscribed: 'To the man who nearly made me kill my grandmother', explaining in a letter that Félicité so resembled his grandmother that he had been on the point of strangling her while she was asleep. Small wonder that Mauriac was to write an essay on 'The responsibility of the novelist'. Fernand had been taken directly from life — not a difficult derivation, since, as Edmond Jaloux pointed out in his review, the provinces were full of such human wrecks 'frightened and cowardly, comic and touching.'[1] Here, as in Le Baiser au Lépreux, Mauriac is in perfect command of his subject and his style. The concentration is never relaxed, and gains from a setting which never changes. The Landes are held at a distance which the story demands. Around it only 'the tulip-trees, poplars, planes, and oaks shook their dripping leaves against the rainy sky,' and 'the warmth of other summers burnt in the bottles of Yquem, and the sunsets of years gone by reddened the Gruaud-Larose.' Now and again the moralist in Mauriac peeps out, but to enlighten, not to edify:

> She began to realise that the absent are always in the right, for it is they who do not counteract the workings of love. If we look

[1] Le romancier et ses personnages, 1933.

at our lives, it seems that we have always been separated from those that we love the most; perhaps it has always been enough for the person we adore to live at our side for him or her to become less dear to us.

This was almost a literal transcription of a passage from his diary:

> Perhaps it is always enough that a creature we love should live beside us, not perhaps that we should love them less, but that we should no longer realise that we love them.[1]

The greatest novelist will generally leave us to imagine the lives of his characters before we have met them and after they have gone upon their way, whether in this world or the next. In *Génitrix,* a masterpiece of its kind, Mauriac prescinds nothing of their future itineraries. 'With *Génitrix'* he noted in his diary 'I know the meaning of celebrity. Publishers, reviews, and newspapers are competing for my copy. The money is coming in.' At the same time, however, Claude, now ten years old, was taken seriously ill with pneumonia, and Pierre Mauriac hurried to his bedside from Bordeaux. The danger quickly passed, and the boy went to recuperate in the Gironde where his father joined him, hard at work already on *Le Désert de l'Amour.* In Paris he had lunched at Prunier's with Raymond Mortimer, who assured him that in England the partisans of French policy in the Ruhr were 'stupid country squires who knew nothing of French civilisation.' Since Mauriac had not shaken hands with a German since the war, Mortimer may well have found him on the side of Poincaré and the country squires. If this was his rule he broke it, however, when Gide introduced him to Ernst Robert Curtius who had admired *La Robe prétexte* very far beyond its deserts. Gide was then being attacked on many sides for the publication of *Corydon,* where his homosexuality was openly avowed. In conversation with Mauriac he spoke with a certain nostalgia of the prison cell where the pacifist, Gustave Hervé, was expiating his anti-militarist opinions. In the same way Gide compared himself to Oscar Wilde as a martyr in the homosexual cause – though, as Mauriac was later to observe, the martyrdom which had brought Wilde to Reading gaol had not kept Gide from Stockholm and the Nobel Prize. Mauriac did not share the indignation of his co-religionists over the case of Gide. In reply to a questionnaire on the subject, he declared that the normal man also sins seventy times against nature; and that although inversion is natural for those inclined to it, 'nature itself is fallen and everything natural is not therefore in conformity with the will of God.'[2] The problem, for Mauriac, was not

[1] *Journal d'un homme de trente ans. O.C. IV,* 271.

[2] *Les Marges,* January – April 1926.

between one kind of sexuality and another; it was the choice of resistance or submission to any importunity of the flesh. An entry in his diary of the previous year betrays an awareness that in his contacts with other people he was dissipating his time and also, perhaps, his affections. 'What a disproportionate place absurd people can occupy in my life ... a hand held a little longer than it should have been.'[1] If that was all there was to it, the hand had a great deal to answer for.

[1] *Journal d'un homme de trente ans. O.C. IV*, 271.

GOD AND MAMMON

1

Mauriac spent all that summer of 1924 in the chalet at Saint-Symphorien with his mother and Claude. The circumstances were propitious for the novel he had in hand. Now in his fortieth year he felt the onset of middle age, and one of the three principal characters in *Le Désert de l'Amour*, Dr Courrèges, was a man of fifty-two, still suffering from the *crise de quarante ans*. The second was his son, Raymond; and Mauriac, with Claude, still convalescent, as his daily companion, brooded over a relationship which becomes less articulate, though not necessarily less close, as the years go by. The third character was inspired by a woman he had once seen passing by in her victoria, solitary and unashamed among the cushions. The uncle of one of his schoolfellows was said to have been her protector, and Mauriac remembered his mother's comment: 'Ces femmes-là, tout de même!' This was the genesis of Maria Cross, and the germ of Thérèse Desqueyroux.

Maria, a former schoolmistress of modest antecedents, is twenty-seven years old. Having lost her husband she had taken a post as secretary to Victor Larousselle, a wealthy and dissolute business man, whose wife is dying of cancer and therefore no longer capable of entertaining his associates. He instals Maria in his house at Talence on the outskirts of Bordeaux, where she acts as his hostess, and later becomes his mistress more through indolence than desire. Dr Courrèges, who lives near by, attends her in the course of his duties; falls obsessively in love with her; is brought closer to her by the death of her little boy; and hopes from one visit to another for an opportunity to declare his passion. But he is a man of regular habits, imprisoned by a family — mother, wife, son, daughter and son-in-law — with whom he has nothing in common but the servitude of the daily round. Refusing to confide in each other, they are strangely confident of surprising each other's secrets. 'Like a crew embarked for a lifetime on the same ship, the instinct of self-preservation makes them careful to ensure that no fire breaks out on board.' They are as distinct, and as inseparable from one another as 'the stars that make up the Milky Way'.

Raymond Courreges is only seventeen and still at school — evidently at Grand-Lebrun, for we recognize the plaster walls of the indoor playground and the treatise on obstetrics which earns him a magisterial rebuke. This is 'the age of impurity' of which his angelic features show no trace. At once diffident and ambitious, he dreams of adventure in Spain, but finds it closer at hand. Returning daily from school in the same tram that takes Maria Cross to the cemetery where her boy lies buried, he exchanges looks with her, and eventually they fall into conversation. She invites him to her house when Larousselle is away on business, more attracted to him than she realises, and playing with the idea of a semi-maternal relationship. Much to Raymond's disappointment she insists on showing him photographs of her son, and on his second visit he tries to take her by storm. Her sentimental dream is shattered, and she sends him about his business. He proceeds on a career of sexual conquest, but carries the memory of this humiliation like an open wound. With his father, incapable of such gross importunity, the case is different. Maria respects Dr Courrèges more than any man she knows, but she is bored by him. Alone in her salon, with its tattered draperies – a dingy mixture of luxury and indigence – she is bored by everything, even by her books. Neither the son nor the father is aware that they share the same obsession.

Seventeen years later Raymond meets Maria Cross in a Paris bar. She has married Larousselle and become deeply attached to his son, Bertrand. Her hair is now cut short, but she shows little signs of age; she has the same 'wide, calm, forehead' that we shall presently recognize in Thérèse Desqueyroux. Raymond's passion is excited afresh, but he stirs in Maria Cross no feelings whatever. He is trying to inflame her memory when Victor Larousselle, drinking at the bar, collapses on his stool. Raymond helps to bring him home to Maria's bare apartment, and Dr Courrèges, who happens to be in Paris at the time, is called to his bedside. In him, too, the sight of Maria revives a longing which, in contrast to his son, he believed that the years had deadened. Could they not meet again? But Maria was now so rarely in Bordeaux. Well, perhaps they could write . . . . The next morning Raymond sees his father off in the train from the Quai d'Orsay, and the 'désert de l'amour' stretches out, interminably, before them both.

The novel begins and ends with the meeting in Paris; and now and then, but not too often, as the story is told in retrospect, we are brought back to it. Mauriac's management of time is masterly. The canvas is broader than in any of his previous work, and the organisation more complex; but the book loses nothing in concentration and one does not notice the sleight of hand. Mauriac had taken the title from Rimbaud – never far from his sympathy in these years of stress – and, as he admitted, it might have served for any novel he ever wrote.

For epigraph he could well have substituted for the last line of Feste's song: 'Journeys end in lovers' *missing*'. The character of Raymond was suggested by the memory of a schoolfellow who appeared to share the same conviction that, up to the day of his death, he would be able to excite the passion of 'many another Maria Cross, of whom he would become in turn the wretched satellite'. Here is yet another Daniel Trasis, just as Larousselle is another Dupont-Gunther, but there is no indication that Raymond's lubricious fingers will ever find their way into a stoup of holy water. The deeply moving portrait of Dr Courrèges was born not of experience, but of presentiment.

> The characters in our books do not always belong to our past; they are often an image of ourselves that we project on to the screen of the future. In our novels we are, to some extent, our own prophet. I am astonished to discover in myself, now that I am old, the features of the characters I conceived in my youth or my maturity. They are not always the fruit of memory; more often than not I have ended up by meeting them.[1]

Although the book never forsakes its objectivity, the curtain is raised for a moment on Mauriac's personal drama at the time he was writing it. Raymond stands aghast at the thought of his father's frustration, although he cannot give chapter and verse for it.

> The essential is to know whether debauchery would have freed him from his passion. Fasting exasperates it, indulgence only makes it stronger. Virtue irritates it and keeps it awake. It fascinates and it frightens us. But if we give way to it, our weakness will never be proportionate to our frantic need. He should have asked his father how he had lived with this cancer. What, in the last analysis, is a virtuous life? Where are the loop-holes? What is God able to do about it?

It is the measure of Mauriac's art, and the measure of the 'desert' that he invites us to traverse, that in the end the characters are left where they were at the beginning, except that Maria Cross, veiled in her own ambiguity and always viewed, as it were, at a certain distance, now has her marriage lines for whatever they are worth. The doctor and his son – 'related through Maria Cross' – are scarcely related to each other. The doctor will go on living, besieged by his family, until he dies of *angina pectoris* – one of those living corpses against which Raymond had risen in adolescent revolt. But Raymond is no more alive than he. 'One can be old at any age' Mauriac wrote in a later preface

---

[1] *Bloc-Notes IV*, 92.

to the novel; he also admitted that 'The sort of rancour that family life had built up inside me, and of which no trace remains today, expresses itself here already.'

> The incommunicable solitude of human beings whom the ties of blood and the lottery of marriage bring together under the same roof compose the better part of the book, in my opinion, with the stormy atmosphere of Talence and the dreary, flat countryside which holds Bordeaux in its dusty embrace.[1]

Shortly before his early death, Jacques Rivière told Mauriac that *Le Désert de l'Amour* was 'the novel I should like to have written'; and in one of the last letters Mauriac received from him he discerned how much of the author was in the novel, and yet how fully the novel had digested it.

> I, whose profession and perhaps whose gift it is to see directly into the mind of the writer, realise very well how much of yourself has gone into it, all those fragments of the soul that you have left lying about. But that is because this is my business. In reality, the book is completely detached from you, and lives with a life of its own. All your characters are established down to the last detail. There is no trace of that imaginative laziness which occasionally possessed you in your previous books, so that parts of them were dead — or rather, they were passages where the author alone was active. In *Le Désert de l'Amour* everything that happens belongs, as of right, to the characters; you have had the patience to let each of them express themselves totally in act or in thought. The composition is also very remarkable; I mean by this that the events are utilised with the happiest economy. . . . The lives of the characters develop in a way that is at once perfectly distinct and perfectly combined; there is that reciprocal repercussion of one person upon another, without which a novel cannot exist, and yet one can see how each develops in its own desert. I don't know how you manage to do this, but the success is remarkable.

When *Le Désert de l'Amour* was published serially in the *Revue de Paris*, a fellow novelist, Jacques Sindral, declared that Mauriac had not only surpassed himself but anyone else in France writing fiction at that time. Charles Du Bos compared his progress to 'a Garonne which in the course of three years discharged on to its banks *Le Baiser au Lépreux*, a polished, irreproachable pebble; *Le Fleuve de Feu*, the most ambitious

---

[1] *D'autres et moi*, 251.

of his previous works . . . . . *Génitrix*, an etching, here and there too heavily underlined, ... and now, as its stream broadens out, like its estuary in the Gironde, what is up to date its author's masterpiece.'[1] Mauriac may well have regretted that the criticism of Du Bos, as he put it with slight exaggeration, was 'an admirable soliloquy, intelligible to only a dozen people in Europe.'[2]

The book was awarded the *Grand Prix du Roman* by the Académie française – an imprimatur which settled, once and for all, the question so anxiously on the lips of the author's relatives in Guyenne: 'Do you think you will succeed?' For anyone who saw the adaptation of the novel for the television screen by Pierre Cardinal, Maria Cross will always be Christiane Minazzoli and Dr. Courrèges will always be Pierre Dux. 'We no longer called him anything else but "Doctor" ' Mauriac was told 'and we didn't even realise we were doing so.'

2

Celebrity had gone to Mauriac's head only in the sense that it had given him seriously to think about his vocation as a novelist. In a long short story, *Un homme de lettres*, published first in the *Nouvelle Revue Française* and then by Les Editions Lapina (1926), he gave a warning both to himself and to others. For the central character, Jérôme, he borrowed certain traits from a fellow novelist, Jacques Chardonne. Jérôme leaves his mistress, Gabrielle, because she loves and protects him too much, for Berthe, a married woman with two children, who loves him less and protects him not at all. In the end he leaves Berthe in order to be alone with the literary booty he has collected from them both. The story is told with much accomplishment, and aroused the envy and admiration of Roger Martin du Gard – perhaps because it does not vibrate with Mauriac's usual intensity. As the epigraph suggests, Montaigne is here his mentor. He wrote in a dedicatory letter to Bernard Barbey: 'I have enlarged out of all proportion certain defects of which we carry the seeds, maybe, within us; and it is no bad thing to drag the monster into the light, put it on a table, and contemplate the wicked beast which we have pampered all too fondly, and which we might have turned into ourselves . . . . . But this is a danger that we need not fear, my dear Bernard. We know the sweetness of a home, for two young wives have taught us to hate the ferocious mystique of aestheticism. Let us learn how to safeguard the power of loving. Passion is more essential for us than for other men.

---

[1] *La Nouvelle Revue Française*, April, 1925.
[2] *Bloc-Notes IV*, 144.

Let us love that we may not lose our humanity.'

It was some years since curiosity had led Mauriac to the assizes in Bordeaux where a woman was standing trial as a poisoner. The image of that white face in the dock remained with him until it assumed, by way of Maria Cross, the features of Thérèse Desqueyroux. Yet more than memory was here at work. When the author was asked whether he could say, as Flaubert had said of Madame Bovary: 'Thérèse Desqueyroux — c'est moi', he admitted that she was 'made up of everything that in myself I have been obliged to overcome, or circumvent, or ignore.' As we shall see, her destiny, left obscure in the last pages of the novel, continued to haunt him, as if she were a living person, and as in fact she has haunted so many readers. This presence, which a notable film has done much to emphasise, derives in part from her ambiguity. She belongs, not to a psychologist's case-book and certainly not to a psychiatrist's couch, but to the central 'mystery of things'. She is not a monster, but a victim of circumstance and environment. Her crime is not a *crime passionnel*. True, she is not in love with her unimaginative husband; the memory of her honeymoon is too painful, and the contrast between his normal attentions and 'the patient inventions of the dark'. Nor is she in love with the young Jewish consumptive who opens her eyes to horizons wider than the *Landes* and to riches other than the resin which she, too, carries in her blood. She is not a *femme fatale*, although her charm is generally remarked upon. The prisoner of a milieu governed by family pride and possessions, she espies a way of escape and follows it — almost automatically. Noticing that Bernard Desqueyroux has thoughtlessly taken a double dose of Fowlers Mixture, with its powerful ingredient of arsenic, she does not stop him. From that it is only a few steps to falsifying a prescription, and finding herself in court on a charge of attempted murder.

The novel has become justly famous; nevertheless it got off to a false start. Mauriac had at first conceived Thérèse as a Christian, sending to a priest the written confession of her crime. Her husband, Pierre, is less gross a character than, as Bernard, he eventually became. He tries to share her musical and literary tastes, but to no avail. The instincts of the flesh 'transform the person who approaches us into a monster that bears no resemblance to him. . . . If I had loved him, I should have loved the smell of his clothes when he came back from shooting, and even the smell of his breath after he had taken his aperitif. . . . So it was no use for my sad Hippolytus trying to be an Adonis. . . . You would have said the days were too short for his devoted attentions to make me forget his endless, and patient, and unimaginable inventions when it was dark.' Thérèse does not finish her confession — 'but there, I am straying from what I have to say' — and presumably the novel was to have completed her story, although she would no longer have related it herself. Mauriac published this fragment, under the title *Conscience, Instinct Divin* in a private and limited edition 'Les Introuvables' (1927), and included it in his Collected Works (Vol. III).

When a lecturer in French from Exeter University[1] was preparing an edition of the novel for academic use, Mauriac escorted him from Malagar to Bazas, the former seat of a bishopric and the principal town in that section of the *Landes*. Thirty-five steps lead up to the sombre portico of the court house, and it is here that we meet Thérèse as the book opens — narrowly acquitted through the perjured testimony of her husband. No scandal must sully the family's good name, or injure the prospects of her father in the forthcoming elections. The façade of convention must be preserved. But when she returns with the intention to confess and the hope of forgiveness, she is isolated in a rarely inhabited house of the Desqueyroux, only appearing publicly at her husband's side for Mass on Sunday morning. Endlessly smoking her cigarettes until they, too, are taken away from her, and in the charge of two unsympathetic servants, she wastes away in an atrocious solitude. Finally Bernard decides that she will do better to disappear, returning only for such formal occasions as the tyranny of convention demands. He accompanies her to Paris, and then asks her why she had acted as she did. Her reply leaves her motives in a mystery which she cannot explain, and which Mauriac does not elucidate. 'I was only conscious of being cruel' she tells him 'when my hand was hesitating. I blamed myself for prolonging your suffering. I had to go on to the end, and quickly. I yielded to a dreadful sense of duty.'

In praising the book as the work of a great novelist, Edmond Jaloux measured the risk that Mauriac had taken. It was a case of that 'motiveless malignity' which Coleridge ascribed to Iago, and which the record of other women poisoners confirmed. Thérèse was in some way predestined to do evil; her fall was vertiginous, like the incestuous passion of Phèdre; it could only be explained by a Jansenist reading of human nature. Was this in Mauriac's mind when he associated her crime with all that, in himself, he had been forced 'to overcome, circumvent, or ignore'; why he described the book as one that could only have been written by a Christian; and why, in a later novel, he imprudently followed Thérèse beyond the point where he should have left her — lonely and laughing on the pavement, and powdering her nose? Her future movements, like her past motives, are, of set purpose, left hanging in the air. A similar uncertainty seemed to hang over the novel as a whole. Would its density dissolve under the questions which it raises

[1] Dr. Cecil Jenkins.

but does not answer? It has not done so, although Mauriac in pursuit of
his favourite heroine still left her 'dreadful duty' in the dark.

Thérèse has no knowledge of what lies in front of her; Elisabeth
Gornac in *Destins* (1928) knows only too well. Thick-set and in her
fiftieth year, she has become 'one of those dead persons that the
current of life drags along with it.' Yet she has experienced, almost
grotesquely, the power of love for which Thérèse Desqueyroux was
famished. Did Thérèse try to poison her husband because she had,
literally, nothing else to do? Elisabeth Gornac had known Bob Lagave
as a boy. He would often stay with his peasant grandmother, Maria,
who lives across the road from the Gornac property — as unmistakably
Malagar as any other *locale* in the Mauriacian map. Bob is the victim
of his own physical charms, and in Paris they have earned him an
unenviable reputation. (These pages are spiced with the satire which
Mauriac had not indulged since *Préséances*.) When the book opens,
Bob is recovering from pleurisy with his grandmother, but very much
under the care of Elisabeth Gornac. She is a widow, living with her
ailing and avaricious father-in-law, and she has one surviving son, Pierre,
for whom she has little more than a formal affection. Her maternal
feelings — less purely maternal than she imagines — are centred on Bob
Lagave.

Bob has formed an attachment to Paule de la Sesque, the daughter
of parents very much his superior in the social scale. She drives over
from Arcachon to see him, and Bob informs Elisabeth that they are
unofficially engaged. While they are out for a moonlight walk Pierre
Gornac arrives at the house unexpectedly, and after Bob has returned
to his grandmother, conceives it his duty to warn Paule of the scandal
attaching to his name. The girl leaves a letter for Bob, telling him that
she needs more time for reflection and will return in three weeks. Bob
writes to her, but receives no answer. Elisabeth surprises him one day
when he is the worse for drink, and he attempts to take her in his arms.
At last he yields to the importunity of some Parisian friends, who have
sought him out, and agrees to drive with them to Deauville. On the way
their car crashes into the gates of a level crossing, and Bob is killed.

Paule de la Sesque returns, too late, and informs Elisabeth that she
would have lived with Bob if she could not marry him. Pierre, convinced
that he had acted with the best intentions, cannot escape the conclusion
that they had led to the worst result. He tries to console himself with the
knowledge that Bob had at least drawn his last breath in a presbytery;
and leaves for Africa to follow in the footsteps of Charles de Foucauld.
Elisabeth Gornac, her father-in-law now dead, is alone with her vineyards and the memory of a passion which she had not recognized and
which, had she known it, her inherited scruples would have refused.

Destins, though it was badly served by its title, is a powerful and moving novel. Mauriac had used the technique of the cinema to illustrate the background of his characters, and in Elisabeth we are shown the tragic dimension of a life shaken out of its emotional routine and then frozen once again by the shock of what it has discovered. The prototypes of mythology stalk behind these 'destinies' intertwined among the arbours of Malagar. Bob Lagave has much of Narcissus or Ganymede, and Elisabeth of Juno. As Mauriac wrote, 'the whole landscape is at the mercy of the gods'. He had known Bob Lagave in 1920 at 'Le Boeuf sur le toit', and he was also 'le jeune homme' whose features he had traced in the essay published by Hachette. The novel is at once an 'anthem for doomed youth', and an anthem for doomed age, for it is the tragedy of Elisabeth that 'our body has not the same age as our heart'; that when she awakens to love she is a heavy middle-aged woman; and that her passion is surprised by her own son, 'a bitter and gloomy young seminarian'. Often, when he was still a child, Mauriac had the presentiment of such a passion as hers, stifled in the depths of a lost countryside, and in a house visited by nobody. He adds, significantly:-

> The two lads, opposed to each other . . . are both drawn from my own substance and incarnate my own deep contradiction. This was not my intention in creating them; it was in no way deliberate. But it is a fact that after thirty years I recognize myself in both of them — 'frères ennemis' but born of the same flesh.[1]

They represented 'the *fleuve de feu* that was overflowing its banks in the Paris of 1925, and the pure, icy stream that ran between the elder-trees of the *Landes*, when I was a child.'[2]

It was this 'deep contradiction' that was now festering to a crisis.

3

Only in a limited sense is it possible to give chapter and verse to what has been called 'the crisis of 1928' — a crisis which had been gathering since 1925, and was not to be resolved until 1930. The contradiction was not merely between whatever of Bob Lagave and Pierre Gornac confronted each other in François Mauriac, but between a life outwardly happy and brilliantly successful, and a life inwardly tormented. Whatever gossip or slander may have suggested, Mauriac was the subject of no public scandal. No classic love affair, like Paul Claudel's liaison with Ysé of *Partage de Midi*, troubled either himself, his family, or his

---

[1] *D'autres et moi*, 246-8.
[2] *Bloc-Notes IV*, 70.

friends. What he may have done or, more probably, dreamt of doing, remained his secret. It seems probable that, as he entered upon middle age, the desires which his fastidious scruples and sincere piety had generally restrained became increasingly exigent, and that they could not be satisfied within the limits of a happy marriage. There was nothing unusual in this 'crise de quarante ans'; what was exceptional was the intensity with which he felt it, and the corresponding intensity which it gave to his work. Since he was a Catholic, the Catholics expected him to edify with spectacular contritions and death-bed repentances. As an artist, he knew that it was his business to interpret life as he saw it, both in others and in himself.

There is, of course, nothing in Mauriac's writing which today would bring a blush to a school-girl. He confined himself within established decencies, not without a certain sense of self-sacrifice. 'If I had not been a Christian, no one could have better depicted the physical aspect of human passion.' His work is all the stronger for this restraint. If a writer wishes to convey the force of sexual passion, the last thing he should do is to describe it. Mauriac was a master of suggestion. But the modern reader is still puzzled by these agonies of conscience; and Mauriac cannot be understood, either as a writer or a man, unless one realises that, for him, the moral code, as the Church laid it down, was imperative; and that its deliberate infraction cut one off from God. The sins of the flesh might not be the most heinous, although they were certainly the most frequent. Nevertheless Mauriac was convinced that they were at the root of many other moral disorders with which they had apparently nothing to do. He is not to be accused of hypocrisy because he professed one thing and may have practised another. He should rather be admired for publicly confessing to a contradiction which was nobody's business but his own.

The title of *Destins*, which might have been given to any novel by any novelist, reflected this crisis in the destiny of its author. It was when he sat down to write the book that Mauriac felt the furthest removed from the faith which he professed. This alienation is evident in the cruel portrait of Pierre Gornac, and in the hardening of Elisabeth after the death of Bob. Her religion leaves her unconsoled. Both here, and in the preceding novels, as Charles Du Bos pointed out, Mauriac was like a man taking a steam bath where 'through the power of his poetry, everything is bathed in an irresistible halo of lyricism, even, and perhaps especially, those things which make us shudder.' This was a comment, not a criticism; it merely drew attention to Mauriac's connivance with what another side of him would have condemned. Du Bos added that 'while Mauriac the novelist gained at every point from his Catholicism, the Catholic in Mauriac gained nothing from his partner and only reaped the hatred which in *Destins* would one day rebound upon the Catholics, and against them.'[1] Even when he was in a 'state of grace' Mauriac avowed that his characters came 'from the more troubled depths of his being'; and General de Castelnau, who spoke for Catholic susceptibilities, declared that such 'morbid works do not find their way into my own house, or into the houses of my children.'

Among his intimates at this time was the young Julien Green, who eventually occupied his seat at the Académie Française. In his *discours de réception*[2] Green recalled the gaiety of Mauriac 'in a corner of the Place de l'Alma . . . almost deserted at 9 p.m.', and how he would be 'doubled up' with laughter at his own *boutades*. But the mood would change and as they endlessly walked the streets, one or other of them would mutter the name of Pascal. Then Mauriac would repeat, with emphatic pauses, Pascal's condemnation of the flesh. 'Let those who think that man's good is in the flesh and his harm in what turns him away from the pleasure of the senses, get drunk on their belief and die of it.' The empty streets would echo to an anathema which sounded the death-knell of passions they both found it hard to resist. 'For two or three years' Mauriac admitted 'I was like a madman.'

A clue to the conflict can be found in his third volume of poems, *Orages*,[3] published in 1925 in a private collection, 'Les Amis d'Edouard', and then in 1926 by Les Editions de la Sphère, with illustrations by Coubine. Here, if anywhere, Mauriac reveals himself. The fear —

> *L'espace d'un baiser me donnera la mort*

the desperation of disgust

> *En vain nous serons vaincus*
> *Par le Dégoût, ce complice*
> *Du Dieu qui nous aime plus*
> *Que nous n'aimons nos délices*

the lie that is learnt with age

> *Ce mensonge charnel que nous enseigne l'âge*
> *J'en commence d'avoir l'humiliant usage.*
> *Et rôde autour des corps qui ne le savent pas*

the delights of memory

> *Visages exhumés, chaque jour moins distincts,*
> *Ma délectation vous ronge*

---

[1] *François Mauriac et le problème du romancier catholique.*

[2] 16 November 1972.

[3] *O.C.VI.*

the intermittencies of lust

> *Poursuivi de ton flux, si je me voulais chaste,*
> *Je fuyais vainement l'écume défendue,*
> *Mais quand je t'appelais pour que tu me dévastes,*
> *Tu feignais de dormir, mer étale et perdue*

the cushions that console for the absent mistress

> *Mais dans les coussins — vaine proie*
> *Que je n'ai pas su retenir —*
> *Je creuse une place à ma joie*
> *Pour t'attendre et me souvenir*

the torture of the Christian conscience

> *Cachons notre folie à Celui qui la hait*
> *Comment se lèveraient pour calmer la tempête*
> *Ces éternelles mains où j'ai fixé des clous*

the wild appeal to Rimbaud

> *Je porte en moi l'enfer où tu fus . . .*
> *Quand un dernier rayon brûlera mes rideaux*
> *Aurai-je comme toi ce lit encerclé d'anges?*

and desire compared to a David eager to be vanquished by a more subtle adversary than Goliath

> *Providence implacable, en ruses si féconde,*
> *O vous, de mon désir adorable ennemi.*

These are no metrical exercises; the salt of experience is in them, as you taste it in Villon and Baudelaire.

The debate was brought out into the open by an invitation from *La Nouvelle Revue Française* to contribute an essay on Bossuet's *Traité de la Concupiscence*. This appeared on the 1st October 1928 under the title: *Souffrances du Pécheur*. If Mauriac did not afterwards put the *Traité* among his bedside books, it was because every word of it seared him to the core. It was only rarely that he wrote for commission, but in the present case 'an entire destiny crystallised' around this *cri du coeur*. Christianity, he bluntly argued, allowed no rights to the flesh, Bossuet was echoing Pascal when he affirmed that 'God demands *everything*', and Pascal had given it to Him. Marriage might be sanctioned as a sacrament, but in condemning woman to 'perpetual fecundity' it condemned man to 'perpetual chastity'. Bossuet had even described him as 'conceived in the heat of a brutal concupiscence, in the revolt of the senses and the eclipse of the reason. We must combat to our dying day the evil we have contracted in our birth.' Bossuet was no Jansenist, but no Jansenist could go further than this.

Mauriac had visited Tunisia during the season of Ramadan. He had been attracted by a 'practicable religion', and repelled by its social fruits. But it was beyond his power to shut his eyes to what Bossuet had called 'the fragile and deceitful beauty of the body'. He distinguished between passionate love and 'legitimate affections'. When affection became passionate, it turned into sodomy or incest. Physical union was a snare: 'For a few seconds we thought we were only one person and now, once again, we are two; this body and that other body; this wall, this breast which is now shut to us; a closed world of flesh and blood around which we revolve like a wretched satellite.' Only the mystic could lose himself in an incarnate God, and Bossuet had recalled the Magdalen at the feet of her Saviour. 'The tears and the perfume and the hair – He had them all.' Mauriac quoted Chesterton's definition of modern heresies as 'truths run mad', and among them he gave pride of place to the romantic notion of love as 'always holy, always innocent, because it is love.'

Doubtless he was thinking of himself when he wrote of the man incapable of choice, 'who yields a little, and renounces a little', and he envies those who know no law to restrain their appetites. Rimbaud's cry 'O pureté! pureté! C'est cette minute d'éveil qui m'a donné la vision de la pureté' echoed in his mind like the bird-song of a lost paradise. He had many such 'minutes d'éveil', but they did not last. The pleasures of the senses could only be resisted by spiritual delights with which he could not hope to be favoured; by what the Jansenists had called 'the victorious delectation of grace'. Was the repentant sinner renouncing the substance for the shadow? Pleasure was a certainty; what could one oppose to it but the hope of Heaven or the possibility of Hell? If one belonged to the race of lovers – as Mauriac realised that he did – one risked remaining a lover up to the limit of old age. It was a displeasing prospect. Yet Christ was the author of the drama which was tearing him apart; it was He who had precipitated mankind into an adventure which those who had lived before His coming had scarcely foreseen. Moreover, sexual passion was not only wrong; it was ridiculous. One did not need the gravity of Bossuet to show it for what it was:

> All the great works of profane literature have illustrated this tragic absurdity. This dance of mosquitoes, this desperate pursuit of a creature who does not see us, this indifference to the creature who is chasing us and is herself pursued.'

Mauriac did not deny the validity of the Christian ethic; he merely denied that it was accessible to the majority of men. The delights of concupiscence, once enjoyed, were constantly revived in the imagination. A single transgression represented a thousand others. Concupiscence was not limited to certain acts; the cancer was general, and the infection everywhere.

Souffrances du Pécheur was not, as we shall see, Mauriac's last word on the subject; but it came, like the appeal of a drowning man, to startle the readers of *Thérèse Desqueyroux*. It was a cry to those of his fellow-men who had their life-saver's certificate. These were not lacking. Others had reacted against the cult of drugs, alcohol, and homosexuality prevalent in Paris at that time. Jean Cocteau, reeling under the death of Radiguet, had been reconciled to the Church through the mediation of Pierre Reverdy and Jacques Maritain. It was a hasty return followed by a fairly quick relapse. Charles Du Bos, Henri Ghéon, and Jacques Copeau – all of them intimate friends of Gide – had fortified themselves against the Gidian equivocation by rallying to a truth that was unambiguous. The morning found Max Jacob on his knees in the Sacré-Coeur, even if he had spent the night elsewhere on Montmartre. In a word, Catholicism was fashionable. Mauriac had only frequented the fringe of this 'paradis artificiel', but the 'sauve-qui-peut' of those who had escaped it echoed his despair and prefigured his salvation.

He remembered an earlier time when Robert Vallery-Radot had taken him away from Paris, almost by force, and installed him in a country hotel. Now it was Jacques Maritain who publicly answered the semi-asphyxiated cry of *Souffrances du Pécheur*. Mauriac went occasionally to the philosophical retreats at Meudon, but he was allergic to the vocabulary of Thomism. Only when the mystical doctrine of St John of the Cross was the subject of the gathering did he feel at home. Neither dogmatic theology nor pure philosophy was his *forte*; he rallied to the reasons of the heart rather than the head. Nevertheless Maritain's aesthetic sensibility was too acute not to appreciate Mauriac's problem – how to purify the spring and still to describe the muddy waters; to reconcile two standards of truth. But it was Charles Du Bos who came to his aid at the decisive moment. His preoccupations were more nearly the same as Mauriac's; he knew him well; Mauriac had twice attended the *Décades* of intellectual discussion at Pontigny where both Gide and Du Bos were prominent; and Du Bos had himself only recently been converted. On the 6th November 1928, only four weeks after the publication of *Souffrances du Pécheur*, they met for lunch at the 'Petit Durand' in the avenue Victor-Hugo. Always a striking pair, Mauriac had reminded one observer of 'a bored greyhound' and Du Bos 'with his customary funereal face seemed to have received the ashes the same morning.'[1] But on that day Du Bos' mood was anything but Lenten. Mauriac found him

> on fire with the return to God, and the bliss of recovering the sacramental life. It was Polyeucte returning to the temple and preparing to overthrow the statue of Gide. On the other hand I had reached low-water mark, and I could not sink any further without dying. But I was suffering, and this made me docile to the advice given me by Du Bos.[2]

Du Bos owed his conversion to the abbé Jean-Pierre Altermann, a remarkable though in some ways a singular priest, himself a recent convert from Judaism, and it was to him that Mauriac now went. Altermann was an intransigent Thomist, standing – as Mauriac put it – 'on the frontier between the two Testaments'. His were the shoulders best fitted to bear the weight of Mauriac's anxiety, and he became his spiritual director. Together with Du Bos they founded a quarterly review, *Vigile*, elegantly produced, published by Grasset. Regularly Mauriac, Du Bos, and others would attend the Mass, celebrated by Altermann to the exquisite plainchant of the Benedictine Sisters in their chapel of the rue Monsieur. He was a persuasive and inflexible director, and many were the young women whom he sent to the convents for which he considered them best suited. But when he showed himself equally inflexible over the contents of a literary review, difficulties arose. Du Bos, whose standards of criticism were just as inflexible, could not tolerate so dictatorial a censorship, and the review ceased publication.

One characteristic of Altermann irritated Mauriac almost beyond endurance – his particular way of turning the other cheek. If Mauriac shocked or scandalised him – perhaps by some trivial remark about St Thomas Aquinas – the abbé would heave a deep sigh and murmur: 'I knew that today you would make me suffer', offering up his vexation as a sacrifice to Almighty God. This feature of the abbé – but this alone – Mauriac was to borrow for his portrait of Brigitte Pian in *La Pharisienne*. For the rest he recognized in Altermann the Good Samaritan who had picked him up by the wayside. He invited him to Malagar, and Altermann took him to Solesmes. Mauriac's relatively luxurious habits – first-class on the trains, the best hotels, the *plats de choix* in the restaurants – disconcerted him a little on the part of a penitent from whom he expected at least a façade of asceticism. But Altermann was too discriminating a hunter of prodigal sons not to feel a certain pride in adding Mauriac to his score; and he kept his protest within reasonable

[1] Robert de Saint-Jean: *Journal d'un Journaliste.*

[2] *Nouveaux Mémoires Intérieurs,* 156.

bounds. If Mauriac referred to Père Laberthonnière and his tribulations under the anti-modernist Inquisition, he regarded such aberrant sympathy with a kind of charitable contempt. A celebrated novelist was a useful convert in his cap, but his theological whims were not to be taken seriously.

They went together to Lourdes – still staying at the best hotel. For Mauriac the pilgrimage was at once a stimulant, a tranquilliser, and an ordeal. It stimulated his faith, tranquillised his desires, and put his aesthetic sensibilities to the test. The crowds declaiming the Rosary at the Grotto or making the Stations of the Cross – hideous effigies in zinc – the statue of the Virgin from which even Bernadette had averted her head in disgust, the commercial *bondieuserie* of pious knick-knacks – all this was a far cry from the angelic plainchant of the rue Monsieur. Léon Bloy, the passionate pilgrim of La Salette, had always been distrustful of Lourdes, if indeed he had ever been there. Huysmans had regarded it with horror. Each had been the victim of his temperament. As Mauriac wrote: 'There is such a thing as holy anger; there are no such things as holy temperaments.' It was Barrès, the spiritual dilettante, who had declared that there were 'places where you feel the breath of the Spirit' – and Lourdes was one of them.

Mauriac had the authority of his brother Pierre, a Professor of medicine, for one of the more remarkable cures. A young woman, mortally ill with tubercular meningitis, had been completely restored to health by absorbing a few drops of Lourdes water in a convent far removed from the *piscine* from which it had been taken. Mauriac's grandmother and one of his aunts had heard the story of the Apparitions from the lips of Bernadette herself only eight years after she had seen them. If Descartes and Montaigne had both knelt at the shrine of Our Lady of Loreto, it was not for François Mauriac to let his taste for liturgical luxury prevent him kneeling at the shrine of Our Lady of Lourdes. If 'Christian democracy' had a meaning anywhere, it had a meaning here. Christ had never flattered a generation asking for a sign, but when the sign had been given them, who were they to question it? Questions there had been in plenty, and Bernadette had answered them. Now, three quarters of a century later, the occasional cure and the numberless conversions returned the questions to those who had doubted, not to those who had affirmed.

Mauriac gave his impressions of Lourdes in *Pèlerins*[1] (1932) through a dialogue between a fervent believer and a slightly troubled sceptic – Huguenot and humanist. Augustin is an undisguised self-portrait. He is the young man who, as a boy, had ritually kissed the Druidic oak;

[1] *O.C. VII.*

watched the pilgrims from Bordeaux venerate the Black Virgin of Viridis; and then, in the 'crise de quarante ans', sat in the back pew of a chapel where he had never been before, waiting for a sign. It had not been given him. But three years later, when God and the abbé Altermann had done their work, he realised, as he knelt one day in the chapel of the rue Monsieur, that it was here that he had asked for a sign, and that he had only to stretch out his hand to touch the chair on which he had previously sat. The example of Pascal, for whom no devotion was too popular, ratified his own devotion to Lourdes, and also to Lisieux. A pious contemporary of Pascal had observed that 'the grace of God can be recognized in great minds by little things, and in ordinary minds by great things.' Mauriac found God more easily in solitude than in society, but the Christian, like other men, could not remain for ever in his room. If he went on a pilgrimage he left his room, but God went with him.

It was natural, at this time of painful, if salutary, transition, that Mauriac should have turned to Racine. He had done so at Malagar during the *grandes vacances* of 1927. There were similarities both of temperament and situation. When, in his admirable *Vie de Jean Racine,*[1] he describes the poet as *frémissant*, he is describing himself. It was said of Racine that, although he had expressed the wish to be buried at Port-Royal, he would never have buried himself there while he was alive. Nevertheless, as in the case of Mauriac, the rigours of Jansenism overhung his youth, and provoked a natural reaction. But where Racine rallied to its doctrines on the threshold of middle age and – apart from *Esther, Athalie*, and the *Cantiques* – wrote no more, Mauriac rallied to a more balanced spirituality and went on writing until his fingers could no longer hold a pen. Where Racine abandoned the theatre, Mauriac courted it – for a time, with considerable success. Racine spent the later years of his life in servile flattery of Louis XIV, but stood finally in the shadow of the sunshine which had warmed him. If an unfriendly critic complains that Mauriac served General de Gaulle with no less fidelity, he was at least faithfully rewarded. It would be true to say of both men in their maturity, as Mauriac said of Racine, that they were 'père de famille et bourgeois, sans ostentation ni gêne.'

Mauriac knew 'what it was to live, from his earliest years, in a kind of familiar terror, in the presence of a God whose eye is upon us, even in our dreams.' The hymn chanted at his first Communion began with the words: 'Tabernacle *redoutable*'. The coincidence of Easter and spring was responsible for the tensions of any religious education, and Racine's adolescence had been troubled by it. Each of them had a heart 'ardent

[1] *O.C. VIII.*

et faible'. Each had yielded to 'the instinct which leads very young men to seek the friendship of those who are in the way of success, and to swim in their wake.' It is easy to imagine Mauriac, in some modest hotel, having asked for a chamber pot, being annoyed when he was brought a dish-warmer. Bossuet had been severe on writers whose profession it was to describe the passions; the debate still went on within the Church, and Mauriac, like Racine, had suffered from its irritations. He knew, but vainly pleaded, that one could not 'bring people to a better understanding of mankind without serving the cause of the Catholic religion.' Again, like Racine, he was 'irritable in proportion to his tenderness. He would put up with nothing from other people because there was one person from whom he would put up with everything.' If his family suspected little of his internal torment, it was perhaps because 'the most sincere of men is instinctively insincere with his children'. And if Racine, as he approached the apogee of his achievement in *Phèdre*, showed a little less irritability, it was because he already felt 'the pleasant and passing influences which the Académie française never ceases to radiate from afar upon those who venture to approach it.' Mauriac would not have very long to wait.

He was writing from the heart when he observes: 'We don't always know when people like us, but we nearly always know when they do not'; and when he attributes to Racine, through Phèdre, 'the certainty, fatal to human happiness, that carnal love is evil, and the evil that we cannot help committing'. The pages on *Phèdre* are of a piercing insight, because Mauriac himself is pierced by them. 'Two protagonists: Phèdre and God. A poet brings human love to trial before the judgement seat of God.' When Louis XIV heard recited the following couplet of Racine

> *Je ne fais pas le bien que j'aime,*
> *Et je fais le mal que je hais*

he turned to Madame de Maintenon and remarked 'Madam, I know both those men very well.' François Mauriac knew them too.

The *Vie de Jean Racine* was greatly admired by André Gide, although the admiration was double-edged:

> 'You show a greater advance here in your knowledge of mankind, perhaps, than in any of your novels; and I think I prefer the author of *Racine* to the disturbing author of *Destins*, even . . . But for all the involutions of your specious thought, the Catholic point of view of the ageing Racine and your own point of view as a Catholic novelist differ to such an extent as to be positively opposed. Racine thanks God for His clemency in accepting him as

His own *in spite* of his tragedies which he wished he had not written and which he talked of burning . . . . You, on the other hand, congratulate yourself that before Racine died God spared him the time to write his plays, and to write them *in spite* of his conversion. In fact, what you are searching for is the *permission* to write *Destins* — the *permission* to be a Catholic without having to burn your books; and it is this that makes you write them in such a way that you will not have to disown them on account of your Catholicism. This reassuring compromise, which allows you to love God without losing sight of Mammon, causes you anguish of conscience and at the same time gives a great appeal to your face and a great savour to your writings; and it ought to delight those who, while abhorring sin, would hate not to be able to give a lot of thought to it. You know, moreover, what the effect would be on literature and especially on your own; and you are not sufficiently Christian to cease to be a writer. Your particular art is to make accomplices of your readers. . . . Doubtless if I were more of a Christian I should be less your disciple.'[1]

Gide published this letter in *la Nouvelle Revue Française*, and Mauriac raised no objection to his having done so — although Gabriel Marcel had written that it was 'difficult to discredit more perfidiously the Christianity itself of M. Mauriac.'[2] Further correspondence, however, gave Mauriac the opportunity to clarify his position. He had been 'inoculated' by Christianity; he had not 'chosen' it. 'I shake the bars all the more violently because I know they are indestructible.' But he felt that Gide's analysis, which was anodyne in a private letter, might appear differently on the printed page. They met shortly afterwards, and Mauriac hoped that he had given Gide proof of his personal affection. 'For me you remain the adversary in the noblest understanding of the word — the one who could have got the better of me — who could still get the better of me.'[3] What Gide admired in Mauriac was — as he saw it — the compromise between the writer and the man; what Mauriac clung to was his resolution to end the compromise between the two men at war in him.

I am 43 years old, and I can no longer be torn in half . . . The question is to know whether the process of growing old should not be a process of sanctification. Shall this flesh of ours, which nobody can love, turn us away any longer from the Spirit which

---

[1] *God and Mammon* (1936), 18 (English edition).

[2] *L'Europe nouvelle:* 30 March, 1929.

[3] *Cahiers André Gide 2.* May 1928, 78.

is not bound by time and which is also — supremely and uniquely — made for love — the Spirit which is love itself?[1]

So far from being condemned to intellectual stagnation, the mind of the practising Christian was nourished by an inward purity:

> That I can assure you. My intellectual life is far richer since I have been living in a more Christian way; my curiosity is greater; and I am much more interested in ideas. We know only too well, alas! that when we are not living a good life, there is only one thing, at bottom, that interests us.[2]

In 1931 Mauriac added *Bonheur du Chrétien* to *Souffrances du Pécheur* and published them together. Only in the former did he now recognize the man he had become — still a cripple but now walking with crutches. 'Just as the morning light consumes the desert, so this morning the little Host rises, is lifted up, radiates, and takes possession of this creature with its quiet power.' Here was a 'mysterious economy whose laws escape all investigation, unforeseeable correspondences, secret compensations, and stunning gifts.' The real suffering of the Christian was not, as he had once suggested, the inability to satisfy his desires with an easy conscience; it was the failure to be a saint. Cybele and Christ were reconciled at last:

> At the flight of a bird, the Host is no further away from me than it would be in a cathedral. Cybele is purified by Him that I do not see; she closes upon Him, hiding Him under leaves and stones; she contains Him; the rays of the monstrance are vines and forests.[3]

Madame Jean-Paul Mauriac died in the summer of 1929. In fact she had been dying for the past four years, walking slowly with her stick and avoiding the slight slope that led down to the terrace at Malagar. Only her practical concern for the vintage distracted her from the contemplation of eternity; and then her fingers would close once again upon her rosary. She never suggested that François' books had troubled her; only, after reading an essay of his on Bordeaux, she remarked: 'I did not realise that you had been such an unhappy child.' Neverthless she must, he felt, have suffered from seeing 'the eccentricities of a grandfather attributed to a great-aunt and monsters inhabiting the honourable old house between its arbour and its meadow.' But there was never

[1] Ibid., 80-1.

[2] Ibid., 83. 11 May 1931.

[3] *O.C. VII*, 266.

a reproach, never a complaint.

> Every Christian mother is a resurrection of Saint Monica. In our infinitely smaller way, we were still a mother and her son at the window or on the edge of a terrace, and the same sun that shone upon Ostia shone upon our humble Malagar. She could not die until I was in the hands of God. In the dining-room, when we came back from Mass, she still had a joy in serving us, and pouring out the coffee with her poor deformed hand.[1]

François was not at Malagar when she died, but he was told of her last words. 'It is this light that I am sad to be leaving, and these trees.'

[1] Ibid.

SOUS LA COUPOLE - Académie

1

The effect upon his writing of the crisis Mauriac had just been through was of much concern alike to himself and to other people. He was a penetrating critic of both, and indulgent only to the latter. In *Trois Grands Hommes devant Dieu*[1] – essays published in 1929 and 1930, afterwards collected in a single volume (1947) – he scrutinised Molière, Rousseau, and Flaubert. Molière had taken on Pascal's 'wager' in favour of belief, and discovered comedy in the man who worried about his soul. Fashioning himself on Gibbon's 'rational voluptuary' who adhered 'with invariable respect to the temperate dictates of nature', he found himself suspected of incest; and those who knew them both compared his taciturnity to the good humour of Pascal – and Pascal had the excuse of chronic ill health to put him out of temper. Having recognized the fatal domination of the senses and the impotence of reason to control them, Molière could not reconcile himself to the discovery. Even the despair of the *misanthrope* was turned to ridicule – for the 'Roi Soleil' had to be amused, and if Molière shared the desperation of Arnolphe he was obliged to conceal it behind a satiric smile. Was Pascal's search for the meaning of life in a separation from the world any more unreasonable than Molière burning his candle at both ends? But, just as he had the genius of the theatre in his veins, so he had its charity and its courage in his heart. When he was at the end of his tether he insisted on acting for an audience of fifty poor working men. It was their day off; what would they do if he did not appear? He showed to his public the compassion he had refused to his characters.

Rousseau had rightly been called the 'father of the modern world', and Mauriac, scenting the contagion, did not spare him. The envy that preached the gospel of equality; the tenderness that abandoned five children to the public care; the hypocrisy that pretended they would be the better off for his desertion; the corruption of conscience worshipped as a 'divine instinct'; the corrosive lie which transmuted good into evil; the cult of 'sincerity' which had found its latest neophyte in André Gide – all this was a seductive counterfeit of the virtues it essentially

[1] *O.C. VIII.*

denied. Mauriac himself was something of an 'esprit mobile', but he accompanied the 'promeneur solitaire' with his eyes wide open, comparing Rousseau's 'All I shall need to be happy is myself' with St John of the Cross: 'We shall be judged according to our love'.

In the case of Flaubert, Mauriac preferred the man who idolised his art to the man who exploited it. But Flaubert's meticulous observation did not go deep enough; it stopped short of the soul. Or rather, he had nothing of his own to oppose to his immersion in the characters he had conceived. It was one thing to say: 'Madame Bovary, c'est moi'; but he had said the same thing of Bouvard and Pécuchet: 'They possess me to such an extent that I've become one of them, and it's killing me.' But Flaubert had the grace to admire Voltaire and detest his progeny; 'the people' he said 'who laugh at the great things'. Flaubert gave himself away in the admission: 'I hate life; I am a Catholic' – for he was alienated from Catholicism by contempt. Only with Madame Arnoux in *L'Education Sentimentale*, and in *Un Coeur Simple*, did he overcome it; and it was not in the patient search for an adjective or an assonance that his art, considerable as it was, betrayed its weakness, but in turning an instrument into an idol, and in maintaining himself at one remove from life. The greatest novelists – and Mauriac quoted George Eliot, Tolstoy, and Dostoievsky – had not been content to sit on the bank while the flotsam and jetsam of human experience drifted down the stream. This was certainly not the stance he had chosen for himself. Gide, while admiring these essays, thought them 'clever rather than just'; here and there Mauriac seemed to be 'finding what he was looking for, and nothing but what he wanted to discover'.[1]

In a further essay (*Le Roman*, 1928) Mauriac examined what he called 'the crisis of the novel'. Of course there is always a 'crisis of the novel', and what Mauriac wrote on the subject in 1928 is hardly different from what he might have written today; except that the 'nouveau roman' had not yet come to distract the reader from the study of human beings to the contemplation of inanimate objects. The crisis was due to the change in social convention and moral beliefs. If it was of no consequence whether A slept with B, the area of inward or outward conflict was considerably narrowed. The genius of Proust had enlarged the area of sensation, but the novelist would try to improve upon Proust at his peril; he would do better to supply the religious or metaphysical dimension which in Proust was missing. Here Mauriac invoked the influence of Dostoievsky, not only because Dostoievsky believed that man had a soul, but because he shattered the idea that man was all of a piece. He had shown that, more often than not, contradiction was the

[1] *Journal*, 9 April 1930. *O.C. VIII.*

clue to character. This intuition that man was chaotic rather than consistent challenged the tradition of the French novel, handed down from Balzac to Bourget, and its effect upon Mauriac can be seen in Thérèse Desqueyroux, and in other characters still to be examined. Mauriac did not go so far in this direction as his great contemporary, Georges Bernanos, but it is safe to conclude that neither Mauriac nor Bernanos would have written as they did, or been accepted as they were accepted, if Dostoievsky had not shown them the way. Other novelists — Colette, for example, whom Mauriac ardently admired — had illustrated the 'misère de l'homme' of which Pascal had written; but Mauriac was almost alone in defining it as the 'misère de l'homme sans Dieu'. Such a definition could not be expected of Colette; nevertheless 'this pagan and carnal writer leads us irresistibly to God.'

Here, the reader may object, Mauriac was speaking for himself. As a practising novelist, he had to meet the challenge of Verlaine: 'Ah! tout est bu, tout est mangé. Plus rien à dire!' There would, in fact, be plenty to say; but he resolutely set his face against any conception of the novel diverted from its proper purpose which was 'the understanding of man'. To throw light on what was 'most individual, particular, and distinct in the heart' of a human being was his essential business. But in doing so he must set his face against nothing in the tradition of the French novel, and yet enrich it with the contribution of foreign masters, Russian and Anglo-Saxon, and particularly of Dostoievsky. 'We must leave to our heroes the illogical, indeterminate, and complex characteristics which are proper to living creatures; and at the same time continue to construct and to organise according to the genius of our race — to remain writers of order and clarity.' By these standards he was content to be judged. He maintained with Ramon Fernandez — who was a critic and also a philosopher — that 'a novel that succeeds is the most artistic of all literary genres precisely because its aesthetic equilibrium is more interior, and more independent of fixed and apparent rules.' The difficulty was 'to reconcile the liberty of the creature and the liberty of the Creator' — for Mauriac had described the novelist as 'the ape of God'. And the French novelist, in dictating the behaviour of his characters, too often resembled 'the God of Jansenius'. Speaking for himself, Mauriac was 'never so reassured about the value of my work as when my hero forces me to change the direction of the book in hand, pushes me, and draws me on towards horizons which at first I had not glimpsed.'

Some of these themes were taken up on a more personal note in Dieu et Mammon (1929). How to reconcile the 'utility-sense of the apostle and the disinterestedness of the artist'? It was not that he wished to evade the 'cross' he had accepted; this would be nothing more than 'a fleeing from one's own self and a losing of one's own self, for our special aspect is given us by our sorrow and our special contours are fixed and checked by our cross.'[1] He did not wish to be 'embogged half-way up Mount Tabor, incapable of advancing or escaping'. Yet it never occurred to him that he should cease to write; still less, as Gide suggested, ask anyone's permission to do so. The world was still waiting for 'the miracle of a writer who is reduced to silence by God'. Even Racine, though he had renounced the theatre, had not completely laid down his pen.

The writer's urge to communicate derived from his unwillingness to remain alone. Baudelaire had compared artists to lighthouses. 'They light a great fire in the darkness, and they set light to themselves so as to attract the greatest number of their fellow-beings to them.' Mauriac was agonisingly aware of his responsibility. Must he falsify the truth to avoid giving offence to pious ears? Yet he knew from his correspondence that his most severely censured novel[2] – he did not specify which – had exercised the strongest religious influence on his readers. It was all very well for Maritain to say: 'purify the source'. Maritain was a philosopher dealing with concepts; Mauriac was a novelist dealing with creatures, drawn from a knowledge of the world and a knowledge of himself – often, as he said, 'from the most troubled depths' of his being. Maritain, in replying to Mauriac,[3] recognized the difference. The novelist should not be compared to a scientist observing phenomena; his characters would have no life unless they existed in him, and he in them. Nevertheless his public was much wider than the philosopher's or the scientist's, and his influence for good or evil correspondingly greater. Maritain scented a Manichean tendency in Mauriac of which the later novels show less trace. There need be no limit to the novelist's connivance with his characters. But it was one thing to understand why a person had behaved in a certain way, and quite another to insinuate a moral approval or disapproval of what he had done. The moralist – or the immoralist – must not trespass upon the rights of the imaginative artist.

Dieu et Mammon was a direct reply to the letter of Gide, discussed in the previous chapter. Many years later, on the occasion of the book's republication, Mauriac tells us how he was at first unaware of the 'aspic' hidden in the bouquet. Nothing, he wrote, was more important than *Dieu et Mammon* for an understanding of his personal history. Gide had intervened at a moment when the issue was still in doubt. If Mauriac was ever to renounce his Christian faith, he was then at the cross-roads where he might have taken the wrong turning. He described the book as

[1] *God and Mammon*, 38 (English edition).

[2] Probably *Destins*.

[3] *Roseau d'Or*, no. 32.

a 'hearth covered with cinders which gave out their sparks, and the fire was re-kindled a little later on.' The struggle had grown less intense, but it had never ceased altogether. Even old age had not arrested it; it merely seemed further off.

> From a promontory which overlooks the ocean and the night we sometimes turn our head in the direction of the plain where a battle of phantoms is being waged; but it is only in thought and in desire that we any longer take part in it.[1]

Ce qui était perdu (1930) was described as a 'novel of transition', but if this meant that it fell between two styles, the criticism was hardly justified. It was vulnerable, however, on another count. Mauriac held that, with *Les Anges Noirs* et *Le Noeud de Vipères*, it was one of the only three novels of his that could, without restriction, be classified as 'Catholic'. Here he was walking on slippery ground and with less assurance than he was afterwards to show. The fear of scandal and the wish to edify are too apparent. The action is confined to Paris, and to the milieu of 'Le Boeuf sur le Toit' which he knew so well but rarely treated. The interest is skilfully divided between six characters. Hervé de Blénauge is as repellent an individual as you will find in any of Mauriac's novels, where he certainly does not lack competitors. At once cowardly, ruthless and devious, he is consistently unfaithful to his wife whom he has married only for her money. Irène de Blénauge is asking Nietzsche for a meaning to a life threatened by cancer or tuberculosis, according to the rival diagnoses. An essentially noble character — and admirably drawn — she devotes much of her time to the sick and needy, and repays her husband's neglect with magnanimity. Only at the end does his mother force him to recognize his own likeness. 'Now you see yourself, and know yourself.. . . You realise that mud is mud.' Madame de Blénauge is a rigid Catholic, visiting Irène whenever she gets the chance, and working like a beaver for her salvation. For Irène — as for Anna de Noailles — 'The Catholic Church is my mother-in-law.' Hervé, having arranged to spend the week-end with his mistress, reluctantly agrees to stay at home and read aloud to his wife. When she falls asleep, he seizes the opportunity to escape; but the closing of the door wakes her up, and in despair she takes an overdose of gardenal, reviewing her past life in delirium. These pages are among the finest in the book; only at the end does Mauriac's desire to edify betray him. Was it likely that, in her search for love, she should 'recognise, see, and at last call upon this love by a name which is above all other names'? It was not impossible; but while all things are possible

---

[1] *Mémoires Intérieurs*, 248-9.

to God, all things are not prudent for the novelist. Irène was too good a woman for her suicide to rob her of salvation; and Mauriac would have done better to leave her as he had left Thérèse Desqueyroux on the pavement, but with rescue more certainly at hand. It was in her character that she should call upon somebody, but not that she should call upon His name. What others might condemn, or conceal, as a suicide was in reality a sacrifice to the Unknown God.

This scene is followed by another equally fine, but similarly flawed. Madame de Blénauge seeks out a priest and accuses herself in confession of having forced Irène into marriage with her son, and of having allowed her to die alone. The priest consoles her with the following words: 'I can only tell you again what the Master inspires me to make you understand: "She was absent, but I was there".' The priest had every reason to give hope to his penitent, but would he have claimed the authority of so direct an inspiration? Again, he might have done so; but again, though a little less implausibly, Mauriac forces the note.

Irène, Hervé, and his mother compose only one side of a diptych. Hervé's friend, Marcel Revaux, also has a wife and a mistress. (Hervé's mistresses are so numerous as not to be worth the naming.) Marcel is a novelist who has exhausted such powers as he possessed; Tota, his wife, is a country girl from Entre-Deux-Mers, attracted by a drug addict, William Turner; and his mistress, Maria Chavès, is in a clinic undergoing a cure of disintoxication. Both Marcel and Maria are on friendly terms with Irène, and Maria depends on her to complete her cure. A breath of fresh air is brought into this hot-house of marital discontent and frustrated desire by the arrival of Tota's brother, Alain Forcas, on his first visit to Paris from the Gironde, and the bedside of a father incurably ill and ferociously anti-clerical. Alain is only nineteen, and we already suspect in him the stirrings of a religious vocation, so alien does he appear to the surroundings in which he finds himself. But if Alain is in love with God without knowing it, Tota is in love with Alain without knowing it. The horrifying suggestion is insinuated by Marcel. Charles Du Bos admired the delicacy with which Mauriac had raised the theme of incest, although Mauriac wished that he had explored it in greater depth. He had taken his cue from Augustine's 'Etiam peccata serviunt'; God made use of our worst inclinations. Tota's passion is half-reciprocated, again unconsciously, but for Alain this 'pays sans chemin' is not a 'pays sans issue', and it is not long before he perceives the exit. Where it will lead him we shall discover in *Les Anges Noirs*. The character is beautifully drawn; certain features of it were borrowed from a young priest he had known in Paris, afterwards to be killed in 1940. Mauriac had wished to show 'the possibilities of deviation at the root of sanctity'.[1] Nevertheless, of all his novels, *Ce qui était perdu* left the author with a sense of a lost opportunity. He felt that it was only 'the sketch of what could have become a great book'; and regretted 'a kind of timidity before a frightening theme'. It did not frighten André Gide. 'I shall never dare say to Mauriac that far from giving me a disgust and horror of the incest which his characters seem likely to commit, he only makes me ardently hope that they will in fact commit it – at least for such a reader as myself.'[2] Mauriac remained, however, justifiably attached to Irène de Blénauge:

> I have always had a predilection for these eager and noble souls who, in their search for God, come up against the false God of their bourgeois milieu; the idols of a conformist religion intervene between them and the Trinity, and their atheism is the unconscious homage they pay to the infinite Being. Written at a time when I was most preoccupied with religion, *Ce qui était perdu* visibly suffered from the desire to edify, combined with the fear of giving scandal.[3]

Just as Mauriac looked forward to what might become of Alain Forcas, he was still haunted by Thérèse Desqueyroux. As Alain is walking along the boulevard, he sees a woman seated under a lamp-post. Her throat, visible above her chinchilla fur, seems offered to the executioner's knife; and her repeated sighs suggest that she is ill. Alain recognizes the accent of the Gironde, and they fall into conversation. She asks him to find her a taxi and they walk together in the direction of the rue Royale. When he enquires the cause of her suffering she replies – as ever mysteriously: 'From somebody' – with a peculiar emphasis. She stops at the point where the trees come to an end, and indicates a bench. 'We sat there one evening last July. It's all over.' Then she gives Alain her card: 'Thérèse Desqueyroux, 11 bis, quai d'Orléans'. 'Oh' he replies casually 'that's a name from our part of the world.' He does not meet her again, but we shall meet her – and more than once.

2

Anything that Mauriac wrote about another writer was in the nature of a personal encounter, whether it were a man like Racine whom he was glad to meet or like Rousseau whom he could not help meeting. Pascal had walked at his side ever since he had sat at the feet of Fortunat

---

[1] Interview with Jean Amrouche.

[2] Letter to Roger Martin du Gard, 2 June 1930 (*Cahiers André Gide* 2, 230).

[3] *D'autres et moi*, 254.

Strowski in Bordeaux. As a writer he had taken from Pascal his curiosity about human nature, the rapier thrusts of his polemic, and the glacial purity of his style. It was the moralist, not the mathematician, who attracted him; nevertheless, as he wrote in *Blaise Pascal et sa soeur Jacqueline* (1931),[1] 'Grace has never prevented a geometrician from arguing.' In the case of Mauriac it only fortified the taste for argument. If Pascal had something in common with Racine, Jacqueline was like a character out of Corneille. Without the genius of her brother she had the greater strength, and an easier approach to sanctity. Mauriac was still at grips with the 'démon de midi'; Pascal was for a long time at grips with the demon of pride. He confused the *libido sciendi* with the *libido dominandi*, and was not immune, Mauriac suggests, from the *libido* with which he himself was so well acquainted. Had he not reminded the Queen of Sweden that 'the power of kings over their subjects was only an image of the power of superior minds over minds inferior to them'? His youth, like Mauriac's, had been studious and withdrawn; perhaps, at the age of thirty, he had yielded to the same seduction of a society of which he could never feel completely a part. At every turn of his prodigious career, Pascal was a lover — 'even' he had written 'in those things from which it seems that love has been separated.'

Mauriac was speaking for himself as well as for his subject when he wrote that

> In lives naturally turned towards God there is nearly always a time, more or less long, of weariness where everything worldly appears attractive to the soul; it forces itself to pleasure as vainly as others force themselves to heroism and sanctity; it admires what is beneath it and envies what is too low for it to gather up.

Mauriac had suffered too much from a Jansenist upbringing not to be alert to the angelic pride of Port-Royal. He saw the doctrine of predestination for the monstrous aberration that it was; and saw, too, that the 'passion of opposition' was essential to the genius of Jansenism, as indeed it had been to all the greater heresies. It had notably served the sublime polemic of Pascal; and when Mauriac turned to polemics himself he recognized its dangers. Pascal had recognized them too. 'The desire for victory is so natural, that when it is disguised by the desire to secure the triumph of truth, one often takes the one for the other, and one thinks one is seeking the glory of God where one is in fact seeking one's own.' Mauriac knew, like any other Catholic, that the conscience can be deformed as well as reassured by casuistry.

> If certain casuists are ridiculous when they cheat with God and

[1] *O.C. VIII.*

oppose an imbecile and cunning procedure to His justice, the
Jansenists are even more repellent when they assign limits to the
infinite mercy and decree its laws. And the infallible Church has
condemned them both . . . One only has to live in the provinces
to realise the ravages of Jansenism in this respect. How many
frightened hearts have been severed from what should have been
their strength and their joy!

Mauriac admitted that, for all the verve of the *Provincial Letters*, the
Jesuits were in the right against Pascal, and for this reason one could
forgive him for 'clearing the way to Voltaire'. If the life of François
Mauriac presents something of a paradox, he had laid his finger on
much that was paradoxical in the life of the Franch writer whom, with
Racine, he admired beyond all others. Attached as he was to the most
terrifying theology of grace, Pascal needed the sensible consolations of
religion; not for him the 'dark night of the soul'. The scourge of his
century, he still possessed its graces and its ways. Continuing to believe
in the God of Port-Royal who had sentenced the majority of mankind
to eternal damnation, he yet lived in closest union with the God of
mercy incarnate in Jesus Christ. Feeling himself obliged to resist or to
compel attraction, he could still, three months before his death, after
attending Mass at Saint-Sulpice, regard with pleasure and astonishment
the beauty of a young girl. The clergy of Saint-Sulpice were the sworn
enemies of Jansenism, and on this occasion their ministrations had a
salutary effect. If Pascal was 'one of us', Mauriac understood the reason.

This Jansenist is a son of Montaigne. Montaigne was his real
master. It was not from Jansenius that he learned his knowledge
of the human heart. . . . Pascal throws a tragic light on the valleys
and mountain tops of the same heart and the same nature that
had attracted the observation of Montaigne. His lightning tears
open the brassy sky, and bathes the human landscape where the
author of the *Essais* walked without fear. What was only a hollow
becomes an abyss, and what was only a mountain touches the sky.

In his next novel, *Le Noeud de Vipères*, (1932) Mauriac showed how
largely he was indebted to them both. Here, he felt, he had most nearly
succeeded in achieving what he had set out to do. With *Thérèse
Desqueyroux*, this has proved the most popular of his works, and it is
in some respects the most characteristic. The title indicates, accurately
enough, a subject sombre in the extreme. Mauriac's new found security
of faith in no way modified his view of human nature. With relentless
realism, and brilliantly assured technique, he takes us down into the
depths; even, indirectly, into 'le plus trouble de moi-même'. The setting,

once again, is Malagar, although the 'knot of vipers' resembles no family that had ever lived there. Only for the central character did Mauriac admit having taken certain features from his father-in-law. Louis — whose surname we are never told — relates his own story in a letter to his wife, Isa, who has quite unexpectedly predeceased him. The letter is found, uncompleted, by his son, Hubert — and Hubert is allowed a pejorative gloss upon its contents. Louis' grand-daughter, Janine, however, who has been close to him during his last days, confirms the sincerity of what she rightly supposes to have been his final dispositions. The man who had passed his life in a 'knot of vipers', very largely of his own creation, had in the end, like Irène de Blénauge, called upon 'the name which is above all other names'. Why do we believe in his appeal more readily than in hers?

The answer would appear to be that grace is given to one according to one's needs — not necessarily according to one's deserts. Or, more exactly, Irène, through a lifetime of self-abnegation, had already received grace, though she was not aware of it. She had called upon Nietzsche, which was better than calling upon nobody, and another had answered her appeal. The Louis of *Le Noeud de Vipères* had called upon nothing. He had reversed the second great commandment and, with one or two significant exceptions, hated his neighbour as himself. Mauriac plumbs very deep in revealing self-hatred as the root of the hatred he inspires in other people; and the avarice which accumulates its bonds and bullion as the image of a heart which he refuses to unlock. The only son of a widowed mother, of fairly humble birth, clever at school and later a brilliant advocate, with no physical graces but a considerable fortune, Louis marries a girl from a consumptive family, only too relieved to find her a husband but obviously ashamed of his inferior social standing. Louis believes that she loves him until he discovers, shortly after their marriage, that she had given her heart — though nothing else — to the partner of a previous flirtation. He never recovers from this disillusionment. Isa is punctilious in her religious devotions, to which he is bitterly hostile, and has no thought for anyone but her children. Louis, for his part, is consistently and casually unfaithful — with a particular preference for prostitutes because, in contrast to the waiters in a restaurant, he is not obliged to give them a tip! He has, however, a natural son, Robert, by a former mistress. Knowing that his *angina pectoris* may at any moment bring his life to an end — for he is 68 years old when he sets out to tell his story — he lures Robert into a scheme to defraud his family of their inheritance only to discover, a few days later, that Robert, frightened of the possible judicial consequences, had revealed the plot to two members of the family in exchange for the promise of a secure income. Louis then learns that his wife has died, and that Janine has been deserted by her husband. This is the turning point in his itinerary of hate.

He knows perfectly well what his family think of him, which is no worse than what he thinks of himself. They call him a 'crocodile'. Nevertheless Mauriac is careful not to redeem even the worst of his characters without exposing some patch of ground upon which grace can operate. Louis was astonished when a young seminarian, engaged as tutor to the children, had told him that he was a 'good man'. He does not recognize 'goodness' in his devotion to his daughter, Marie, and in his grief when she dies young; nor in his affection for his nephew Luc, who is killed in the Great War; nor in his understanding of Janine — so different from the attitude of the other 'vipers' — when her husband leaves her. It is in a rediscovery of himself, whom he had hated, that he finds himself defenceless against the faith which he had always derided, not least because its practice by those around him was so pharisaical. Even his wife was not the immaculate *dévote* she had appeared, for among the cinders in the grate he retrieves some pages from her diary which reveal her jealousy of his attachment to Luc.

Le Noeud de Vipères is a powerful and deeply moving novel. Mauriac excites our pity for Louis in proportion as Louis does not ask it for himself. The book was praised to the skies and sealed the author's reputation. It was now clear that the French novel could stand a fairly stiff dose of metaphysics without any damage to its sales. The doors of the Académie seemed already ajar when, in the spring of 1932, the blow fell.

Mauriac was leading a regular life, and his general health had improved. He drank less — though he had never been a heavy drinker — and he no longer went to bed so late. On the eve of a lecture, however, he suddenly found himself hoarse and consulted a voice specialist. After a lengthy examination a second, and more expert, opinion was called in. Professor Hautani did not mince his words: Mauriac must enter hospital for an operation the next day, and there were eighty chances in a hundred — but no more — that he might be cured of what was evidently diagnosed as cancer: 'I was standing there in the gentle light of springtime, full of strength and vigour. Familiar sounds came from the street outside. My wife was waiting for me at home.'[1]

The operation was successful, but Mauriac emerged from it with his voice permanently impaired. He spent some time in hospital, trying to take Pascal's advice on the 'bon usage des maladies' and drawing much comfort from his faith. As he became convalescent — 'a convalescence doubtful, threatened, and in which I only half believed' — the taste for

[1] *Nouveaux Mémoires Intérieurs*, 163.

life returned to him as strongly as ever. 'I became, as I approached my fiftieth year, a young man once more.'[1] After an exhausting treatment under the rays, it was to music that he now turned – the chamber music of Mozart, which was new to him, and the Archduke Trio of Beethoven with Cortot, Thibault, and Casals. From now on, if a doubt crossed his mind as to the existence of God, a phrase of Mozart would remove it for him. After living for some time in the shadow of death, he had discovered a new lease of life, and a new reason for enjoying it. When Hautani visited him at Malagar six months later and declared him cured, he was torn between relief and scepticism. Afterwards he went with Claude for a short holiday at Font-Romeu in the eastern Pyrenees.

He was not alone in wondering if the cure would be permanent; but only three days after the operation he was elected President of the Société des Gens de Lettres, and now his election to the Académie, already probable, became an early and foregone conclusion. 'We must not let him go' Henry Bordeaux urged upon his colleagues 'without making him one of us.' But Mauriac feared that he would not be accepted unless his voice were strong enough to make the required *discours de réception*. Nevertheless, on the 1st June 1933, he enjoyed what is known as an 'élection de maréchal' – for a Marshal of France is chosen by a unanimous vote, and spared the slightly humiliating procedure of inviting it from quarters where it may be refused. Henry Bordeaux – an almost embarrassingly *bien-pensant* novelist – and Paul Valéry were his 'godfathers', and at 1 p.m. on the 16th November he rose 'sous la coupole' of the Institut de France, a slim and elegant figure in his 'immortal's' uniform, to occupy the seat left vacant by the death of Eugène Brieux. There was a roll of drums, and the *garde républicaine* presented arms as he entered the amphitheatre. Mauriac had dutifully done his homework. He did not pretend that Brieux's social dramas had for years been his bedside reading or his favourite theatrical entertainment, but he paid a generous tribute to the warmth of heart and strength of purpose which had inspired them. Brieux was too obviously a child of nineteenth-century scientism to make an appeal to a child of the Catholic revival; and the gulf between a son of the people and a scion of the *bourgeoisie* was not easily bridged. Nevertheless Mauriac shared Brieux's reaction against the cult of the *poètes maudits*, though he reminded his listeners that one of them was called Baudelaire and another Verlaine. Much of Brieux – and not the best of him – was unashamed social propaganda; he had with reason been described as 'le conférencier de la pièce' – and Mauriac was quick to apply the warning to himself. If he were asked why he did not also write plays, he confessed that he

[1] Ibid.

found the difficulty 'insurmountable'. Before long, however, he would prove able to surmount it. For the rest, he neither disguised nor paraded his religious beliefs, meeting Brieux on the words of one of his characters: 'When one has breathed the air of the temple for a long time, one can never get it completely out of one's lungs.'

It was an occasion for compliments, and in his speech of welcome André Chamieux did not spare them. He recalled, as Mauriac himself had begun by recalling, the priceless patronage of Barrès; emphasised the tension between Mauriac and the characters in his books — the 'mixture of sensuality and mysticism which is troubling and not always agreeable'; but he was strangely insensitive to Mauriac's love of nature. After the session a banquet, presided over by André Maurois and Henry Bordeaux, was held in honour of the new academician. General Gouraud with his Father Christmas beard was among the guests. Mauriac had come through the ordeal with grace and courage; it must have been painful for him to speak at all; and there was no malice in the witticism of Jean Cocteau: 'He had every voice except his own', since he had, unknowingly, taken the words out of Mauriac's own mouth. Claude Mauriac, sitting beside the abbé Mugnier, described what was left of his father's voice as 'rough, distinct, beautiful, and moving'; and Mauriac himself remembered how he had read the last pages of his text 'like a horse that gets a whiff of the stable — I set off at the gallop.'[1] A touching souvenir of the occasion was the gift of a seventeenth-century terracotta statue of St Francis of Assisi, which was taken to Malagar in 1940 and always stood in his study. It did not matter that he had been named after St François-de-Sales.

[1] *Le Temps Immobile*, 132.

THÉRÈSE REDIVIVA

1

Between his convalescence and his election to the Académie française, Mauriac wrote the only novel of his that can properly be described as autobiographical. There was no certainty that his cure would be permanent, and he did not wish *Le Noeud de Vipères* to stand as his last word on the subject of the family, or indeed as his last essay in fiction. The family in *Le Mystère Frontenac* bears certain obvious resemblances to that in which François Mauriac had grown up, and the principal character, Yves Frontenac, is a self-portrait – though 'darker and more desperate, as I might have been if I had not founded a happy family myself.'[1] It is not a flattering picture, and in reviewing a novel 'devoted to the family and its virtues', Edmond Jaloux confessed his surprise that the author had 'not felt obliged to make the central character of his story less completely egocentric'. Of story there is in fact very little, and not a great deal of mystery, for the Frontenacs are no more mutually devoted than many other families of their kind – and rather less so, by all accounts, than their acknowledged prototype.

Only two of the other characters are taken directly from life. Blanche Frontenac differs in no respect from the author's mother, as he has described her elsewhere. Widowed at an early age with five children – three sons and two daughters – she has renounced all thought of re-marriage, and gives herself wholly to her religion, her family, and her good works. She is not hardened, but narrowed, by her sense of duty, and her scruples torment no one but herself. Of limited intelligence, but practical in the management of her property, she captures nevertheless the affection of her youngest son who has met Maurice Barrès, published a volume of verse, and is surprised when people have not heard of André Gide. Even when she echoes the old reproach: 'Diseur de riens!' – the words are tenderly spoken. She loves, but does not understand her son, and is only relieved when he confesses himself shocked by a blasphemous song heard in a Paris night club. Dying of cancer, she takes the words out of the mouth of Madame Jean-Paul Mauriac; for all that she will miss will be the trees in whose shade she had liked to sit at

[1] *D'autres et moi*, 260.

116

Bourideys — which is just another name for Malagar. In the novel, as in real life, this relationship between mother and son had been at once intimate and incommunicable, and it is here transcribed with *pietas* but with no trace of sentimentality. Memory had only sharpened its contrasts.

Blanche's brother-in-law, Xavier Frontenac, is a portrait of Louis Mauriac who had acted as guardian to the children after their father's death. In the novel his function is the same. This was a case where blood was thicker than unbelief. When Xavier pays his regular fortnightly visit to Bordeaux, Blanche omits the night prayer recited in common, and Xavier is horrified at the thought that his nephews should ever learn that he keeps a mistress in Angoulême. For he, too, is rigorous in his own way — with a 'peasant and republican' probity; and he will at least light his candle before the household gods. The children are devoted to him, and of course they eventually discover his secret. When he is close to death, they meet the faded and nondescript Joséfa whom he had been ashamed either to marry or to desert. Xavier is the victim of 'his timidity, his phobias, his inadequacy, and his obsessive anxiety', and he excites pity rather than contempt.

The clue to the 'mystère Frontenac' is not, however, the clue to the 'mystère Mauriac'. There was no parallel in François' own life to the close relationship between Yves and his elder brother Jean-Louis. Neither he, nor the second brother, José, found their prototypes in the Mauriac family. It is Jean-Louis who discovers Yves' literary gifts and brings to him, in Paris, the news of their mother's death to spare him the shock of a telegram. It is Jean-Louis who understands him despite a radical difference of temperament. Where Yves spends his days in a giddy pursuit of pleasure, Jean-Louis is conventionally married and runs the family business on socially progressive lines. Here there is, indeed, a certain mystery in the affinity of apparent incompatibles, and Mauriac explores it with a delicate perception. On the one hand

> Jean-Louis did not foresee that the years would go by, that he would be the subject of a thousand dramas, that he would have children and would lose two of them, that he would make a big fortune, and that as his life drew towards its close it would crumble away — but through it all the married couple would still talk to each other in words as simple as those that satisfied them in this morning of their love, during this interminable déjeuner, where the wasps buzzed in the fruit dishes, and the ice pudding collapsed in its pink juice.

François Mauriac had now behind him twenty years of married life, and although he had once shared the feverish ambitions of Yves Frontenac, and had since realised them to the letter, a passage from his

Journal of 1934 shows that he appreciated what Jean-Louis and his wife — who certainly lacked the brilliance of Jeanne Mauriac — had to look forward to.

> Still, after many years, to have so much to say to one another, from the most trivial to the most serious, without any desire to astonish or to be admired — what a wonderful thing that is! No more need of lies; man and wife have become so transparent to each other that lying can no longer be of any use. This is the only love that cherishes immobility, that feeds on the habitual and daily round.[1]

A passage describing Yves Frontenac's reverie, as he stands at the window looking out on to the pines of Bourideys — which is only another name for Saint-Symphorien — is curiously prophetic. Is this what Mauriac himself was feeling when his personal future, and the political future of Europe, looked uncertain?

> He awaited everything and invited everything, even suffering, but not the shame of surviving over a number of years the loss of his inspiration; of relying on tricks to sustain his fame. And he did not foresee that he would express this drama, day by day, in a diary that would be published after the Great War; he would resign himself to this, for it would be some years since he had written anything. And these agonizing pages would save his face; they would do more for his reputation than his poems; they would charm, and agreeably trouble, a generation given over to despair!

Did Mauriac already have an inkling of what his role was to be after a second Great War, although matters more important than his own reputation would be the subject of his polemic or his introspection?

Edmond Jaloux was right. Yves Frontenac is deplorably egocentric, and no one could acquit — or indeed wish to acquit — his prototype of a passionate interest in himself. A certain egocentricity is an ingredient of compulsive literature. What would be left of St Augustine or Chateaubriand if they had not been interested in themselves? The fascination of *Le Mystère Frontenac* is to conjecture how far Mauriac in his middle age has transformed — and not for the better — the Mauriac of his adolescence and early youth. Here, for example, is the Mauriac whom religious belief had imprisoned rather than liberated:

> Why have they taught us to doubt the existence of nothingness? What cannot be remedied is to believe, in spite of everything

[1] *Journal I,* 38.

and against all the evidence, in eternal life. This is to lose the refuge of nothingness.

When Yves Frontenac hears the appeal of a love 'which would have united you to all other men in charity', he shakes his head and asks God to 'leave him alone'. There were many times, no doubt, when François Mauriac had done the same. Had he been, like Yves, a young man for whom love was a 'torturing imagination'? Had he so organised his life in those last years of the 'belle époque' that no evening should be without its engagement? Had he been — or was he still — alternately a brilliant and a lugubrious guest? Were his sentimental adventures so abortive? At least there is no reason to suppose they had led him to attempted suicide. Mauriac does not judge his milieu in *Le Mystère Frontenac*; for him, as for Yves, Blanche and Xavier, it remains in some sort sacred and untouchable, aureoled 'with a poetry from which they could not escape', and which the novelist conveys by his evocation of place and season. Yet there is no prettifying of the family album. Yves Frontenac, like his author, has one eyelid lower than the other; and Uncle Xavier, as he looks at his nephews under the lamplight, sees the 'bare knees with their scratches and cuts, the unwashed legs, the hob-nailed ankle-boots, and the broken laces tied together in knots' — the poetry of the commonplace, and the perennial images of the nursery.

2

It was a time for stock-taking, and in the same year (1933) Mauriac lifted the curtain on the creative process of the novelist in an essay, *Le Romancier et ses Personnages.*[1] With the deliberate exception of *Le Mystère Frontenac*, he had proved that 'the novelist begins to take shape in us at the same time as we begin to detach ourselves from our own feelings.' In that conventional family of Frontenacs, he had been the spy — the traitor unconscious of his treachery — who captured, registered, and retained unawares the obscure complexity of daily life. He never conceived a novel without having clearly in his mind, down to its minutest detail, the house and surroundings where the action would take place. He admitted the monotony of atmosphere to which his choice of theme, place, and milieu condemned him; nor was it enough to reproduce, in one book after another, the properties he had known since he was a child. He invaded the houses of his neighbours, using as a theatre for some drama of intolerable tension the salon where old ladies had once offered him 'the finest muscat grapes, cream pastries,

[1] *O.C. VII.*

quince *pâtes,* and a large glass of slightly sickly *orgeat.* '[1]

It was one thing to observe, another to transform. Thérèse Desqueyroux owed something to the poisoner he had watched at the Bordeaux assizes, but who had nothing in common with the character who did not herself know what had driven her to crime. If she had been living in Paris she would have known quite clearly, but in Paris it was 'difficult to imagine a rural world where a woman understands nothing of herself, once her feelings stray ever so little from the norm.'[2] Similarly, the central character of *Le Noeud de Vipères,* and the principal outlines of his story, were the fruit of observation; but once the character began to move he became totally different from his prototype. The novel was essentially the story of a recovery, and it finished when the author had 'restored to my hero, to this son of darkness, his right to love and to illumination, and, in a word, to God.'[3] Both he and Thérèse Desqueyroux were exempt from the one vice that Mauriac found it hard to put up with in a human being: 'complacency and self-satisfaction'.[4]

If he were criticised for a monotony of characterization as well as of atmosphere, he accepted the charge and justified it. In Balzac and Tolstoy, Dickens and Dostoievsky, the same types recurred from one book to another. This was particularly true of *The Idiot.* And in his own case the principal character of *Le Noeud de Vipères* recalled, feature by feature, the principal character of *Génitrix* — and the echo was quite unintentional. It was the mark of a genuine novelist — the guarantee so to speak of his paternity — that the creatures of his imagination should exhibit a family likeness. Yet Mauriac was troubled by what appeared to him the inevitable bankruptcy of the novelist's art.

> On the one hand it claims to be the science of mankind — a swarming world which both persists and passes away — and all it can do is to isolate from the swarm, and fix under its magnifying glass a particular passion or virtue or vice which it amplifies out of all proportion: Père Goriot or a father's love, Cousin Bette or jealousy, Père Grandet or avarice. On the other hand — the novel claims to describe for us the life of society, and yet it never reaches individuals except by severing most of the roots which attach them to the group. In the word, the novel isolates and immobilises a passion in the individual, and it isolates and

---

[1] Ibid., 290.
[2] Ibid., 292.
[3] Ibid., 299.
[4] Ibid., 300.

immobilises an individual in the group. And you can say that in doing so the painter of life expresses the contrary of what life really is.[1]

This might be so, but Mauriac was encouraged by the survival – he would not have claimed the immortality – of certain of his characters. As always, he came back to Thérèse Desqueyroux. Why had she tried to poison her husband?

> The question mark has done much to preserve her melancholy shade in our midst. Several readers have looked to Thérèse for a light upon their own secret, or perhaps sought her as an accomplice. These characters are not sustained by their own life; it is our readers, and the anxiety of living hearts, that penetrate and animate these phantoms, allowing them to hover for a moment in some provincial salon, around the lamp where a young woman is lingering over her book, and pressing the paper knife against her burning cheek.[2]

The secret of Mauriac's art was an intimacy with his characters, and like other intimacies it could not be forced. 'Why don't you draw some good people?' he was often asked; but he generally made a mess of his good people. 'Try to raise their moral stature'; but the more he did so, the more obstinately they declined even the most modest elevation; 'You never write about the people' objected the democratic reader, but Mauriac replied that it was absurd to write about a milieu that one did not know. He compared his attitude towards his characters to that of a 'strict schoolmaster' who found it hard not to show a secret preference for the more unmanageable pupils. At least he had Biblical warrant for his favouritism. The intimacies of literary creation raised problems of a moral and psychological order. The dispersal of the novelist through so many characters, and the ever closer identification with them, imperilled the unity of his personality. 'How much of him is left after these multiple and contradictory incarnations?' Proteus, in reality, was nobody, because he had the power to be everyone. Just because the novelist held himself open to every impression, at the disposal of any subject, the contradictions and the multiplicity of his creation must be organised around an 'unchanging rock'; or to be more precise, around an unchanging Person. *Le Romancier et ses Personnages* is a fascinating exercise in self-examination, but Mauriac was presently to discover that the public confession of these intimacies could not be undertaken without risk.

[1] Ibid., 296.
[2] Ibid., 297.

In his next novel, _La Fin de la Nuit_ (1935), he yielded to temptation, and the temptress was Thérèse Desqueyroux. He confessed that whereas in the novel that bears her name she had imposed herself upon him, in the sequel he imposed himself upon her,[1] and he was to pay dearly for the indiscretion. Everything essential had been said about Thérèse; what happened to her, how she lived and died, could have been left to the imagination of her many readers — just as Mauriac had left her on the pavement, powdering her nose. But he had fallen in love with her, and could not leave her alone. The book was greatly damaged by a preface, which Mauriac suppressed in the collected edition of his works. Here — with an eye on the Catholic readers who had so violently attacked him over the past twenty years — he apologised for not converting Thérèse on her death-bed. In fact, he tells us, these pages were written and then destroyed, because he could not 'see' the priest who could have heard her confession. Later on, in Rome, he did see him; and he held out the prospect of telling how Thérèse 'entered into the illumination of death'. Edward Sackville-West, who has written with keen perception about Mauriac, expressed the hope that he would do no such thing[2] — and the hope was realised.

It is fifteen years since we last saw Thérèse, except for that momentary glimpse in _Ce qui était perdu_. Living alone in Paris, with only a maid to look after her, she is visited by her seventeen-year-old daughter Marie, who is in love with a student, Georges Filhot. He is reluctant to engage himself in marriage, and his parents — wealthy farmers in the _Landes_ — do not encourage him to do so. The Desqueyroux are less prosperous than they once had been, and the cloud that still overhangs their name lowers still further the price of their daughter in the marriage market. Marie now extracts from her mother the truth of what hitherto she had only heard vaguely hinted at, and Thérèse promises at the same time to settle her private fortune on Georges and Marie, should they eventually get married. When she meets Georges he falls under her spell — for she still has the remnants of beauty beneath a skilfully applied cosmetic. The ambiguity of this brief relationship illustrates what Mauriac had written in his preface about

> the power given to creatures the most burdened with fatality — the power to say no to the law that crushes them. When Thérèse, with a hesitating gesture, brushes away the hair from her ravaged forehead, so that the boy she charms shall be horrified to look at

[1] _D'autres et moi_, 252.
[2] _Inclinations_ (1946), 235.

her and shall remove himself from her presence, this gesture gives its meaning to the whole book. The unfortunate woman renews it at each encounter, never ceasing to react against her power to poison and corrupt.

As the book proceeds, her heart condition worsens and her neurasthenia turns into something not far removed from insanity. She imagines that the police are after her. Eventually Marie brings her back to her husband, and to what had once been her home in the *Landes*. It is there we take leave of her, after she has more or less forced the betrothal of Marie to Georges. One has the feeling that Thérèse should have died, if not hereafter, then at least elsewhere — though, in fact, she is still living when the novel comes to an end. It is as though Mauriac felt that she was someone about whom the last word could never be said. He certainly had great difficulty on saying it.

La Fin de la Nuit is less important for itself than for the stringent criticism it provoked from Jean-Paul Sartre. This did not appear until four years later, in February 1939; but it will be convenient to discuss it here. Twenty pages of closely reasoned, hostile dialectic in the *Nouvelle Revue Française* must have appeared to Mauriac like a betrayal in the house of his friends. The article affected, and even discouraged, him deeply, for it was a *mise en question*, not only of *La Fin de la Nuit* but of his whole practice as a novelist. Sartre was not yet the social prophet and philosopher he was shortly to become, but he was already a voice to reckon with; and in a climate of literary opinion that was rapidly changing under the threat of war and the stress of political tension he sounded a sharp discord amid the plaudits of the Académie française. The 'Immortal' was to receive a rude reminder of his mortality.

The article was entitled 'M. François Mauriac et la Liberté'. Sartre began, so to speak, by taking the ball into Mauriac's court. He did not hold it against him that he was a Christian novelist; on the contrary he maintained, quoting Dostoievsky to his purpose, that Christian belief should be to the novelist's advantage because it was based on a belief in free will. The novelist must create a dimension of time like that of the reader in which 'the future is yet to make . . . do you want your characters to come alive? Then see that they are free.' His business was 'not to explain but to *present* actions and passions which are unpredictable'. When Mauriac spoke in his preface of the 'fatality' that weighs upon Thérèse, and against which she recurrently reacts, he was apparently thinking of vices inherent in her nature. 'When liberty accepts Nature, fatality begins its reign. Or she may reject Nature, and remount the slope. Thérèse Desqueyroux *is* free.' Free, according to the preface; but not, as Sartre sees her, in the novel, where Mauriac switched back and forth between the notion of a creature struggling against tendencies in her own nature and a destiny imposed upon her from outside; in other words between the natural and the supernatural. If Sartre's criticism was well founded, Mauriac would not have been the first Christian to be caught by the problem of predestination and free will, nor the first to find it insoluble.

Sartre further accused Mauriac — and not in this novel alone — of identifying himself with a character and then considering it from outside, whether with his own eyes or those of other people. He gave the following as one example:

> She heard nine o'clock striking. She must wait a little longer, for it was too early to swallow the pill which would guarantee her a few hours of sleep; *not that this was a habit of this careful and desperate woman,* but this evening she could not deny herself the relief.

Who described Thérèse as 'careful and desperate'? Clearly not Thérèse herself. Mauriac had exchanged the liberty of his heroine for his own omniscience, and indeed he had compared the relationship of the novelist to his characters with the relationship of God to His creatures. Sartre categorically denied this. The novelist could be the witness or the accomplice of his characters, but he could not be both at the same time. And he could not be their judge. God viewed everything in the light of eternity, but once the novel escaped from the dimension of time it deserted the only atmosphere in which it could survive. In allowing his characters to do so, Mauriac destroyed their consciences; and *La Fin de la Nuit,* which he intended to be an illustration of liberty, was in fact an illustration of servitude.

By the time that Sartre mounted his attack, Mauriac had written his first play, *Asmodée,* and Sartre understood why the theatre had tempted him. It suited the quickness of his temperament and the classicism of his method. I have already described him as the most Racinian of novelists. But Sartre contrasted the dramatic construction of his dialogue with the stylisation of talk proper to the novel; to the hints, stammerings, and repetitions out of which Dostoievsky, Conrad, and Faulkner had woven the illusion of life and time. French classicism was both 'eloquent and theatrical', and the reaction against it was in full swing. Sartre sympathised with the reaction where Mauriac did not; and an opposition, initially aesthetic, was to become evident in other fields as well. But whatever justice there was in Sartre's criticism, Mauriac had sinned in good company; and it was going a little far to declare that '*La Fin de la Nuit* is not a novel' and that 'M. Mauriac is not a novelist'. Sartre delivered the *coup de grâce*

With Madame François Mauriac, at the time of his
election to the Académie française, 1933.

In Academician's robes, 1933.

Mauriac's widowed mother with her five children, *c.* 1892.

Aerial view of Malagar.

when he turned the Divine analogy against his victim:

> A novel is written by a man for men. In the sight of God, who
> penetrates appearances without pausing over them, there is no
> such thing as the novel, and no such thing as art, because art lives
> by appearances. God is not an artist; and neither is M. Mauriac.

It has seemed right to give the Devil's advocate a hearing, but I think
that Mauriac himself undervalued *La Fin de la Nuit,* and I prefer to
endorse the opinion of Edward Sackville-West that the two books that
relate the story of Thérèse compose 'a nearly faultless work of art'.[1]

4

In writing of *Les Anges Noirs* (1936) Mauriac admitted to a broadening
of his canvas 'under the influence, no doubt, of the English novel, for
as a reader I have always preferred those very long stories, very long
and very slow, of which time itself forms the thread, to stories organised
according to the rules of French classical tragedy — characters, and then
catastrophe. But I only like them when they are written by the Anglo-
Saxons and the Russians. With the exception of Proust, there is no
"roman-fleuve" in French which I enjoy as such.'[2] By a *"roman-fleuve"*
Mauriac did not, of course, mean a 'stream of consciousness', but a
novel which never looked like coming to an end.

Les Anges Noirs is certainly not a *roman fleuve* by these standards,
but it is more ambitious, both in its aim and execution, than anything
Mauriac had hitherto achieved. It is the nearest he ever came to Dostoievsky — a novel of action as well as emotional tension and metaphysical conflict, saturated in an atmosphere propitious for the confrontation of Heaven and Hell. Mauriac claimed that with *Ce qui était perdu*
and *Le Noeud de Vipères,* and with these alone of his novels, it de-
served to be described as 'Catholic', because it was based upon Revelation. What he meant by this was explained in a preface to the book
when it appeared in the Collected Edition of his works.

> The cycle of Alain Forcas is the novel of the reversibility of
> merits, and it is also the novel of vocation. Alain, chosen and
> called from the midst of a world doomed to damnation, suffers
> and pays for all my wretched protagonists. But *Les Anges Noirs*
> illustrates another idea which obsessed me at that time; that in
> the worst criminal there subsist certain elements of the saint that
> he might have become, and that in the purest human being

---

[1] *Inclinations,* 235.
[2] *D'autres et moi,* 262.

hideous possibilities lie concealed. Gradère, perverted from child-hood, sacrilegious, a pimp, procurer, thief, blackmailer and assassin, belongs none the less to the world of the spirit. He is no stranger to the pious Alain, for he is a citizen of the same invisible city. Burdened with every sin, he communicates with the supernatural from below. Beside him, Alain Forcas, brother of a debauched and incestuous sister, only escapes from the sin for which he seems to have been born by cutting himself off from the world, putting on the dress which makes him an object of ridicule, and throwing himself into the arms of God. If *Les Anges Noirs* has a merit in my eyes, it is because the metaphysical system which the book expresses nowhere appears in an abstract form; I see it as the most carnal of my novels, the most deeply rooted in the mire of human experience . . .[1]

It was the first time that Mauriac had described a murder, and al-though certain critics found this unconvincing — wrongly in my opinion — when he looked back on the novel after twelve years, he was surprised at his ability to do certain things of which he had not believed himself to be capable. 'I could have succeeded, like another, along the road which Simenon has made illustrious, and perhaps if I had known Graham Greene a little sooner . . .'[2] Gradère in *Les Anges Noirs* belongs to the same family as Pinkie in *Brighton Rock*, but does he deserve to die in his bed, at peace with God and men? Has Mauriac justified so drastic a reversal of merits? It is upon our answer to that question that our estimate of the novel must depend.

In a long prologue of seventy-two pages Gradère tells the first part of his story in an unfinished letter to Alain Forcas. The opening sen-tence gives us a necessary clue. 'I have no doubt, Monsieur l'abbé, as to the feelings of horror I must inspire in you.' Alain is now the parish priest of Liogeats in the *Landes* where Gradère is co-proprietor of the château, and he is the spiritual director of Mathilde Desbats who had once been in love with Gradère, but whom he had deceived by first seducing, and then marrying, her cousin Adila. His natural son by Adila, Andrès, has been brought up by Mathilde after Adila's death, and is now expected to marry her daughter Catherine. The price of this alliance is the sale of certain properties to Symphorien Desbats, and Gradère arrives at Liogeats for the signing of the contract. Alain Forcas is despised in the locality for giving shelter to his sister, Tota Revaux, whom we have met in *Ce qui était perdu*, and whose incestuous love for her brother has been discreetly emphasised. She has now left her

[1] Ibid., 255.
[2] Ibid.

husband, and Alain is doing his best to rescue her from drugs and debauchery. But rumour has it that she is not his sister but his mistress.

The prologue relates Gradère's fall from innocence into crime until he is now the victim of blackmail at the hands of the prostitute with whom he lives in Paris. He is now fifty years old, and his features have scarcely altered since the time when the women would embrace him in the street as he came out of school. This awareness of his own charm, and 'the desire, at first instinctive, and then more and more conscious, to utilise it' have been his undoing. What, therefore, induces him to confess his infamy to a priest from whom he neither expects nor wishes absolution? It is the nagging curiosity about his own nature, as to which he has no illusions, and the certainty that Alain can alone understand him. 'You are a child, I told myself, and even a little child, but you are forewarned. And I feel that what has been preserved in you has also been threatened.' He feels that 'one can penetrate the supernatural from below'. The conclusion of the book is thus adumbrated, however faintly, at its opening, although much will have happened in between.

What happens is murder. Catherine Desbats surprises everyone by refusing to marry Andrès, whose liaison with Tota Revaux has come to her knowledge. Symphorien Desbats is suffering from a severe heart condition, and a shock might be fatal to him. In that case why might not Andrès marry Mathilde? 'You will not forget' insinuates Gradère 'that I have secured your happiness at a time, now very near, when even the night will no longer separate you from Andrès.' Consanguineous marriages were a useful preservative of property in the *Landes,* and, after all, Mathilde and Adila had been only cousins. Symphorien, though he knows nothing of this idea, senses his danger, and knowing that Gradère is in flight from the blackmailing threats of his mistress, discovers her address and invites her, anonymously, to Liogeats. Catherine will meet her at a certain time off a certain train. Mathilde reveals the plot to Gradère who imitates Aline's voice on the telephone and thus postpones her arrival. When she comes on the day originally fixed, he is at the station to meet her, protected from identification by an umbrella. He then leads her through the pines and the drenching rain to the edge of a sandpit into which she stumbles, and there strangles and buries her.

Although he had been observed, the previous night, leaving the house with a shovel, the crime cannot be brought home to him. Nevertheless he lives in an aura of suspicion. Catherine picks up a brief notice of Aline's disappearance in a newspaper, and Gradère avoids the family, taking his meals in a café. Tota Revaux has returned to her husband, and Catherine and Andrès engage themselves to be married, though Catherine is under no illusion that her passion is reciprocated. Meanwhile, along this sinister itinerary, Gradère and Alain have been brought closer together. Shortly after his arrival at the château, Gradère had discovered a pile of twigs and greenery heaped up outside the door of the presbytery; knowing that this was a habit of the peasantry when a couple were about to get married, he had realised its impudent application to Alain and his sister, and had cleared it away overnight. Later, he slips his epistolary confession under Alain's door. The priest receives it coolly, and when he meets Gradère merely tells him that he is at the disposal of souls who seek his help. But as he begins to read it by the light of his oil lamp . . .

> His great temptation, the mystery before which Tota's brother had so often lost heart, the mystery of evil — here he was, this evening, holding it all in his hands under the blue cover of a little lined notebook. He read it straight through up to the point where Gradère, obsessed by the devil, quoted the saying of the old priest. 'There are souls which are given to *him*.' 'No' he protested aloud 'no, my God, no!' Alain did not believe that any soul had been given to *him* . . . But whence did this power come to him? To whom did he owe this principality?

Gradère continues his letter squatting on the edge of the sandpit, where the body of Aline lies rotting in the damp earth. He is drawn there 'not by remorse, but perhaps by the horror of his solitude'. From a long walk in the rain he catches a pleurisy which brings him coughing to the door of the presbytery. A window opens, and Alain Forcas gathers him up, hardly any more a man, but 'simply an object, without speech or words or gesture; a stone although the light of the lamp now fell upon his face.' He spends four months under Alain's care, watched over sometimes by Andrès. He does not give himself up to justice, although he is tempted to do so. The crime has not been discovered, and he answers the commission sent to question him about the disappearance of the woman who had been his accomplice in so many other crimes. He dies peacefully and reconciled; and as a sign of grace, and of gratitude to the man who has rescued him, he makes Andrès promise not to pursue Tota with his famished importunity. For in saving the father Alain Forcas has also saved the son.

> On the worn steps, where the moon shone upon every wrinkle, they remained standing face to face. And at that moment, a simple look and a pressure of the hand were enough to tell how much they loved one another.

Edward Sackville-West found it difficult to accept Gradère's change of heart. I do not feel this difficulty, hesitant as I am to differ from so fine a critic, because the change has been so carefully and subtly prepared for. The content of the novel would have warranted a book twice its length, and in other hands would doubtless have done so. Gradère's life of crime is powerfully suggested, but only in its final instance described. Whether he is telling his own story, or the novelist is telling it for him, the ambiguity of evil is wonderfully conveyed, and the elements combine to reinforce it. The pine trees of the *Landes* are here a prison into which the sun never shines. In this 'Catholic' novel it is the odour of sin that one inhales, and only rarely the odour of sanctity, as one 'penetrates the supernatural from below.'

PLEASURES AND POLITICS

1

With a growing family the Mauriacs had moved, in 1930, from 89 rue de la Pompe to an apartment at 38 avenue Théophile Gautier, close by. In the salon stood the grand piano, for Jeanne Mauriac was a sensitive player, and since his operation music was for François a solace, and almost a sacrament. Even more than literature, it cemented his friendship with Georges Duhamel. He carried the vivid picture in his mind of an evening at Valmondois, not far from his wife's home at Vémars, and a young girl[1] at the piano to whom Duhamel was 'prompting an *andante* which came to birth, lingered an instant, and then gushed forth like an unfrozen stream.'[2] Here was a friendship less controversial than the friendship with Gide, less complicated than the friendship with Cocteau. Spiritually, Duhamel was a casualty of the Great War, and music – Bach and Mozart in particular – was his defence against unbearable memories, as it was Mauriac's defence against intellectual doubt.

One summer, in June 1935, when the Mauriacs and the Duhamels were on holiday at Estoril, the voice of Georges Duhamel came down the telephone: 'I have found your *rondo*.' It was a *rondo* of Mozart they had been trying to recall the previous evening, and it only needed Duhamel's voice to bring it back to mind 'like an infant newly brought to birth'. Duhamel was married to Blanche Albane, the unforgettable Olivia of Jacques Copeau's *Twelfth Night*, and Mauriac remembered how she had recited a poem of Paul Claudel as they were sailing up the Tagus, and how the young Portuguese girls, one by one, came up from the bowels of the ship, drawn by the beauty of her voice.[3]

Mauriac was not a compulsive traveller, but music drew him to Salzburg, for so long as Toscanini and Bruno Walter were free to present their contrasting interpretations of *Don Giovanni*. For Mauriac this opera *buffo* laid bare the logic of damnation, and it was Walter, with his more romantic approach, who, without adding anything to the

[1] Cécile Goeffroy Dechaume (the Hon. Mrs Edmund Howard).

[2] *Journal II*, 152.

[3] Ibid.

work, had wrested from it the last iota of its 'appalling secret'. The voice of the Commendatore brought an echo of Pascal's 'Nous l'avons entendue, cette voix sainte et terrible', when he was describing the miracle of the Sainte-Epine. The nemesis of pleasure — seen here as 'the expense of spirit in a waste of shame' opposed to 'the marriage of true minds' — was illustrated as nowhere else in music because there was in Mozart something of the angel and something of the child, and this had enabled him to see 'with direct eyes' into 'death's other kingdom'.[1] His lucidity was pitiless, whereas the choral intervention at the close of Beethoven's Ninth Symphony was seen as covering up the composer's suffering with a desperate — and unjustified — affirmation of joy. The voices could lie, sublimely, where the instruments could not.

Mauriac's response to music was passionately subjective, and not exclusively classical. It might be a visit to the *Bobino*, a favourite music hall of his youth, with a coat over his left shoulder to conceal the rosette of his Légion d'honneur; or with his wife and Claude to the cabaret *Chez Agnès Capri*. His children were now old enough to become his friends, and the relationship with Claude was particularly close. When Claude said that he lacked the sense of sin, his father replied: 'The present generation can be easy on that point. I had enough of it for two of them.' He went on to regret the exaggerated Jansenism of his youth and the more so that it had not prevented him from sinning. He had sought a thousand excuses for indulgence — the effect of milieu or heredity — and what had it all amounted to? 'How we romanticise our feelings! When I look back on the dramas of my sentimental life, I realise how artificial they were. A whole symbology of passion which had no connection with reality.' Passion was rarely divorced from jealousy, and for Mauriac jealousy was 'a hateful and atrocious thing'.[2] Claude gives a vivid impression of his father listening to Wagner:

> The memories gather, and in his heart there is a sequence of emotions where joy is mingled with sadness. Sometimes he seems to wake up, and his face comes alive. He passes a weary hand across his chin. Then he takes flight again, comes down to earth, is off once more into the seventh heaven, with eyes raised and mouth half open in an expression of radiant and helpless wonder.[3]

Furtwängler's *Tristan and Isolde*, with Melchior and Frieda Leider, reminded him of Gide's observation that the Devil collaborates in every work of art, and here, standing on the steps of the Opéra, he could

[1] T.S. Eliot.

[2] *Le Temps Immobile*, 277.

[3] Ibid., 299.

exclaim with the Rimbaud of *Une Saison en Enfer*: 'J'ai avalé une fameuse gorgée de poison.' It seemed to him 'the greatest miracle of human genius that people to whom the experience of love has not been given can shed the same tears, in the second act of *Tristan*, that they would have shed on such a night, if they had known what it was like.' But let them find consolation in the thought that this love song – 'the most sublime that flesh and blood has ever uttered' – is in reality a funeral dirge; 'what Tristan and Isolde are fleeing in death is the horror of loving each other less, the shame of no longer loving each other at all.'[1] Nothing could shake Mauriac's fidelity to *Carmen*. One Saturday evening he took his four children to hear it at the Opéra-Comique where it survived, not without difficulty, a fairly mediocre performance, and confirmed the impression it had left on Nietzsche – that 'the basis of love is the *mortal hate* between the sexes'. When would Bruno Walter 'restore the work in its pristine grace and its everlasting youth'?[2]

Mauriac was in Madrid during the last days of the monarchy, dining with a Grandee of Spain who, like himself, was 'a model for El Greco'. The ambassador of a foreign power was within earshot, and the Grandee remarked: 'To think that these people look upon us as apes.' The time was shortly to come when Spain would inspire very different comparisons. In December 1935 Mauriac was in Rome as correspondent for the *Figaro*. Laval was trying to forge his own Axis with Mussolini, and Mauriac as a friend of the ambassador, M. de Chambrun, met them both at an elegant and icy banquet in the Palazzo Farnese. Mussolini, who was being handed Abyssinia on a silver plate, assured him that he would read his articles. More edifying was a private audience with Pius XI, and Mauriac discerned beneath the purple of his successor 'the burning soul of a humble priest' – a rather flattering impression of Cardinal Pacelli. Rome had always been holy; the Duce had made it hygienic. 'At the mere sound of his voice, poor districts are abolished, and workers' dwellings, as fine as any in London or Paris, arise like mushrooms.' Suburbs were replacing the open country; in the heart of the city 'the broken imperial column'[3] now stood upon its feet; and the baroque churches 'extricated from the hovels which had hemmed them in since their birth, now appeared shivering and as if ashamed of their nakedness.'[4]

Yet Mauriac felt himself in some sense a stranger in Rome. He was not stirred, like Maurras, by vestiges of the ancient *imperium*, and

[1] *Journal II*, 42.

[2] Ibid., 56.

[3] T.S. Eliot.

[4] Ibid., 87.

still less by contemporary attempts to emulate it. He was impressed, but hardly moved, by the façade of ecclesiastical triumphalism. The Christianity he cherished was buried deep in the catacombs. It was in Greece, where he went in 1936, that he felt more at home. Here, on the pediment of Olympia, was

> the beauty born of a moment's equilibrium between the omnipotence of the flesh and the omnipotence of the spirit. But for a moment only . . . a few yards separate this Apollo from the Hermes attributed to Praxiteles; and here already is grace and prettiness, attraction and trouble. Here, maybe, Gide could have meditated on another *Corydon*, and Proust another *Sodome et Gomorrhe*. The problem would have been disentangled from physiology.

It had not remained so disentangled for long. The hideous results of 'man's desire to possess what he admires' had only proved that 'the law of nature is the law of God. Left to itself, nature has no law because it has no will. The Greek vice comes up against an interdict, and more than an interdict, an execration.' For Mauriac there was 'no more serious mistake than to see in Greece the fatherland of reason opposed to the supernatural. The secret of its power over the heart and mind springs from God . . .' It had 'the sense, the taste, the passion of the divine — but its god is only man writ large. Man must be accepted for what he is.' Mauriac was speaking from his own experience when he wrote that 'Christians brought up in the struggle to kill the old man so that the new man may be born, feel the tragedy of this acceptance, of this effort to adore in God all that one has adored in man'; and when he recognized in the Parthenon 'la part mutilée de mon être.'[1]

2

There was still hope for Europe in that July of 1934 when the Mauriacs, with sundry members of their clan, were staying at Le Moulleau near Arcachon, in an old chalet which had once been rented by Gabriel d'Annunzio. 'Climbing roses embraced the trunks of the pines, and huge, miraculous dahlias grew out of the sand. They were lovely summers in those days . . .' They were still lovely in September 1936 when Mauriac, with Claude, Claire and Luce, found Venice *en fête* for Prince Humberto, and the music at Florian's was as sweet as the ice-creams. But they were not to remain lovely for very long. François Mauriac was not a political animal, in the sense that politics were his

[1] Ibid., 189-195.

constant and professional preoccupation, as they were for Charles Maurras and even, to some extent, for Georges Bernanos. The ministries of the Third Republic played their time-dishonoured game of musical chairs, and its mutations did little either to season or to disturb the *douceur de vivre*. Heads were shaken over the decline of parliamentary eloquence. 'We dream of Jaurès' cymbals and Briand's cello, as we dream of Sarah Bernhardt's golden voice.'[1] But the rise of Hitler at the head of a renascent Germany, the insolent pretensions of Mussolini, and the growth of Fascism in France itself in opposition to the power of a Communist party subservient to Moscow, forced Mauriac not, as yet, to commitment but to an anxious consideration of the political scene. Even a visit to Salzburg in 1935 was clouded by the flags lowered in mourning for the murder of Dollfuss. Mauriac was more conscious than ever of his divided heredity. On the one hand, his father had signed his name 'Jean-Paul Mauriac, soldat de la République', and his uncle had been a convinced anti-clerical and Dreyfusard. On the other hand, his mother's family had combined piety and anti-Dreyfusism. François had sided with the one in politics and with the other in religion. His flirtation with the Sillon, ill at ease as he felt himself in that *milieu ouvrier*, had left him with basically democratic sentiments; and although he had surmounted the 'crisis of 1928', he remained restive under the paralysis of Biblical exegesis and theological speculation which had resulted from the anti-modernist inquisition. Both in matters of Church and State, therefore, he leaned slightly to the left. This was not always appreciated by those whose attitude he shared. 'Monsieur Mauriac' said André Marquet, the Socialist mayor of Bordeaux 'you are a traitor to your class.' Nevertheless his place in the literary and social establishment labelled him, broadly speaking, as a man of the right, and it was not a label that he was in any hurry to discard.

Paul Valéry – a friend whom Mauriac admired 'this side idolatry' – had learnt the following lesson from the first World War; that 'civilisations are mortal'. It was the sense of this fragility that now prompted Mauriac to journalism. There was nothing new in eminent writers contributing to serious newspapers and reviews, but more often than not they presented only a shadow of themselves. Mauriac resolved from the start 'to put the whole of myself into the slightest article, like Picasso in one of his drawings'.[2] His first instinct was one of self-protection. The rule of law and the sovereignty of reason, common to all the nations of Western Europe and the particular heritage of France, were threatened as they had not been within living memory. The

[1] *Nouveaux Bloc-Notes,* 136.

[2] *Mémoires Politiques* (1967), 17.

situation had changed since the *union sacrée* which had cemented the fissiparous tendencies of the French during the first World War. The enemy was now within the gates and even — where Mauriac could watch it at close quarters — 'sous la coupole'. The sapping operation resulted in the rejection of Paul Claudel because he had served the Republic, and the election of Charles Maurras because he had done all he could to destroy it. The riots of the 6th February 1934 very nearly succeeded in doing so. The Republic, largely through its own fault, was losing the last vestige of authority, and dictatorship was the order of the day.

Mauriac was not looking for a dictator, but he was looking for a man. One of his friends, François le Grix, thought he had found him in Philippe Henriot. 'He has everything for the part; beauty, youth, eloquence, and faith. There's nothing he lacks; all one needs is to make him popular.' Such miracles, observed Mauriac, could not be had for the asking. Henriot was a deputy for Bordeaux, and Mauriac, at the invitation of his brother, Pierre, had met him at Saint-Symphorien. He appeared more interested in butterflies than in politics. Later he became notorious, but hardly popular. After serving the Vichy government, he was killed by the French Resistance and earned a Requiem in Notre-Dame. Another friend and admirer, Ramon Fernandez, perhaps the finest critic of his day, had succumbed to the dubious and demagogic charms of Doriot. 'Do not dare' he wrote to Mauriac after the riots of the 6th February 'defend the government and the extreme left in a drawing-room. An urgent and unanimous ostracism will sentence you on the spot.' Did Fernandez really suppose that the *salons* counted any more? 'Of all the consequences of the 6th February this seems to us the least worthy of engaging the attention of a philosopher.'[1] The old categories of right and left had lost their meaning; the Jacobin of 1793 had turned into the National-Socialist of 1934. Drieu la Rochelle, whom Mauriac remembered with St John's Gospel beside his bed, also recognized in Doriot the leader he was looking for. Mauriac and Pierre Brisson, the director of the *Figaro*, had lunched with Doriot, and they had both been horrified by Drieu's illusions. Many others were sharing them. 'The deepest definition of Fascism is this' Drieu had observed. 'It is the political movement which leads most openly and radically towards the restoration of the body — health, dignity, fulness, heroism — towards the defence of man against the large town and the machine.'[2] Drieu was to pay dearly for his naïveté; but Mauriac was also looking for his man:

[1] Ibid., 45.
[2] Quoted by Alistair Hamilton in *The Appeal of Fascism*, 216.

We are waiting for a man, or men, in whom the idea of the nation and the idea of society will be reconciled and incarnate. Their will to work for the greatness of France, and in doing so to restore the power of the State, will not distract them from seeking the remedy for those ills from which the working class is principally suffering, but which today are no longer its painful privilege.[1]

— a man who would realise that 'the art of politics is the use of events, the reasoned exploitation of chance, in the service of a plan matured over a long period of time.'[2] Mauriac was quick to recognize the man when he eventually appeared, for the destiny of Charles de Gaulle could not have been foretold more succinctly.

Mauriac was a liberal, very much as the word is understood in Britain, and he remained one, opposed to the totalitarian state in any form. When Maurice Thorez held out the hand of friendship to the Catholics of France in the name of working class solidarity, and reassured the peasants that a Communist government would not expropriate them, Mauriac could equally understand why the 'main tendue' should be grasped and why it should be declined. But this caution did not confine him to neutrality; distrust of one's allies was no excuse for refusing to face one's enemies, particularly while all the trumps were still in one's own hands. On the outbreak of the Spanish Civil War in July 1936, Mauriac was at first hesitant. Meeting Léon Blum at Vichy, he advised him not to burn his fingers in a fire that might spread so easily. But the Nationalist attack upon the Basques, and José Aguirre's cry on the radio: 'We did not want the war, we were thrown into it', changed his attitude overnight. As generally happened, a strong element of the subjective entered into Mauriac's *parti pris*; the Basques were his neighbours in the Gironde, and they straddled the Pyrenees. He remembered them from his childhood — 'with their stubborn foreheads, fiercely playing ball against the wall of the playground.'[3] Moreover, of the parties engaged they were the only innocents. A legal government had given them their long desired autonomy, and when they declined to revolt against the government, the rebels treated them as enemies. A people with so large a percentage of practising Catholics did not find it easy to believe in 'gesta Dei per Franco', and Mauriac, with Maritain, Bernanos, and a few others, shared their scepticism. In refusing to join the clerical hue and cry in France and elsewhere, these men did much to save the honour of Catholicism; and Mauriac was

[1] *Mémoires Politiques,* 46.

[2] Ibid., 48.

[3] Ibid., 83.

confirmed in his refusal by Verdier, the Cardinal Archbishop of Paris.

He signed the manifesto against the bombing of Guernica, and the Popular Front had seen to it that the Church should also have its martyrs. But Mauriac still reserved his protests for the Basques:

> It must not happen that when the Basque people wake up from their nightmare, they can say that only the enemies of the Church have succoured them; it must not happen that the priest and the Pharisee who pass by without turning their heads are Catholics; nor that they should have reason to believe that the Good Samaritan wears a hammer and sickle on his turban.[1]

Mauriac realised – as his fiction had abundantly demonstrated – that 'there is no hatred like the hatred between members of the same family. The most frightful injuries always come to us from those who are close to us in faith and culture.' In the early summer of 1939 Gabriel Marcel, who was a liberal with a markedly English label, observed to the present writer that the mutual feelings of François Mauriac and Henri Massis were indistinguishable from hate – and here were two men who would communicate at the same altars. Mauriac, in fact, never avowed anything like hate to Massis – only the antagonism 'between two casts of mind which will always be opposed to each other within the same faith.'[2] But it was no longer a question of merely intellectual debate. With the Front Populaire in power – of which Mauriac was no supporter – France itself looked ripe for civil war.

He wrote his articles either in *Le Figaro* or in *Sept*, a weekly paper run by the Dominicans and finally, after its opposition to Mussolini and Franco, suppressed by the Master-General of the Order – in exchange, it was said, for Italian support in the restoration of Santa Sabina. As a consequence of this, a school-teacher wrote to Mauriac that she had decided to become a Protestant. *Sept* was succeeded by *Temps Présent*, edited in the same spirit by laymen, and therefore exempt from ecclesiastical control. Asked to define its purpose, Mauriac denied that this was political. It was rather 'the penetration by the Gospel of those milieux which appear most hostile to it';[3] and around this 'the mobilisation of the Christian intellectual forces'. But the time had gone by when politics and religion could go their separate ways. Mauriac saw how many Frenchmen preferred the foreigner to their domestic opponents: 'Better Hitler than Léon Blum' ran the secret refrain. He had become President of the *Amis des*

[1] Ibid., 81.

[2] Ibid., 97.

[3] Ibid., 97.

Basques, but he was too ashamed of democratic impotence to take the chair at a meeting in support of the Austrian Catholics, for what was the point of meetings when Cardinal Innitzer had accepted the *Anschluss* with a 'Heil Hitler!', in which neither irony nor despair were audible? But he later became President of the Austrian Catholic refugees.

> The murdered countries die without a cry . . . all the peoples of the earth turn towards this nation of France which is divided, paralysed, haggard, and as though absent from itself. They prompt it to its part and sometimes they insult it with the contempt of a disappointed love.[1]

In July 1938 Mauriac took his younger son, Jean, on pilgrimage to Verdun; was the butchery to begin all over again? It was the moment to correct Hamlet's 'The rest is silence' to 'The rest is prayer'; but Hamlet had already given an unheeded motto to the western governments, neither of whom could say, or would have wished to say: 'The readiness is all'. Like so many others, Mauriac applauded the Munich agreement at the time: 'I was thinking of my two sons, and it was the provisional appeasement of this anxiety which at first prompted me.'[2] But he was not deceived. Was it by chance that the edition of *Mein Kampf* for sale on the boulevards had been expurgated of any passages threatening to France, and even of a chapter on the right use of lying? Was it true that a grossly anti-Semitic pamphlet, also for sale on the boulevards, had been translated, word for word, from the German, and that the translators were German too? In April 1939 Mauriac attended a luncheon given by the *Figaro* at Larue's. Among those present were Paul Reynaud and the Rumanian Foreign Minister, Titilescu. Rumours of a Nazi-Soviet pact were in the air, and a bad meal did nothing to improve the occasion – although, as Mauriac pointed out, there was some excuse for this, since M. Titilescu had not turned up until 2.30! When he recalled those hours he had spent as a boy poring over *Le Monde Illustré*, and the flag of Hohenzollern Germany flying over Strasbourg cathedral, he was not disposed to give any Germany the benefit of the doubt. But the German victory he principally feared, because it would be mortal, was

> the victory over the French mind. What is here at stake is something infinitely larger than France herself. We cannot repeat it too often: whether we like it or not, and whatever our faults, our failures, our betrayals, we remain none the

[1] Ibid., 105.
[2] Ibid., 108.

less, in face of triumphant Nazism, the depositaries of a treasure, of a pearl without price . . .[1]

France was divided between those who were prepared to sell the treasure, and those who would be divided about the best way to keep it and even disagreed as to what kind of treasure it was. In the meanwhile parties were lining up as they had lined up in defence of Dreyfus or against him, and Mauriac must have recognized the old faces after nearly fifty years. *Plus ça change* . . .

3

André Gide had also been diverted from literature into politics, or at least into a concern for the social problem. This had led him to the Soviet Union, where his disillusionment matched the naïveté of his expectations. On his return he confessed it in a book[2] whose patent sincerity disconcerted only those who had shared his sympathies. He was on terms of friendship not only with François but with Claude Mauriac, and it was largely thanks to Claude's initiative that he accepted an invitation to spend a fortnight at Malagar in the summer of 1939. The story of this visit has been told in detail by Claude in his *Conversations avec André Gide*. It was a remarkably successful *ménage à trois* between two eminent writers who talked, and a younger writer who listened and recorded what he heard. He could not have done so more perceptively.

Careful preparations had been made for their guest's reception. Roses, writing paper and books — Simenon and Balzac — were placed in his bedroom. Both Gide and Mauriac were spontaneously and characteristically themselves — at once friends and adversaries. Claude noted how the face of their guest would light up 'at the same time with pride and humility. A triumphant irony deforms his features and gives them an appearance slightly comic, and a little, just a very little, demoniacal.'[3] Gide's curiosity was insatiable; it extended even to a handsome young Annamite glimpsed in a café at Langon. If he had been abroad, he would have sought his acquaintance . . . Meals were taken out of doors under the trees, and the conversation generally turned on religion or politics. Gide's atheism was vulnerable; to Mauriac it seemed to be based on the fear of belief rather than on the certainty of its opposite. Gide opposed Christianity and Catholicism. There was a colony of Spanish refugees near by, and Mauriac could not

[1] Ibid., 110.

[2] *Retour de l' U.R.S.S.*

[3] *Conversations avec André Gide*, 117.

help agreeing that General Franco had made the name of Christ hateful to millions of their fellow-countrymen. They were hoping to get away to Santo-Domingo, and Gide warmly sympathised with their plight, even condescending to give them his autograph — a favour he rarely bestowed. Of the political crisis which threatened — and produced — a European war within a few weeks there was little talk. It seemed as if these two men who had given their lives to matters of the mind and the spirit were savouring every moment of a respite that was not long to last; and that their young companion realised that he might not survive its rupture.

Gide's appearance and behaviour belied his seventy years. In the morning he would be found at his gymnastic exercises, hardly out of breath when he rose from the floor; and in the afternoon he would go off for a long walk on the banks of the Garonne. He was, as always, carefully though casually dressed. One day he appeared in a wine-coloured suit made out of material given him as a present in the Soviet Union. It was among the happier souvenirs of his visit, and he was a little shy to exhibit it. On the Sunday he decided not to accompany Mauriac and his son to Mass; just as well, observed Mauriac, since the stupidity of the sermon, and Massenet during the Consecration, would only have fortified his unbelief. Gide respected Mauriac's religious convictions, but chiefly because they set him in opposition to the majority of his co-religionists. Mauriac replied that these were differences within the same Church, and among people who believed fundamentally in the same things. He was sensitive to his position as a *porte-parole* of Catholicism, and wondered if he dared publish the poem — *Le Sang d'Atys* — on which he had long been intermittently at work. Fragments of this had already appeared, and when he read other parts of it aloud, Gide's enthusiasm knew no bounds. Yes, of course it was a pagan poem, and Mauriac emerged all the greater for it. For Claude 'it revealed to me yet again the essential feature of his character that I am too inclined to forget; that he was consumed by love.'[1]

There was much reading aloud during the long evenings. Mauriac read the story of the Creation and the Fall from Genesis; and Gide remarked that there were *two* trees in the Garden of Eden — the tree of life and the tree of knowledge — and it was only the fruit of the second that was forbidden to man. Did this mean, asked Mauriac, that God was frightened of man's free will? It meant, replied Gide, that God was threatened by the discovery of conscience. Gide, rather mischievously, chose the story of Ammon's incest with Tamar, and the sparing of Sodom and Gomorrah. 'He mimed each detail, filling in the silences with a smile, a shake of the

[1] Ibid., 155.

head, or a gesture of the hand. Here was no longer the tenderness of my father, but a pitiless insight, the hammer strokes of an implacable voice.'[1] Then there were the daily expeditions by car; to Saint-Symphorien and the Druidic oak; to Sauveterre-de-Guyenne where the Mauriacs originally came from; and the village of Mauriac, with its notable tympanum on the little romanesque church. One day François' three brothers came over to luncheon. It was not easy to keep politics out of the conversation — news had come that a hundred Basques were to be executed — but care was taken not to affront Pierre Mauriac's passionate attachment to the Action Française. So the days passed with Gide revealing himself rather more intimately to the younger of his two hosts, no doubt because Claude was the more easily impressionable. François, though still vulnerable in many ways, had his mind made up; Claude shared his guest's anxious uncertainties. Nevertheless François Mauriac and André Gide were brought closer to each other than they had ever been before or were ever to be again. 'I like him' said Mauriac 'because he is upright, lucid, and courageous';[2] or again, on reading a passage from his *Journal*: 'He is a man, naturally incapable of lying, determined that nothing about him shall remain hidden. This exigence, one has to admit, gives back to him a kind of miraculous virginity.'[3] Gide wrote thanking his hosts for '15 days of perfect idleness, without a moment of boredom.'

He had persuaded them to accompany him on a visit to the Vicomtesse de Lestranges near Châtellerault, and from there Mauriac sought the cooler air of the mountains. On the 8th August he returned 600 kilometres for the funeral of Charles Du Bos at La-Celle-Saint-Cloud. The bell was tolling for more than a beloved friend. Just as surely as the Nazi-Soviet pact then in active preparation, it sounded the death-knell of an epoch; and when Mauriac rejoined his son for the *décade* at Pontigny, it must have seemed, in that sanctuary of enquiring minds — now that its chief priest had departed — as if its god were also being taken away.

[1] Ibid., 40.

[2] Ibid., 137.

[3] Ibid., 179.

NEW HORIZONS

1

The *Vie de Jésus* (1933) is not one of Mauriac's more important books. It is rarely among any author's more important books. The Gospels are beyond literature – which is not to say that they are illiterate; just as they are beyond history – which is not to say that they are unhistorical. It is idle to suggest that Tacitus or Thucydides would have told the story better, because they could not have told it at all. For commentary and meditation and exegesis there will, of course, always be room, and on the first two of these Mauriac has plenty to say. On the latter he follows his masters of the Biblical school in Jerusalem. He takes the Gospels as he finds them, but what he adds to the narrative does not sharpen their trenchancy. We used to be invited to read the Bible as 'literature'; and considered as pure literature, or as pure history, it is easy to pick holes in it. As poetry you may prefer Virgil or Isaiah; and a good historian would not have allowed the discrepancies in the account of the Resurrection to get by. A psychological novelist would have turned Jesus into an enigma, and tried to explain Him – or explain Him away. Mauriac realised that if He was enigmatic it was not only because He was more intelligent than other people, but because he was God.

Certainly the narrative gains in comprehensiveness by being related, at choice, from both Synoptic and Johannine sources. Modestly written as it is, it tells us incidentally a good deal about François Mauriac himself. How acute, for example, to have seen that what induces the unbelieving world to tolerate Jesus of Nazareth is its ignorance! 'If they knew Him, they would not put up with Him.' He is a little hard on Nicodemus who reminds him of people who make their Easter duties in some distant parish, so that nobody will notice them. He sees that in Palestine, as in the world today, the sayings of Jesus lost Him as many souls as they gained. There is a vivid image of John the Baptist burning, like a flame, between the Old Testament and the New; and of the Church rising, as it were, from the ground when Jesus makes His promises to Peter. Childhood is more than infancy; it is 'a conquest of maturity'. Here – as so often, one imagines, in his own life – Mauriac evokes the works of Christ to another François:[1] 'I am not He who condemns to eternal punishment; my name is Jesus.' Very moving is the picture of the woman taken in adultery. Why was Christ writing on the ground, and what was He writing there? It did not matter what He was writing; He merely wanted to spare the woman the immediate embarrassment of looking at her. Every Christian knew from 'a cruel and blessed experience' that sin is slavery; and one could agree with Nietzsche that Christianity, if not a religion for slaves, was 'at least a religion for slaves that have been emancipated.' The Second Coming of Christ might be interpreted as the unexpected coming of Christ into the lives of individual men and women. Golgotha, on the evening of the Crucifixion, was a reminder of 'the odour of warm and moist earth, of the emptiness, and weariness of the flesh that I used to feel as a child, after the last bull had been killed, and everyone had left the arena, as if my own blood had been impoverished by all the blood that had been spilled.' He had told Julien Green how the sweat stood on his brow when he went to confession, and now the single word – 'Mary' – of the resurrected Christ to the Magdalen recalled how he, too, as he knelt in some chance confessional, 'had often heard the unexpected and overwhelming word; and suddenly received from a man unknown, gentle and humble of heart . . . the gift of a divine tenderness, and a consolation that was in no man's power to bring.'

The book was much criticised. Some thought that Christ was shown as too neglectful of His mother, some that His anger was emphasised too strongly; in reality the anger was a stumbling block, and Mauriac had underlined it to test his own faith. Again it was objected that the evidence of the Holy Shroud at Turin, for what it was worth, had been overlooked, and that Jesus was presented as too ordinary, or even insignificant, a figure. Mauriac replied that His majesty appeared whenever He wished to demonstrate it; and that His most persuasive likeness was in Rembrandt's 'Supper at Emmaus' – a painting Mauriac had never tired of contemplating in the Louvre. On the other hand the book had troubled many consciences, and he was moved by a letter from 'a poor unknown priest whose name would tell you nothing'.[2]

2

La Fin de la Nuit was not, after all, the end of Thérèse Desqueyroux. Mauriac could not resist delving, yet again, into the lost years and the locked drawers. In *Plongées* (1938) he showed his favourite heroine in

[1] St. François de-Sales.
[2] *O.C. VII.*

two episodes; first in a psychiatrist's consulting-room, and then alone, seized with a sudden passion for an adolescent, in a hotel. *Thérèse chez le docteur* is remarkable for the technique of its narration. The interview is overheard through the eavesdropping of the doctor's wife. Elisée Schwarz is an Alsatian Jew with advanced ideas, whom Thérèse had met in a night club. He had then promised to see her at any time she chose to call. She phones for an immediate appointment, and will not be put off on account of the lateness of the hour. Catherine Schwarz, stung by jealousy, protests but to no avail. She learns, with her ear to the door, that Thérèse has broken with Jean Azévédo, the consumptive she had visited, seven years ago, in the *Landes,* and is now in love with a man called Philippe. But it is still the 'désert de l'amour'. Philippe is living under a threat of blackmail and has suggested that Thérèse shall poison his persecutor, as she had once tried to poison her husband; matters can be so arranged that she can do this with perfect security. Then they can get married – also with perfect security because each will have a hold over the other.

> Save me, doctor . . . he gives me no respite. I shall end by giving way. He is a terrible person, and yet he has the face of a child. What is this power that sometimes possesses people who look like an angel? [One thinks of Gradère]. Only a few years ago they were still at school. Do you believe in the Devil, doctor? Do you believe that evil is a person?

This question only excites agnostic laughter, to which Catherine shuts her ears. Presently she hears a cry of terror; it is her husband calling her by name. She rushes into the consulting-room and finds Schwarz cowering behind the desk, and Thérèse leaning against the wall with her bag open and her right hand hidden. Schwarz imagines that she has a revolver, but when Catherine cautiously seizes her wrist only 'a packet, wrapped in white paper' falls on to the carpet. It merely bears a chemist's label. Thérèse leaves, and Schwarz explains to his wife what had happened. Having told him her story, Thérèse had asked him for a cure. He had tried to make her understand that he had already done her a considerable service in allowing her to talk; that she now saw things more clearly, and could get what she wanted from her man without doing what he was asking of her. On hearing this, she had called him a thief. 'You pretend to cure the soul, but you don't believe in the soul. A psychiatrist means a physician of the soul, and you say that the soul does not exist.' Thérèse, explains the doctor, clearly has a tendency towards the lower forms of mysticism . . . but if Thérèse is disillusioned, so is Catherine Schwarz. She greets her husband's explanation with a laugh: 'It has taken me twenty years, but it's over at last. I'm free. Elisée, I don't love you any more.' The story, written in 1933, is told with severe economy, as Mauriac throws the light alternately on the twilight existence of Thérèse, on her relationship with the doctor, and on the doctor's relationship with his wife. It is curious that he could 'see' the psychiatrist in whom Thérèse was able to confide, but not the priest. Yet he knew far more about priests than about psychiatrists.

In *Thérèse à l'hôtel,* written in the same year, she tells her own story. Philippe has committed suicide, and she is alone at Cap Ferrat, where she is free to exert or to experience fascination. As, later, in *La Fin de la Nuit,* the *homme fatal* is an adolescent. Here, perhaps, will be the tenderness she has looked for but never found. 'We are all tender, men and women alike, when we are in love; never when somebody is in love with us.' The sight of this youth in the restaurant with his family, reminds her of Bernard sitting opposite her and wiping his lips after he had drunk, so that it was almost a relief when he complained of the light in his eyes and came to sit beside her. She was reading *Lady Chatterley's Lover,* and she had seen the boy dipping into the book which she had left on a table in the hall. This was the limit of any interest he had shown in her. Presently they make a casual contact, and she supposes from his fixed attention that her conquest is secure. She is quickly disillusioned. 'The only point of critics is to dispense one from reading books of this kind'; and later, with a candid brutality, as their conversation becomes more intimate: 'I don't imagine you to be better than you are . . . I'm rarely deceived by a face. I don't think I've ever been mistaken in dealing with people of a certain age.' He goes on to warn her against 'angelic faces; the bad angels are beautiful, aren't they? The great thing is to realise it. And as for people who have had a very full life . . . yes, you can read it all in their faces.' She replies that her own would horrify him if he knew it, but he disclaims any mission either to understand or to forgive.

Thérèse tries to reassure herself that her spell has worked once more, for the boy is still regarding her with a passionate concern.

> 'Sometimes, in society' he continues 'certain men and women give me the physical sensation of their spiritual death. Do you understand what I mean? As if that soul were already a corpse. Well, in your case . . . I would wager that your soul is very sick, fearfully sick, but still alive. Yes, bursting with life. Since I've been looking at you, I've been haunted by the contrast between your life as it may have been up to now, and the possibilities. . .'

She fences with him a little, and in the evening they meet again. He tells her that she does not understand the meaning of happiness or love; that she has everything before her, and does not know it. At last she breaks out at him. 'I detest you'; and he replies 'I love you.' It is the word, but not the thing, she has been longing for.

> I have nothing more to expect of love; I know no more of it now that I did when I was young. All I know of it is that I desire it; a desire which possesses and blinds me; which throws me on to the road to destruction; that hurls me against the wall; that makes me stumble in the quagmire, and lays me exhausted in the muddy ditch.

The two stories compose a diptych. Thérèse had found a better psychiatrist than Dr Schwarz, but she was still waiting for a priest.

Insomnie dates from 1927 – the years of crisis. The fragment of an uncompleted novel, it first appeared in a limited edition under the title of *La Nuit du bourreau de soi-même,* and this aptly describes it. As a reverie of obsession, it stands effectively by itself, and is of particular biographical interest since Mauriac admitted, in later years, that he found it 'almost intolerable to re-read'. It expressed 'the sufferings of a lover as I still conceive them.'[1] Light is also thrown on the circles he had once frequented, and from which he had not always been willing or able to escape.

> These self-styled intellectuals are not even capable any more of remaining still for a moment under the lamp, of reading a book, of staying in their room. With no concern for other people, they can no longer bear the sight of their own face; their own sickly personality narrowly confines them, and at the same time becomes so importunate that they struggle to smash it, and to lose it in the emptiness of the dance.

If no other night-club is open, perhaps it will not be too early to go on to Les Halles? The brief moment of physical union only masks an 'irremediable discord', and all the sleepless victim of desire and jealousy can do is to expel from his heart 'this hateful sensibility'. But he is still waiting, as the self-torturing reverie comes to an end, for the ring of the telephone or the footstep on the stair. The refrain is familiar; by now we know it by heart; but the feverish power of the writing makes *Insomnie* worthy to stand beside certain pages of Proust, where another insomniac is tortured by the comings and goings of Albertine.

In *Le Rang* two Girondin cousins meet at a funeral and converse in a café. One of them has sacrificed and impoverished himself in order that his mother and sister can maintain the appearances to which they imagine

---

[1] *D'autres et moi,* 266.

that their rank in society entitles them. The story is a ferocious retrospect on a pharisaical piety and a certain *esprit de famille* which Mauriac held in abhorrence, although he was himself a happy 'family man'. In *Un Conte de Noël*, the narrator is Yves Frontenac. He recalls a Christmas Eve in the play-ground of the school — evidently the Grand-Lebrun. The boys are separating for the holidays. One of them, Jean de Blaye, still has his hair in curls, modelled on those of Little Lord Fauntleroy, familiar from the *Saint-Nicolas* of 1898. The others are teasing him, and there follows a debate as to whether the Child Jesus really comes into the bedroom on Christmas Eve and leaves the presents in the boots laid out to receive them. This is what Jean has been told by his mother, and he is convinced that his mother cannot lie. Yves returns home, like his author, to the room with the ancestral portraits which is only entered on Christmas Eve. Here are the lighted Crib, and Herod's castle on the top of a mountain made out of brown paper. The great bell of the Tour Pey-Berland is booming its summons to Midnight Mass. Yves' mother — *alias* Madame Jean-Paul Mauriac — tells him that he must go to sleep; otherwise the Child Jesus will not come. When she returns from Mass he is still awake, but he keeps his eyes closed, hearing only the silken swishing of her skirt. Nevertheless, since she carries the Host within her, he is satisfied that she has not deceived him.

After the holidays he finds a different and a disillusioned Jean de Blaye. His mother had only been joking, but she will not make fun of him any more — and she has cut off his curls. That is the end of Yves' friendship with Jean de Blaye, and as the years go by, he does not know what has become of him. Then, on another Christmas Eve in a Paris bar, he meets his younger brother, who tells him that Jean has died in Saigon after a bad life. He adds that their mother had kept his curls in a silver box, containing, as she said, a treasure they were forbidden to see. But Jean had forced the lock — and since then he had forced a good many other locks. This is the moment when Yves Frontenac becomes a novelist. He recreates, as he walks home to his student's lodging, the story of Jean de Blaye who 'hated the woman who had brought him into the world because she was obstinately set on reviving the child that he was no longer, and on keeping him the prisoner of his childhood in order to hold him more securely under her thumb.'

Each of these stories is, in one way or another, a 'plunge' into the past. In three of them Mauriac had returned to a character he had already created, and *Insomnie* revealed something of his own torment. He was too scrupulous an artist to 'scrape the barrel'; but it was time to widen still further the horizons already opened by *Les Anges Noirs*.

It was an occasional defect of François Mauriac as a novelist that he was in too much of a hurry. When he was dealing with a single situation and only a few characters, this rapidity was an advantage; but when the canvas was broader and the scene more crowded, it could have a damaging effect. As he freely admitted himself,[1] it did something to impair *Les Chemins de la Mer* (1939), although the book contains some of his finest writing. The story revolves around two families, their individual destinies and their complex inter-relationships. Oscar Révolou has squandered his fortune on a mistress, Régina Lorati, who takes the young Gaston Costadot as a lover. Léonie Costadot, his mother, learning of Oscar's financial failure, forces his wife, Lucienne, to reimburse her for the loss sustained by the Costadot family. Lucienne, with her three children, Julien, Rose, and Denis, hastens to the Chateau Léognan — *alias* the Château Lange, where Mauriac had spent much of his boyhood with his maternal grandmother — and finds that Oscar has committed suicide.

Léonie Costadot also has three children; Gaston who follows Régina Lorati from one music-hall to another; Robert who is engaged to Rose Révolou; and Pierre who writes poetry. In the Révolous' reduced circumstances Rose takes a job in a bookshop; the château is mortgaged to the bailiff, with whose daughter, Irène, Denis enjoys a liaison until he is forced to marry her; and Julien succumbs to a nervous hypochondria which keeps him all day in bed. Robert Costadot finds Rose less attractive now that she works for a living, and breaks their engagement. Léonie, hearing that Lucienne is dying of cancer, wrings from her a reluctant forgiveness, and herself dies suddenly before the woman she has wronged. Pierre, who has much in common with Yves Frontenac, continues to write poetry, goes off to Paris, and then joins the Chasseurs d'Afrique. Julien Révolou dies; Denis and his wife occupy the château; and Rose, after an explosive scene of jealousy with Irène, leaves Léognan to explore, in solitude and sadness, 'les chemins de la mer'.

There was matter here for a novel twice as long as this one. Mauriac was trying to combine the multiplicity of an Anglo-Saxon 'chronicle' with the Racinian economy and tension which came to him more naturally. In the first two thirds of the book he felt — and the reader may well agree with him — that he had succeeded. The slow leakage of Robert's love for Rose, and her total passion for him, is an agonising study of brutality on one side and of heartbreak on the other. It stands out among the summits of Mauriac's imaginative writing. But there is more to *Les Chemins de la Mer* than the two families whose destinies are intertwined. Oscar Révolou had been aided in all his enterprises, commercial and lascivious, by an agent, Landin, of lower station than

[1] *D'autres et moi,* 262.

himself, whom he had known at school. Landin is ambiguous, repellent, and indispensable. He is described as a 'virtuoso of attentiveness'; his eyes are like periwinkles; and his hands 'appeared to have been fashioned by the acts which they had performed, and finally came to resemble them.' As he goes through Oscar's papers after his death, he discovers a memorandum in which his previous employer had confessed his dependence on him, never mentioning him by name, but only by a single epithet: 'l'immonde' – literally, 'the disgusting one'. Landin joins a publishing firm in Paris, which specialises in the discovery and denunciation of moral corruption; and it is in a night-club that Pierre Costadot meets him only a few hours before he is mysteriously murdered. Mauriac was right in finding the character 'heavily significant',[1] and in admitting that he had not allowed space for its development. If Landin was as important as all that, we should at least have been told why he was murdered, and by whom.

When a novelist introduces a poet into his story, he meets the challenge, if not the obligation, to show examples of his verse. Mauriac met this challenge with extracts from *Le Sang d'Atys,* the poem Gide had so admired when it was read aloud to him at Malagar; and he does so the more plausibly in that these were his own thoughts, recollected in maturity, when he was the same age as Pierre Costadot. It is through the mouth of Pierre that he explains the dialectic of the poem:

> For Cybele, who is the earth, Atys is also a world. Just as the Greeks give the stars and the deified elements a human shape, Cybele by a contrary movement sees in the shepherd she adores a world which is unknown to her. I have tried to express this confusion between a planet and the thinking being; between a living body, a poor mortal body, and an earth full of oceans, undulations, mountain-tops, chasms, and forests . . .

> > *Une ligne de sable, un renflement de dune,*
> > *Une frange d'écume et de varechs: la mer . . .*
> > *Le doux trait des sourcils sur ta paupière brune*
> > *Et l'obscure forêt au bord du front désert.*

In these chiselled alexandrines the poetry, latent in Mauriac's fiction, becomes explicit. He had travelled a long way from *Les Mains jointes.* Both in technique and inspiration *Le Sang d'Atys* is a pagan poem, and Maurice Barrès would never have mistaken its author for a seminarian.

Pierre's revolt is against 'a world of which money is the substance'.

---

[1] Ibid., 262.

For those who felt as he did, the choice was not yet between revolution and religious faith; he could find, like Ernest Psichari, a refuge in the discipline of arms. Rose, whom he had comforted in her dereliction, can rise from a prayer that is formal to a prayer that is felt, but a dark night is ahead of her and she is unsure of her navigation. *Les Chemins de la Mer* is a sad book; yet its only taint of morbidity is the hint of incest in Denis' attachment to his sister. Here and there, the moralist in Mauriac comes out explicity: 'We never think of calling our passions by their true names'. His memory recreated the deserted room at Langon, where Jacques Mauriac had died, and into which, like Denis Révolou, he had occasionally peeped, inhaling the 'odour of lacquer and cloves, and contemplating for a long time the empty bed on which the mystery had been accomplished. The curtains of the four-poster had assisted at the event, and each piece of furniture had seen it from where they stood.' The horizons had certainly widened in *Les Chemins de la Mer,* but they had widened within the same hemisphere.

3

On the 7th August 1937 Mauriac spoke to his son, Claude, in accents of despair about his work as a novelist. He felt that it all amounted to nothing. 'I want to write plays.'[1] He had always been attracted to the theatre. Madame Bartet had recited his verses at the Sorbonne, and he had applauded Sarah Bernhardt as Athalie only a few weeks before she died. But the theatre, as he had known it as a boy, was not considered a respectable occupation for a man of letters. Edmond Rostand was the canonised exception to the rule. It was Antoine at the Théâtre Libre, and particularly Jacques Copeau at the Vieux-Colombier, who had restored the stage to literary favour. Mauriac remembered Copeau's *Twelfth Night*; he had been entranced by 'this unique poetry where the bells on the cap of foolery tinkle more lightly than the sighs of love. So many sighs were never mingled with so much laughter to delight the heart.'[2] But it was Copeau's aim to attract new dramatists as well as to revive old ones, and to create an audience which the artifice of 'Sardoodledum' had driven away from the playhouse. Cocteau, Giraudoux, and Jules Romains had all, directly or indirectly, responded to his appeal; Mauriac was a late contender in the field.

His diffidence was equal to his ambition, and it was overcome, first, by his friend Edouard Bourdet, administrator of the Comédie-Française, and then by a performance of *Don Giovanni* at Salzburg. 'There is no

---

[1] *Le Temps Immobile,* 301.

[2] The author's *Shakespeare on the Stage* (1973), 191.

more wonderful stimulant than Mozart' he told Claude 'for the man
who wants to launch into dramatic art.'[1] He lunched with Bourdet at
Maxim's, and confessed his incapacity to invent a plot which would
hold water on the stage. 'All I have are characters.' 'If you have
characters' replied Bourdet 'everything will be all right. Characters are
the only thing that matters. Your play is made.' It was not made quite
as easily as that, and Bourdet's technical assistance was valuable. But
Mozart and Maxim's, in happy coincidence, were responsible for bringing *Asmodée* before the footlights of the Comédie-Française in the
autumn of 1938.

In the folk-lore of the *Landes* Asmodée was a devil who was
supposed to carry off the roofs of the houses; psychologically speaking,
he had been fully occupied in the fiction of François Mauriac. Marcelle
de Barthas is a widow of 38, living in a lonely château with her three
children, a Mademoiselle, and a tutor, Blaise Couture, for the elder
boy. Blaise had been dismissed from a seminary, and had been living
with the family for seven years. During this time he had seduced the
Mademoiselle, and made himself indispensable to Madame de Barthas.
It is high summer in the *Landes*. Bertrand, his charge, has gone to
England, and a young Englishman, Harry Fanning, has joined the household *au pair*. Harry's father is ambassador in Madrid, and his son, himself studying for the Diplomatic Service, already speaks perfect French.
He has often passed through the *Landes* in the Sud Express; it is a part
of the country that he has always been curious to explore. Gay and
open, he captivates the children; Madame de Barthas is attracted to
him; and her daughter of seventeen, Emmanuèle, who is thought to
have a religious vocation, falls in love with him and he with her.

As he and Marcelle return from a walk in the park one evening,
Blaise, crouching unseen on the stairs, overhears their conversation
and suspects their tentative intimacy. The next day he persuades Harry
to go home on some plausible excuse. Harry reluctantly agrees, but is
dissuaded by the children, and Blaise leaves instead. When he comes
back at the end of the holidays, he finds that Harry and Emmanuèle
have engaged themselves to be married. Marcelle, motivated by an
unconscious jealousy, tries to hold Emmanuèle to her supposed vocation,
and vainly seeks support from the curé. To her surprise, Blaise encourages
Emmanuèle to follow her inclinations, for he is jealous of Harry's
attraction for Marcelle. Emmanuèle, in her happiness, sympathises with
her mother for having been left alone on Harry's last evening. But
Marcelle replies 'very bitterly' as the curtain falls: 'No, Emmanuèle, you
see I am not alone. I stay with Monsieur Couture.'

[1] *Le Temps Immobile*, 301.

If there is a fault to be found with *Asmodée,* it is that the nature of Blaise's influence over Marcelle is insufficiently explained. Even after seven years of daily contact, theirs is still the relationship of employer to employed. One is left with the impression that Blaise – a man in the early forties – must exercise power at any cost, sexual in the case of Mademoiselle, psychological in the case of Marcelle. There is something in him of Tartuffe, and something also of a future creation of Mauriac, Brigitte Pian in *La Pharisienne.* The play was directed by Jacques Copeau, and Mauriac only reluctantly agreed to certain changes on which he had insisted. Copeau seemed to be haunted 'by the play that he would have written himself . . . and I had to fight against his perpetual attempts to refashion it according to his own ideas.'[1] Nevertheless *Asmodée* was a clear, though narrow, success. There were two public previews. At the first, in the afternoon, interest flagged during the latter half of the play – perhaps, suggested Léon Blum, because Couture was too odious a character to be tolerable. But the second preview was a triumph with twenty curtain calls, and the author dragged on to the stage. When it was all over the champagne flowed in the Mauriac apartment until the small hours of the morning.[2]

Asmodée has remained in the repertoire of the Comédie-Française, and in 1939 it was produced in London at the little Gate Theatre by Norman Marshall in a translation by Basil Bartlett. Eric Portman was the Blaise Couture, Mary Hinton the Madame de Barthas, and Joyce Redman the Emmanuèle. Mauriac came over to see the production, greeted on his arrival by Charles Morgan in *The Times.* He was entertained to a luncheon at the Savoy, and in the late afternoon James Laver took him to Hampton Court. He found it very evocative to wander through the palace in the twilight. Curious to see the lighter side of London life, he insisted on a visit to the 'Crazy Gang' at the Victoria Palace. He sat in the front row, resplendent in decorations and full evening dress for a subsequent reception at the French embassy, and was the subject of good-humoured mockery from behind the footlights. *Asmodée* was later transferred to the New Theatre, where it ran for two months.

It has proved the most generally acceptable of Mauriac's plays; yet it was not, as he told Claude, at all the play he wanted to write. 'It is just a novel of mine put into dialogue'[3] – and indeed it is easy to see how the theme could have been treated as a novel, perhaps with advantage. It had come too easily to him, theatrical novice though he

[1] *Bloc-Notes II,* 253.

[2] *Vide Le Temps Immobile,* 437-9.

[3] *Le Temps Immobile.*

was. He had been admired for the atmosphere of his novels, and he did not think that his characters would come alive except in a familiar landscape, and in a season of heat and storm. It was an irresistible temptation 'to reconstruct on the illustrious stage of the Comédie-Française the climate of the *grandes vacances* as I used to know them, the moonlight on the pines, the tunes my brothers and I would sing on the hot evenings, as we looked for the stars between the tree tops. I demanded of the *metteur-en-scène* that the children in my play should sing a certain air from a forgotten opera of Gounod — *Cinq-Mars* — because it was this that we used to sing ourselves, nearly half a century ago, before we went to bed, as we took a last turn in the park.'[1] All this was perfectly captured in the production, both in London and Paris, but Mauriac realised, when he saw the play in performance, that its merit lay in the characterization, and its essential poetry in the passions it released. T.S. Eliot felt much the same after *Murder in the Cathedral*; they both looked back to Racine, Eliot to *Bajazet,* and Mauriac to *Britannicus.* Mauriac resolved to confine himself hencefor-ward 'to an action which, moving by degrees to its climax, is sustained only by the interests, the sentiments, and the emotions of the characters.'[2] The result was *Les Mal Aimés,* completed before the outbreak of war, but not produced until after the Liberation. We shall consider it in due course.

[1] *D'autres et moi,* 281.
[2] Preface to *Britannicus.*

WAR AND OCCUPATION

1

The Mauriacs returned to Paris in December 1939, hoping that so unconvincing a war might grind to a halt through the weight of its own inactivity. Nevertheless Claude was mobilised early in 1940, and his father said good-bye to him in the great avenue at Chantilly. Luce Mauriac became engaged to Alain Le Ray, whose subsequent career was notable. After capture by the Germans, he escaped from Colditz in April 1941, and directed the Resistance at Grenoble. François continued to publish his articles, uneasily aware of the lack of leadership. He was looking for the day

> when a French statesman (and why should it not be M. Paul Reynaud) will discover in the circumstances which are strangling us, in the threat of an enemy concentrating his strength to leap upon us, in the saddened or derisive opinions of other nations, the boldness to resolve a ministerial crisis in a few hours, and to present, not so much to the Chambers as to the country, a small team of men chosen from the true *élite* of France.[1]

This was written in March 1940, and for a short time it looked as if it might be M. Paul Reynaud. But when catastrophe came in May, Mauriac, who was then at Malagar, placed a desperate and short-lived hope in Marshal Pétain. He had perhaps forgotten, or chosen not to remember, a curious incident at the time of his election to the Académie. Marshal Lyautey had written to congratulate him, but had expressed his regret that Mauriac should be sitting in the same company as Marshal Pétain. Lyautey, conscious of his indiscretion, had then asked Mauriac to return the letter, but Mauriac had burnt it. Now he wrote of Pétain's assumption of power as 'a supreme proof of love' – an intelligible sentiment in the circumstances. But when a voice on the radio assured him that 'France had never been so glorious', he reacted strongly. The country's only chance of salvation was no longer to dope itself with lies.

He had not heard the appeal of General de Gaulle on June 18th, but

[1] *Mémoires Politiques,* 120.

presently another voice came to him from London. On August 17th
Maurice Schumann addressed a 'Message to François Mauriac'.

> We think of you as a sorrowful image of a distant France.
> Your feet buried in our violated soil, your eyes dazzled by the
> sun that shines upon our invaded vineyards, your heart born to
> experience emotions which it cannot contain, your voice which is
> at once so warm and so broken, there is nothing in you and
> nothing about you which is not an incarnation of our tragedy.
> Just as certain Italian masters show us Christ in miniature, so for
> us you are France in miniature, and a France which is also
> crucified.[1]

Mauriac had already given Schumann the cue for his appeal:

> So let us not deny our love of liberty, let us not abandon
> our defence of the human personality; but let us profit from
> a disaster which has laid us waste, and everything around us,
> to rediscover the true conditions of liberty and individual cul-
> ture. Let us learn how to become once again a sovereign State,
> and free, enterprising, and responsible citizens.[2]

But Schumann reminded him — if the reminder were necessary — that
these hopes could not be realised under the boot of the invader. Quoting
from *Les Chemins de la Mer*: 'Already the bitterness of the wind surprises them, already the taste of salt is on their lips, until the last dune
has been crossed, and the passion for the infinite slaps them with sand
and foam. They have no choice but to lose themselves in it, or go back
upon their tracks.'[3]

Charles de Gaulle and his companions were those who had followed,
literally and metaphorically, the *chemin de la mer*.

Mauriac never wrote another word in support of Pétain, although for
two years he believed — or did his best to believe — that he was playing
a double game. Delegated, as it seemed, from the cemeteries of Verdun,
the Marshal's voice had 'an almost timeless resonance.'[4] Nor did Mauriac
ever move outside the occupied zone. The population of the south-west,
less accustomed to invasion than the inhabitants of Picardy and Artois,
regarded the marching columns on the road from Bazas to Mont-de-
Marsan with curiosity rather than fear. Later, as Mauriac advised them,

---

[1] *La Voix du Couvre-feu* (1964), 19.

[2] Ibid., 20.

[3] Ibid., 21.

[4] *Journal du temps de l'Occupation: O.C. XI*, 310.

they withdrew into the 'reticence of a humble pride',[1] and into what Joseph de Maistre had called a 'souffrance réfléchie'.

For a time he withdrew into it himself, for public expression was strictly controlled. He understood the reasons for the destruction of the French fleet at Mers-el-Kebir, but this was a blow for which he could never forgive Winston Churchill. For the moment Britain had a 'unanimous France' against her. Events, to say the least, were not yet playing into the hands of General de Gaulle, and neither were the men of letters. Paul Claudel had published a dithyrambic Ode to Pétain, and Alexis Léger (Saint-John Perse) from the security of Washington, though he sympathised with de Gaulle, consistently advised Roosevelt to withhold official recognition from the Fighting French. Both these men were experienced diplomats, and their opinions carried weight. Gide was silent, or equivocal; Montherlant — 'prince of artifice and bombast' — continued to 'faire le brave contre Dieu';[2] Giono, Jouhandeau, and Céline were compromised; Drieu la Rochelle was triumphant; and Maurras boasted that 'mes idées sont au pouvoir'. Collaborators or *attentistes*, there was little sign of the *élite* that Mauriac was looking for. Among French writers of the first rank Georges Bernanos was alone, in these early days, to show himself openly and aggressively opposed to Vichy. And he was speaking from the security of Brazil.

On the day of Pentecost, 1940, a particular friend of Mauriac — the young abbé Rémy Pasteau — was killed at the head of his section. He had inspired the portrait of Alain Forcas in *Les Anges Noirs*, and Mauriac had received his blessing on the day he was ordained. Later he used to visit his parish in a poor quarter of Paris which 'not even the twilight could embellish.'[3] At Malagar, in the murderous heat of that summer, one could hear — or fancy one could hear — the stifled breath of the pines that one could not see; and the forest glade at Saint-Symphorien was 'the place where the spear has pierced the tormented body of my country.[4] 'One evening' he wrote 'in the dark winter of 1940, in the *salon* of a remote countryside, we were huddled round a meagre fire. Overhead the boots of the German officer were creaking in the corridor. We were listening to a *reportage* from the London radio — turned low of course — on the Paris streets, and the vendors of popular songs. All of a sudden we heard that wretched old number — "Paris reine du monde" — accompanied on the accordion. This tune from a café concert, more than the most sublime music, tore at our heart-strings.'[5]

---

[1] *Mémoires Politiques*, 127.
[2] Ibid., 135.
[3] *Journal du temps de l'Occupation. O.C. XI*, 347-51.
[4] Ibid.
[5] *Le Bâillon dénoué*, 18.

Even before he had returned to Paris or to Vémars, Mauriac's attitude was not in doubt. An attempt was made to continue the work of *Temps Présent* with a new, four-page literary journal, *Temps Nouveau*. This was edited from Lyon by Stanislas Fumet, with Mauriac among its regular contributors; but it was suppressed by the Germans at the end of July 1941. A month later Mounier's *Esprit* was forbidden. In April of the same year 40 German soldiers were quartered at Vémars for several months, as they had been similarly quartered in 1870. Great damage was done. Family papers were burnt, including letters from Guizot and Thiers; locks were forced and drawers emptied; and an ancestral portrait pierced by billiard cues. When the Germans had gone and the house was made reasonably habitable, Mauriac spent a good deal of his time there. On Thursdays he would come in to Paris for the weekly meeting of the Académie française. Here he found allies in Louis Gillet and Georges Duhamel, but in few others. He would greet Abel Bonnard — who was a minister — with an icy stare; and he had not forgotten how he had once been greeted himself by the egregious Léon Bertrand with 'Heil Hitler!', in the days before 'Heil Hitler!' had become a convenient salutation. André Bellesort, the permanent Secretary of the Académie, wrote for the collaborationist *Je suis partout*. Only his death in January 1942 saved him from Mauriac's public condemnation.

When the meeting was over, Mauriac would gather with a group of kindred spirits in the apartment of a young novelist, Jean Blanzat, at 7 rue de Navarre. This was a centre of the Resistance, and the Gestapo who had an office nearby were well aware of it. Here Mauriac would find Jean Paulhan, Claude Morgan — editor of *Les Lettres Françaises* — Jean Guéhenno, and the Dominican, Père Maydieu, a Bordelais like himself. The courage of Maydieu, and other members of the religious orders and lower clergy, stood in contrast to the caution of the hierarchy. When Mauriac suggested to Cardinal Suhard that he should order prayers for the Jews, the Cardinal replied: 'Fancy asking me to do that!' — though it is fair to remember that the Cardinal later atoned for his pusillanimity. Blanzat would give Mauriac a bed for the night, for he had reason to fear an unfriendly visit to his own apartment — enlarged in 1938 by taking in a flat of the building next door. One day two men from the Gestapo rang the bell, and Jean Mauriac had let them in. They were chiefly concerned with examining his father's typewriter.

Paris had a mute, ironical beauty during the Occupation with the streets under the snow in the moonlight, and the ancient parapets reflected in the waters of the Seine. Were the trees in the Tuileries gardens 'watching over a death-bed, or standing on either side of the entrance, like the angels of the Resurrection? — Sometimes one is tempted to say that Paris, crouching on the bank of its river, covers its face with its hands or hides it in its folded arms.'[1] Victor Hugo was constantly on the lips of those who had not betrayed; and the snow lying on the pavements was an image of their hopes:

> *O libre France, enfin surgie*
> *O robe blanche après l'orgie.*

As Mauriac and Blanzat were crossing the place de la Concorde and averting their gaze from the swastika, they met a convoy of lorries carrying German troops on their way to Russia — and to Stalingrad. Paris was exhausted and hungry, to be sure, but not as the collaborating *Nouvelle Revue Française* had described her: 'like a debauched woman who painfully stretches herself in the morning after a night of obscenity.'

The insults of his enemies — and by now they were numerous — testified to Mauriac's proclaimed sympathies. In June 1941 a lecture at the Théâtre des Ambassadeurs was devoted to 'François Mauriac, agent de la désagrégation française.' A number of his friends were there to boo the speaker. In November 1940 he was compared to a 'licentious sacristan who goes on after Vespers to traffic in dirty postcards'; by another news-sheet to a 'rancorous Hyena'; and a third spoke of 'that pin's head under the two-cornered hat, and that ungainly body of a schoolboy under the green uniform.'[2] A more sinister, though less personal, adversary was Alfred Fabre-Luce who had collected in his *Anthologie de la Nouvelle Europe* texts to serve as guide-lines for a reconstructed continent. These included René Quinton's 'The chief mission of the male is not to reproduce his kind but to kill them.' Mauriac answered this ferocity in the *Cahier Noir*, published by *Les Editions de Minuit* under the pseudonym of 'Forez.' These were extracts from his diary, and on the opening page he had declared his faith in the cause of humanity which others thought irremediably lost. If he were asked to keep his head above the fray, he countered that he would keep it no higher than the Cross — and that was low enough, since it often happened that the dogs ate away the feet of the slaves who were crucified. The slaves were now more evident than the Saviour, and Mauriac had seen them herded into the sealed trains at the Gare d'Austerlitz. Jeanne Mauriac had watched another train packed with Jewish children leave the same station, and when she recalled the scene to a young woman some time after the war, she got the reply: 'I was one of them.' Even the artistic life of Paris, superficially undisturbed, carried its undertones of the unspeakable. On the 8th June 1943 François and Claude attended a concert at the Galerie Charpentier, where Suzanne Balguérie was playing

---

[1] *O.C. XI*, 330.

[2] *Mémoires Politiques*, 21.

With Graham Greene, January 1948.

With Paul Valéry, April 1943.

With André Gide, at Aix-en-Provence, July 1949.

With his granddaughter, Anne Wiazemski, Geneva, 1953.

Satie's *Mort de Socrate*. François observed to his son: 'Everything was there already, and the Last Supper itself, and the disciples' sadness, and the serenity of the Divine victim.'[1]

<h1 style="text-align:center">2</h1>

In February 1943 Mauriac had confided to Claude: 'If I no longer have any wish to write novels, it is because I am the prisoner of an outdated formula. I have not the courage to renew my technique as Verdi renewed it after the appearance of Wagner.'[2] Yet it was only two years since he had published *La Pharisienne* which Julien Green was not alone in considering his masterpiece. This was written 'in feverish haste, during the first weeks of the Occupation, as if I had wished to express myself once more in a novel, before being submerged by the wave of filth that was overwhelming us.'[3] Looking back in conversation with Jean Amrouche, Mauriac himself regarded this study in a loveless religious faith, and in 'the will to power disguised as the right of intervention', as 'one of his most concentrated and successful novels'. Few readers will disagree with him.

The story is told in the first person by a narrator recording, and commenting upon, events in which he himself had taken part. In this he is able to speak from memory, and from oral or documentary evidence; he can speak with his own voice and also, on occasion, with the voice — always unmistakable — of François Mauriac. 'At the point where I then was, Balzac brought me close to life, but inclined to cynicism a mind that was still childish.' Such was the mood in which Mauriac came up to Paris in 1904. He was reading Nietzsche a good deal during these early years of the war, and what Nietzsche had written of the seventeenth century in France was true of Mauriac himself: 'Much of the wild beast in it, and much asceticism to keep it under control'. Echoes of his mother's voice in Gounod's 'Le soir ramène le silence' evoke his own childhood, although Brigitte Pian has nothing else in common with Madame Jean-Paul Mauriac. She is, in fact, the narrator's stepmother: 'one of those people who choose God, but whom God, maybe, does not choose Himself.' One trait of her character — but one alone — Mauriac had taken from the abbé Altermann: 'She offered her left cheek, protesting that it was an excellent thing that she should be thus calumniated and misunderstood, and adding another stitch to the tissue of perfection and merit with which she was totally enveloped, and at which she

---

[1] *Le Temps Immobile,* 81.

[2] Ibid., 85-6.

[3] *D'autres et moi,* 289.

159

worked without interruption.' No other character in Mauriac's fiction, unless it be Thérèse Desqueyroux, imposes itself with the same authority.

If the author had not 'renewed' his technique, he had considerably refined it. As in *Les Chemins de la Mer,* the story is a diptych of destinies closely intertwined. Jean de Mirbel is Louis Pian's — the narrator's — schoolfellow. An intractable subject, over whom his uncle — a former Papal Zouave — has legal control, he is taken away from school and put in the charge of an elderly priest, the abbé Calou, experienced in the handling of similar cases. Disregarding the uncle's advice, Calou proceeds with gentleness and patience. Brigitte Pian and her two stepchildren have a holiday home close to Calou's parish in the *Landes.* Michèle Pian — Louis' elder sister — falls in love with the boy, and he with her. Discovered *tête-à-tête* in a *palombière,* they are reported to Brigitte who forbids any communication between them, although Calou realises that Michèle will be Jean's salvation. Meanwhile Jean's mother pays a rare visit to the presbytery, but obstinately refuses to let the boy spend the night with her in a neighbouring hotel where she has supposedly booked a room. Jean climbs out of his bedroom window to follow her, only to find that she has done no more than leave her suitcase at the hotel, and has proceeded by car, in company with a man, to better accommodation in the nearest town. Here Jean follows her on his bicycle, and falls asleep in the angle of the wall underneath a couple of lighted windows. Presently he is woken by the sound of voices above him. It is one o'clock in the morning, and his mother, with her lover — a fashionable dramatist — are enjoying the moonlight, and preparing to enjoy one another.

The scene is brilliantly described. Jean collapses on the way home, and is found by Calou who has set out in search of him. For some weeks he is seriously ill with pleurisy. Cut off from Michèle, reeling under the shock of that nocturnal revelation, and with only Calou for a companion, he forms an association with the local chemist, a young woman of violently anti-clerical views, who nurses a private grudge against the priest. They disappear together; Brigitte Pian denounces Calou to the ecclesiastical authorities, who remove him from the parish and suspend him from the exercise of his functions; and Michèle leaves her adolescence behind her and, with it, her lost illusions. It was Brigitte Pian's 'pride and her *raison d'être* to take the loftiest possible view of things.' She could now look down with complacency on what she had done to the greater glory of God.

More subtle was her procedure with Louis' tutor, M. Puybaraud, who abandons his quasi-clerical status to marry a schoolteacher, Octavie. Any failure of vocation is a personal defeat for Brigitte Pian. She can do nothing against the *fait accompli* but maintain her grip over the now penniless pair by keeping them at her own expense. When she discovers that they have hired a piano with the money intended for bare necessities, her righteous indignation does much to aggravate the miscarriage from which Octavie dies, and which leaves Puybaraud to fend for himself until he enters a Trappist monastery. But Mauriac redeems his *Pharisienne*, after stripping her of all her pretences, until the moment of triumphant irony when she makes her confession to the abbé Calou — eventually restored to ecclesiastical favour. The secular Brigitte Pian, reading *Adolphe* and *Anna Karenina*, and spending less time upon her knees, becomes spiritually respectable. She even enjoys a Platonic love-affair with a local doctor — a Protestant — and acquires a property adjoining his nursing home. He takes her to the theatre, and awakens in her his own love of music. They discuss theology without any attempt to convert each other. At last he is killed in a motor accident, and she is left alone. Jean de Mirbel, after sowing his wild oats, very briefly, at Biarritz, returns to Bordeaux. He and Michèle are both much changed, but they still recognize the necessity which had brought them together as boy and girl. After Jean has completed his military service they get married; and as for Brigitte Pian, she 'had discovered at last that one should not be like a proud servant, anxious to dazzle one's master by paying what he owes him down to the last penny, and that our Father does not expect us to calculate meticulously our own merits. She knew now that what matters is not to merit, but to love.'

Mauriac was right in seeing *La Pharisienne* as a 'roman de caractère'; and right also, no doubt, in feeling that this kind of novel was going out of fashion. If so, he had no inclination to abet its disappearance. 'There is not a single feature of Brigitte Pian that I have not observed in very devout people, in no way hypocritical and very ambitious for purity and perfection.' He saw the book as the 'story of a saintly priest and a tortured adolescent before that of a proud and hard-hearted woman'; and 'one in which religious experience had been of best advantage to the novelist.'[1] The portrait of Brigitte Pian is formidable, but also compassionate; none of the characters, except the ferocious Papal Zouave, can be described as a 'monster'; and the end of the book is as happy as any book that is true to life has a right to be.

The Mauriacs spent the first winters of the Occupation at Malagar, and once *La Pharisienne* had been completed, François was disinclined for further essays in imaginative literature. The inventions of fiction paled beside the cumulative horror of events. Moreover German soldiers were in occupation of the house, the noise of their accordion in the kitchen threatening to drown whatever music on the radio or gramophone

[1] *D'autres et moi*, 263-264.

might have tempted one to overlook their presence. But Mauriac was never happy unless he were writing something, and an invitation from Flammarion — who had published the *Vie de Jésus* — rescued him from inactivity. Would he consider writing the life of a saint? Hagiography was not his *genre*, and he had no access at Malagar to the books of reference normally essential for such work. Nevertheless the suggestion was opportune. A Jesuit father from Lyon had accused him of 'losing the war', since the reading of his novels 'had discouraged young Frenchmen' from fighting for their country. This was a compliment to his sales that he could well have spared.

But where should he turn on ground that was already so well covered? He was attracted to Margaret of Cortona because her story was little known in France, and because it was all contained in a book written by her confessor. She represented the extremes of profligacy and penitence; her vocation followed the accidental death of her lover by whom she had a child; she was endowed with a beauty which she did everything possible to deface; she had sinned, year in, year out, but she had never lost the faith. 'Just the person for you,' as Flammarion charmingly put it. Madame de Sévigné had written of Racine that he loved God as he had loved his mistresses; Margaret of Cortona loved Him in the same way. But what she sought was not consolation but certitude. Christ spoke to her in numberless locutions that Mauriac cautioned the reader not to take *au pied de la lettre*; as in the case of so many saints, they had so evidently been coloured by the temperament of the person to whom they were addressed. But she was not given the certainty she craved. She knew, as well as St John of the Cross, the desolation of the 'dark night'. 'Separated at once from God and from the world, a creature rejected on every side, she had no presentiment of the final joy that was at hand. On the contrary, the memory of past felicity pierced her to the heart.' She experienced what the great Spanish mystic was to describe two centuries later. 'Their great love does not prevent them thinking that they are not loved in return, for they find nothing in themselves worthy of this love, and they regard themselves as so wretched that they deserve to be hated by God, and looked upon with horror by mankind.'

Margaret of Cortona had followed the classic itinerary of mystical experience. The relation between this and psychological neurosis — if such relation there were — was beyond Mauriac's competence to discuss. He merely followed her step by step. He was far from emulating what others would consider her morbid asceticism, but he was too diffident to condemn it. Never succumbing to despair, he was still conscious, at every moment, of the Christian risk. Salvation could not be taken for granted:

The soul's fate is in jeopardy at every second; yes, its eternity hangs upon a second. It is at the mercy of a lustful look, of a consenting smile, and at any moment it can fall. This is a celestial and infernal game where the immortal part of a man is at risk.

The chief motive of a Christian life — and the time gave it proof — was the sense that life, as one saw it, was unendurable. But this would not take one very far on the road to sanctity. If one had exalted feelings, one was quickly brought down to earth. No doubt Mauriac was speaking for himself when he wrote of the 'abrupt aversion to divine things, the weariness and then the distaste for the liturgy, the relapses and the creeping returns to the confessional — what a wretched and shameful thing is the Christian life when it is not directed to holiness!' The book was a meditation rather than a biography. All this had happened a long time ago, and there were moments when he blamed himself for devoting so much time to a subject so remote from present anxieties. He asked the reader to remember how often he was interrupted by a cautious audition of 'Les Français parlent aux Français', by the 'heavy boots shaking the ceiling' above his head, or by the announcement of a fresh victory for the Reich. *Sainte Marguerite de Cortone*[1] is not a boring book, but the writing of it had been a relief from boredom.

The winters were long at Malagar. In 1941 Flammarion published a volume of essays on the four seasons — *La Guirlande des années.* Gide wrote on spring, Jules Romains on summer, Colette on autumn, and Mauriac on winter.[2] The subject reminded him of chilblains, and sirens moaning in the estuary, and the snow turning the pavements into icy mud, and of exile from the world of nature. If he paid a rare visit to the *Landes*, the tops of the trees were wreathed in mist, and the odour of wet clay was unfamiliar. All the other seasons brought excitement to the flesh; in the heat of summer only the passions were awake. But the winter brought appeasement or insensibility. Mauriac was not yet in his sixtieth year, but he was already beginning to dramatise his old age, and to look forward to a winter that no spring could renew, as it would renew the lifeless landscape of the Gironde. He prayed that in the years remaining to him — and they were not to be few — he might hear 'the immense groaning of men that other men have crucified . . . and that in this last season of our life before the great repose we may enjoy rest no longer, and that the sins of the world may forbid us to relish its delights.'[3] Fortunately for himself, however, and for his family and friends, Mauriac's capacity for enjoyment was not to be

[1] *O.C. VIII.*

[2] *Hiver. O.C. IV.*

[3] Ibid., 349.

exhausted as readily as he then imagined.

3

The Germans were well aware that he was writing for *Les Lettres Françaises*, and a pseudonym had not concealed from them his authorship of the *Cahier Noir*. Warned that he might be arrested at any moment, he moved in the autumn of 1943 from one address to another in the vicinity of Paris. If he ventured into the city he wandered about the streets, or slipped into a café, pretending to read some collaborationist journal, while the profiteers of the black market openly did their sums in a corner. In October he was comparing this clandestine existence to a 'retreat in preparation for death'; and in November — 'Whenever the telephone rings, my ears stand up like those of a hare . . . This vast plain where I'm in hiding is a theatre for the last act of the play. The stage is all prepared for a Shakespearian disembarkation.' He wrote of vague but constant threats, and in December of a walk in the forest of Montmélian wreathed in mist. The windows trembled from the shock of nearby explosions; and the feeling persisted that the tide of danger was 'mounting irresistibly towards my place of refuge'.[1]

As D-day approached tension ran high among the men and women of the Resistance. They feared that Stalin would turn against the West, and that Hitler would produce a secret, annihilating weapon. On the day that Paris was liberated Mauriac, now at Vémars, heard on the radio a voice, husky with tears of joy, reading his own article on General de Gaulle, *Le Premier des Nôtres*, which he had sent to the *Figaro* for publication as soon as this was possible; in the background the bells of all the churches in Paris joining in a chorus of jubilation; and the Germans, in retreat from Le Bourget, who had invaded the house and garden. On the 30th, when Mauriac had sought refuge with a neighbour, Vémars was liberated; and on the 31st Claude and Jean arrived with a car, which the General had placed at their disposal, to bring their father to Paris. The next day he lunched with de Gaulle at his offices in the rue Saint-Dominique, and looked, according to one witness, 'as if he had stumbled upon the Bon Dieu in flesh and blood'.[2] The conversation naturally turned on Pétain. 'I wish' exclaimed de Gaulle impatiently 'that he would retire into his house at Sainte-Marguerite, and that we should hear no more of him.' It was a wish that Mauriac was to echo in the months ahead. But de Gaulle was also interested in André Gide, and in future elections to the Académie. This was more than a meeting

---

[1] *Journal du temps de l'Occupation. O.C. XV,* 354-356.

[2] Claude Guy: *Un autre de Gaulle* (1970), Claude Mauriac, 19.

between a writer and the saviour of his country; it was a meeting between one writer and another. Mauriac had prayed that the 'robe blanche' of a resuscitated France should 'remain like the seamless garment of Christ, that no one could tear apart, and that no force on earth should ever again set against each other the Frenchmen whom General de Gaulle had united in the Resistance.'[1] This hope, too, was doomed to disappointment; but for François Mauriac, Charles de Gaulle was always to be 'le premier des nôtres'.

[1] *Mémoires Politiques*, 147-8.

HOPE DEFERRED

1

Claude Mauriac described the euphoria of the Liberation as an 'ephemeral oasis'; not as a mirage, because it was real while it lasted — only it did not last very long. There was little understanding between those who had resisted in France and those who had resisted elsewhere. Georges Bidault, in charge of foreign affairs, complained to Mauriac that de Gaulle had not even consulted him over the appointment of a new ambassador. The domestic situation was disturbed, with private accounts being pretty roughly settled. Mauriac and Duhamel had both been threatened with death before the year was out in revenge for the murder of Philippe Henriot — a gesture of 'resistance' of which Mauriac had, in fact, strongly disapproved. Their enemies were still at large, and for a time Mauriac was under police protection.

He counted his losses among the men of letters. 'The Voltairian smile, stripped of all its ugliness, where it lit up with a ravishing illumination the fine features of Jean Giraudoux';[1] Jean-Jacques Bernard barely kept alive in a camp at Compiègne; Louis Gillet, the historian; Jean Prévost whom he first met with Jacques Rivière, on the morrow of the first world war, with other contributors to the *Nouvelle Revue Française*. Prévost had not then come of age, but his muscular body 'seemed detached from a fresco by Michelangelo',[2] and Mauriac had asked who was 'this infant Hercules'? In his work for the Resistance Prévost had shown a Herculean strength and courage. On the other side of the barricades, Drieu la Rochelle had committed suicide. His was the tragedy of a weak man betrayed by his worship of force. Claude Mauriac remembered him with his father before the war 'walking round each other, and sniffing each other, with an animal distrust.';[3] and again, during the Occupation, in passionate debate over the dinner table. Drieu was the first of the collaborators, taking over the *Nouvelle Revue Française* in the name of the 'new Europe', and in despair of the Republic. If he had not committed suicide, he would almost certainly

---

[1] *Le Bâillon dénoué*, 151.

[2] Ibid., 44.

[3] *Le Temps Immobile*, 403.

have been shot – although Malraux, who was among the first of the resistants, declared that he would have given him shelter. No doubt the importance, perhaps excessive, which the French attach to the written word explained the summary justice meted out to men of letters. Mauriac met it at the Académie, where Abel Hermant, a fairly innocuous essayist, and Abel Bonnard who had served as a Minister under Vichy, were both excluded from its meetings, although in default of a quorum they could not be formally expelled. Mauriac did his best for Hermant, but felt afterwards that he might have done more.

Of greater consequence was the case of Charles Maurras. This powerful writer and strong, though narrow, intellect had formed an enduring school of political thought in France. Mauriac's own brother, Pierre, was consistently faithful to it. It went by the name of 'nationalisme intégral'. Yet 'nationalisme intégral' had profited by the disaster of the nation, discouraging every effort to redeem it. In his *Cahier Noir* Mauriac had described the followers of Maurras as 'so many Bonapartistes without Caesar, and so many Boulangistes without a General'. For all too many of them doctrinal rigidity had 'dominated and checked the profound racial instinct which should have impelled them to resist the invader – while for many of the working classes the same instinct prevailed over the theoretical internationalism which they professed.'[1] Mauriac received a letter from Francis Yvon Eccles, Emeritus Professor of French in the University of London, pleading on behalf of international opinion that Maurras should be judged with equity. (It is worth remarking that on the single occasion when the present writer met Professor Eccles he was still convinced of the guilt of Dreyfus.) Mauriac passed this letter on to Claude who had stumbled, almost by accident, into the personal secretariat of General de Gaulle. Maurras was then in custody at Lyon, and de Gaulle realised that if he failed to receive a proper trial a large section of public opinion would be permanently alienated from a government whose authority was still precarious. He gave immediate orders that Maurras should be brought to Paris and tried by the Haute Cour. In fact the trial took place at Lyon; it was relatively unprejudiced; Maurras defended himself with brilliant verve, and was sentenced to life imprisonment; and the Maurrasians were never to be reconciled.

This was a case of complicity rather than active collaboration. Yet it was from the *Action Française* that a gifted journalist like Robert Brasillach, writing in *Je suis partout*, had imbibed his virulent anti-semitism. Mauriac had seen Brasillach two days before the Liberation on the terrace of the 'Deux Magots', and wished afterwards that he

[1] *Mémoires Politiques*, 160.

had sat down beside him. Brasillach, who for some time had ceased contributing to *Je suis partout*, could easily have escaped to Spain and forestalled arrest. Instead, he was tried and condemned to death. Mauriac personally interceded for him with de Gaulle, who replied that he had not yet studied the dossier but hoped that he would not be executed. Brasillach, though he had covered Mauriac with insult in his articles, wrote him a moving letter from Fresnes:

> When I was sixteen years old and read your books for the first time, I did not foresee the strange paths that would lead us to this invisible meeting. For myself I should have asked you nothing; it needed the sure and unexpected instinct of a mother, and the devotion of friends, who were not mistaken in their belief that your heart would break down all the obstacles that your mind could set up against it. Our best hope is that we shall meet hereafter in the world invisible; if I wished to doubt it, the chains that I carry, and their noise which accompanies me as I go from my chair to my bed, would remind me of it at every moment. But today it seems to me that, in the world invisible, we shall recognize one another: and for this reason, dear François Mauriac, I send you, from these icy cells, my gratitude and my remembrance.[1]

Brasillach's mother, his brother, and several of his friends called on Mauriac on the eve of the day appointed for his execution. The memory of their supplication turned him cold whenever he recalled it. But he still had reason to believe that his intercession had been successful and it was only when he met Bidault at the Soviet Embassy that he knew that Brasillach would be shot at dawn. Bidault's answer to his enquiry fell like the blade of the guillotine. A photograph of Brasillach in German uniform had apparently sealed his fate; nor was he the only Frenchman to have paraded in colours that were at the same time true and false.

In the case of another writer, Henri Béraud, whom Mauriac had met only once, a plea for mercy prevailed. His article, 'Autour d'un Verdict', had appeared in the *Figaro* and was brought to Béraud in his cell; and of this Béraud was afterwards to write: 'A solitary and ardent voice was heard, and it required great courage. The greatest of all, perhaps; the courage to break the silence amid the universal servitude and fear.'[2] To Mauriac he addressed the following pencilled note:

> A man who had been living his own death for the past five days has stretched out his hand to you, and you have taken it. You

[1] *Un autre de Gaulle*, 87.
[2] *Quinze jours avec la mort.*

have had the courage and the generosity to take it. I have shed my first tears in reading this article which has saved my honour.'

Pierre Laval had little honour to be saved, and when his daughter came to Mauriac for help he could say nothing to encourage her. Nor had he much sympathy for Pétain – 'that aged and living lie with the gold braid on his *képi*, and all those stars on his sleeve'[1] – but he insisted on the distinction between collaboration with the enemy and obedience to a government whose legality had been recognized by every neutral power, including the Soviet Union and the United States. He wished, like General de Gaulle himself, that the trial of Pétain could have been avoided; but whether or not the Armistice was inevitable, its ineluctable consequence was the policy initiated at Montoire. Marshal Pétain was paying for all those who had acted in his name, and perhaps for many who had not. What was to be said of judges who condemned to death a man to whom they had sworn an oath of loyalty? Alike for his admirers and his adversaries. Philippe Pétain would 'remain a tragic figure, eternally wandering, half way between treason and sacrifice'.[2]

> If we have deserved to have Pétain, we have also, thanks be to God, deserved to have de Gaulle; the spirit of surrender and the spirit of resistance, were both incarnate among the French, and they met in a duel to the death. But each of these two men represented infinitely more than himself, and since the humblest of us has a share in the glory of the first resistant in France, let us not shrink from the thought that a part of us, maybe, was at times the accomplice of this stricken old man.'[3]

By January 1945 18,700 cases were being tried by the courts of the *épuration*. But these were 'only the hors d'oeuvre'; more than 50,000 were due to come up. Where was it to end, and what was to become of the national unity for which Mauriac (and de Gaulle) had pleaded? Particularly flagrant was the case of Jacques Bénoist-Mechin, the Vichy ambassador to Turkey. When the tribunal pronounced its sentence of death, one of the jurymen called out to the public: 'We have our dead to avenge!' Mauriac believed that a member of the Resistance had a right to his place in the witness box, but not among the jury. 'These words alone constitute a verdict which judges our false justice, and condemns it.'[4] What was left of Justice when a boy of eighteen was sent

---

[1] *Mémoires Politiques,* 154.

[2] *Journal IV,* 128.

[3] *Mémoires Politiques,* 149-90.

[4] Ibid., 208.

to prison because he had once given the Hitler salute? To Mauriac's objections, Roger Martin du Gard, an eminent novelist and Nobel prize-winner, replied with the arguments of the 'man in the street'. Mauriac admitted that if the Rundstedt offensive in the Ardennes had delivered Paris to Doriot and his gang, as many had feared, he would have heard 'from the depth of my eternity a qualified tribute to my character and my work, pronounced *sous la coupole,* by . . . but let us charitably abstain from mentioning names.'[1] The editor of the Socialist *Le Populaire* accused him of 'putting himself on the side of treason'; could the Socialists not see that 'their only excuse for survival was to defend against Stalinism the humane and Christian principles which we both hold in common – even if this benefits our opponent?'[2] Communist hatred did not always spare the genuine resistant. Colonel de la Roque, founder of the pre-war *Croix-de-Feu* – a quasi-Fascist movement – had directed a network of resistance, and was deported to Germany. On his return, he was arrested and imprisoned in a barracks at Versailles where he subsequently died.

Mauriac wrote with passion because, for the first time, his political allies were in power. The leaders of the M.R.P.[3] – a movement dedicated to the cause of Christian democracy – had been formed in the school of the Sillon. Marc Sangnier was still alive, and Mauriac had the privilege of investing him with the insignia of the Légion d'Honneur. Why did these men keep silent? Why did a man like Emmanuel Mounier, whom Mauriac ardently admired, utter no word of protest? Why did Albert Camus, in *Combat,* enter the lists against him? He was ready to smile when he found himself described as 'Saint François des Assises de Charité-sur-Seine' – the *bon mot* was almost inevitable; but he reminded his readers that 'the saints, more often than not, show themselves to be great realists'; and that 'Father Joseph, the agent and counsellor of Cardinal Richelieu, was very far advanced along the mystical way.'[4] Mauriac did not pretend to be a mystic; he thought, however, that it was 'not too soon to find an issue to this monotonous and bloody labyrinth.'[5]

For these reasons, among others, he had now become a public personality, at a time when he feared that his career was over. 'I have made a mess of my life' he said 'I ought to have been Barrès, and I am nothing.'[6] Yet Barrès was what he had become. His articles appeared in

[1] Ibid., 208.
[2] Ibid., 209.
[3] Mouvement Républicain Populaire.
[4] Ibid., 178.
[5] Ibid., 180.
[6] *Le Temps Immobile,* 433.

the *Figaro* three times a week. He could influence opinion and, through opinion, policy. On the 30th October he organised the *soirée* at the Comédie-Française in honour of the poets of the Resistance, and composed the text which introduced them. This was read by Jean Martinelli, who had won his spurs in the service of de Gaulle. 'Là où est le général de Gaulle, là aussi respire la France' – and de Gaulle was there in a box, 'his tall khaki silhouette framed by the gilt columns.'[1] Poems by Aragon, Eluard, Supervielle, and others were read by the actors of the Comédie against a 'simple tricoloured drapery, and the luminous reflection of a Croix de Lorraine'.[2] Charles Morgan had come over from England to read his *Ode to France*, afterwards given in translation. There could have been no doubt in the mind of anyone present as to where Mauriac had stood, and was still standing; but he was standing, as he always stood, on his own feet.

It was not true, as a writer in *Combat* had suggested, that 'the Resistance was beginning to get on his nerves.' He reminded his critics that the men of his generation had 'grown to maturity in a Europe divided and simmering because a Jewish officer was expiating in prison a crime committed by someone else.'[3] Opposition also came from Pétinist sympathisers. There was an angry confrontation at the Académie, where Henry Bordeaux accused Mauriac of 'trying to extinguish the fires which he himself had lit.' At the Congress of the Front National a delegate protested against his re-election to the directing committee. This inspired a passionate defence by Jacques Debu-Bridel. He reminded the audience that 'the men whom he is trying to save have done their attacks at a time when he was fighting at our side . . . To exclude him from our Council because he asks forgiveness for his enemies would be to commit an injustice, for which no name is too bad, against a great artist who honours us in taking part in our discussions, and a man who did not wait for the invasion to defend the cause of right and justice.' A vote was taken, and Debu-Bridel was supported by 1809 delegates against three opponents and one abstention.

Jeanne Mauriac had returned to Paris for a few days early in September; Luce had joined her husband as he emerged from the *maquis* near Grenoble; Claire was with another *maquis* in the south; Jean had enlisted in the Chasseurs Alpins; and Claude was near at hand to serve de Gaulle, and share his father's anxieties. 'How close I feel to him, one in flesh and one in spirit';[4] and as the year drew to its

---

[1] *Un autre de Gaulle*, 58.

[2] Ibid., 3.

[3] *Le Bâillon dénoué, O.C. XI.*

[4] *Le Temps Immobile*, 59.

close it was not only the Rundstedt offensive that sent a chill down his spine. There were the 'threats, clearer every day, against my father's life.'[1]

Mauriac had not heard the 'Te Deum' of Liberation in Notre-Dame, but he heard it in Strasbourg cathedral. The tall figure of de Gaulle in the choir, and the sound of distant gunfire competing with the organ, were among 'les plus beaux souvenirs de ma vie'.[2] Afterwards he followed de Gaulle into Germany. The myth — and I use the word in no pejorative sense — around which his political thought was to crystallise had already taken shape. At their first meeting the General's physical appearance had given the impression of 'a man stripped to the bone'. There was 'no mask' on the face which he turned towards his countrymen.[3] Like Mauriac himself, de Gaulle had survived his milieu. Nevertheless the war in Europe was not yet over before the new president of the Comité National de la Résistance was showing his hostility to the 'premier des nôtres'. 'Make no mistake about it' Mauriac assured him 'if you succeed in getting rid of de Gaulle, it is not the people who will benefit but the trusts.'[4] Less than a year later, de Gaulle anticipated their wishes.

2

Already, in April 1939, Mauriac had completed the second version of his new play, *Les Mal Aimés,* and read the last two acts to his son. There were phrases that Claude found 'physically wounding'. One, at least, of them, carried an echo of his father's conversation. 'When you don't have the chance of knowing what is evil, you are wrong to let it worry you.'[5] The play turns on a father's possessive love for his elder daughter Elisabeth; his success in persuading her to break with the man, Alain, seven years younger than herself, whom she loves and by whom she is loved in return; and on the marriage of Alain to the younger daughter, Marianne, with whom he had enjoyed a casual flirtation. This distraction of an idle summer had brought Marianne to the brink of suicide; but the happiness she had sought turns to ashes, and so does the sacrifice which had made it possible. Elisabeth, at the last moment, renounces her intention to go away with Alain; and her father, M. de Virelade, can listen to her reading aloud from Balzac or Dumas to his heart's content.

[1] Ibid., 68.

[2] *Bloc-Notes II,* 139.

[3] *Mémoires Politiques,* 164.

[4] *Le Temps Immobile,* 413.

[5] Ibid., 56.

Certain passages, as Mauriac read them, were scarcely tolerable. In the light of Claude's reaction, he slightly modified the character of M. de Virelade, and read the scene again, assuring his son that the most painful speeches would get by if they were gently spoken.

> My father read, miming every speech. Sometimes he looked aside, or smiled, or grimaced . . . he was really in the skin of his characters.'[1]

He had looked for a title in the Book of Job, but the Old Testament left him cold with its expectations of long life and prosperity; so he turned to Apollinaire instead. No title could more perfectly have described the subject, because none of the characters are loved as they wish to be. Even Elisabeth's return is too late for her father's comfort, since he knows that she was ready to abandon him. 'How do people lay down their burdens?' she asks 'mine is attached to my shoulders, and nailed to them'; and Marianne replies: 'I too bend under the burden, Elisabeth, and it is you that have laid it on me.' The last word of desperate irony is with Elisabeth: 'And yet we love one another.'

Towards the end of August (1939) Mauriac had read the revised version of the play to André Maurois and his wife who were visiting Malagar. Between the second and third acts they listened to the news: 'Moscow announces a pact of non-aggression with Berlin'. 'What does it mean?' asked one of the children. 'It means war' replied Maurois; and he adds that the play distilled 'the same atmosphere of moral *malaise* as *Asmodée*.'[2]

François Mauriac's imaginative writing did not unduly flatter his fellow-countrymen; this is one reason, no doubt, why *Les Mal Aimés* was not produced under the Occupation. So frightening a study in emotional frustration would have done nothing to resuscitate civic morale; indeed it could only have confirmed the penitents of Vichy in their diagnosis of national decay. By the summer of 1945, however, it was drawing big audiences to the Comédie-Française, with brilliant performances by Aimé Clariond, Madeleine Renaud, and Renée Faure; and also a good deal of adverse criticism. The fashion was then for plays inspired by Greek legend – Sartre's *Les Mouches* and Anouilh's *Antigone* – and the stuffy bourgeois interior of M. de Virelade's household went against the popular grain. The world had changed, but not the world of François Mauriac. Nevertheless fatality broods over these twisted destinies as surely as it does over the House of Atreus. Mauriac had, in fact, successfully refined his dramatic style; he had done what he

---

[1] Ibid., 56.
[2] *Mémoires, I* (1942), 191-192.

set out to do after seeing *Asmodée* on the stage.

> The characters must talk the language of conversation; the spectator must feel that he is hearing the same words that he uses in ordinary life. But an imperceptible transposition should give the reader the impression that every speech belongs to a work of art. As a dramatist, I want the audience to forget that I am a writer; I don't want him to say, when he is listening to a play of mine: 'That is literature.'[1]

Similarly, T.S. Eliot, in his later plays, set out to prevent his audience saying: 'This is poetry'. Both achieved a simplicity which avoided either rhetoric or slang. They met, during the same summer, at a luncheon in honour of Eliot, given by the *Figaro*; and Mauriac met Gide on the same occasion for the first time since the outbreak of war.

Paul Valéry was also present at that luncheon, for he had recently taken the chair for Eliot at a lecture organised by the British Council. A few weeks later his body lay in state on the Place du Trocadéro, and Mauriac stood with the other Academicians to salute his passing. It was not quite true to say that Valéry had turned his face to the wall, since he had always faced it. But the fact that Mauriac had seen an opening where Valéry did not, had never clouded their friendship. Mauriac did not expect to know what Valéry thought of his latest novel, because he knew that Valéry would not have read it – and the knowledge inflicted no wound to his amour-propre. Valéry was the last, and not the least, of the poets in Mauriac's personal *pléiade*. It did not matter that he had refused the 'bet' that Mauriac had taken with Pascal, for no complacent serenity had calmed 'that noble face, and spiritual in the absolute meaning of the word', which looked down on him from a faded photograph on the walls of his study. Underneath it Valéry had written:

> *Que si j'étais placé devant cette effigie*
> *Inconnu de moi-même, ignorant de mes traits,*
> *A tant de plis affreux d'angoisse et d'énergie*
> *Je lirais mes tourments et me reconnaîtrais!*[2]

'Angoisse' and 'énergie' were common to them both.

The ending of the war in Europe was followed by the visit of the Old Vic company to the Théâtre des Champs-Elysées with Olivier in *Richard III*. As Georges Bernanos had written, 'every great historical drama is Shakespearian'; and to Mauriac the curses of Richard's victims on the eve of Bosworth reverberated from the ruins of the Reich

---

[1] *D'autres et moi*, 282-283.

[2] *Mémoires Intérieurs*, 223.

chancellery in Berlin. Michel Saint-Denis – then better known as Jacques Duchesne of 'Les Français parlent aux Français' – introduced him to Olivier afterwards. Gide was with them, and Olivier seemed a little vague about the celebrity of his two admirers. Anglo-French differences in Syria were putting the *entente* under strain, and General de Gaulle did not attend the performance. On the 25th September Mauriac returned to Malagar. It was two years to the day since he had left it, advised by the Resistance that the Gestapo were on his track.

Mauriac's third play, *Le Passage du Malin*, was produced at the Théâtre de la Madeleine in December 1947. Emilie Tavernas lives with her uninteresting husband and both her mothers-in-law – an improbable incubus, even for a French family. She is the head of a school, liking to exercise her gift of authority to protect the morals of other people. The play turns on her attempt to save an adolescent girl from the attentions of a young man, Bernard Lecêtre. In the event, she falls in love with Bernard himself, and he with her; and they spend a single night together. Bernard is an insatiable – and unsatisfied – *coureur*. 'We belong to the same race, you and I, whether you like it or not. The only difference is that I cannot do without the bodies of those I want to possess. But in fact I never do possess them. One doesn't know what to do with the creature one has held in one's arms, and who gives one nothing of her secret.' As Mauriac puts it: 'Each of the two lovers yields to a reciprocal and similar charm; the charm of what they have always hated and fought against';[1] in the case of Emilie the charm of the senses, in the case of Bernard the charm of the spirit. Each betrays their natural instinct for domination. The play ran for more than 100 performances, despite adverse criticism – not altogether undeserved. The characters of the two mothers-in-law, a clumsy attempt at comic relief, are grotesquely overdrawn. There is something of Brigitte Pian in Emilie Tavernas, if it were possible to imagine Brigitte Pian in the arms of anybody. The play was received on its opening with something less than lyrical enthusiasm; and when a fashionable dramatist of the boulevards observed to Mauriac with glacial insincerity: 'You must be pleased', Mauriac replied: 'Not so pleased as you are.'

On March 13 of the same year (1947) Mauriac welcomed Paul Claudel *sous la coupole*. His speech had a warm and personal resonance, for he had admired Claudel at a time when few others – Jacques Rivière was an exception – either admired or understood him. He recalled Jean de la Ville de Mirmont, in that gasping voice of his, reciting passages from *Connaissance de l'Est*. 'Many people, living and dead, are urging me to speak to you as if we were alone together, you and I.' Mauriac, like Claudel, had caught the whiff of the supernatural in Rimbaud, but they

---

[1] *D'autres et moi*, 284.

had followed their vocation as Catholic writers in ways diametrically opposed:

> There are believing novelists and playwrights whose inspiration springs from the most troubled depths of human nature. The very substance of their work is impure, and their whole life is spent in the uncertain struggle between two antagonistic vocations; on the one hand the call to every Christian, who has received the gift of speech and the gift of writing, to propagate the fire which the Son of Man has come to spread over the earth; and on the other hand the necessity he is under to probe the sounds of human nature until, from one circle to another, he touches the abyss.

This had not been the way of Paul Claudel, but Mauriac declared his preference, among the poet's plays, for *Partage de Midi* and *Le Soulier de Satin* where the note of heartbreak had been sounded. This was more persuasive than his triumphalist Catholicism. The demon of mischief did not always lie dormant in the genius of Claudel; he took delight in his provocations. People had even described him as 'grumpy'; but no, said Mauriac, a grumpy ambassador was surely a contradiction in terms. It was a graceful, generous and perceptive address, though it left some members of the poet's family — if not the poet himself — less than completely satisfied.

In June Mauriac and his wife travelled to Oxford, where the University bestowed on him an Honorary D. Litt. Gide had preceded him by a fortnight, and for the same purpose; in both cases the diplomacy of Dr Enid Starkie had been at work. It was thought unsafe to lodge Gide at Wadham, in such close proximity to undergraduates, so he was put up at an hotel. The Mauriacs were the guests of Lady Phipps, an old friend, at her house in Wiltshire. The Public Orator, Mr T.F. Higham of Trinity, welcoming François in the Sheldonian, referred to three of his novels — *Le Fleuve de Feu, Le Baiser au Lépreux,* and *Le Noeud de Vipères* — and quoted a phrase of Ronald Knox about books dealing with the 'eternal triangle of *amo, amas, amat.'* In a reference to *Les Mal Aimés*, which had just been produced — not very successfully — at the Arts Theatre in London, he spoke of plays in which a fourth character is introduced, of much riper age than the others, and apt to forget the precept of Ovid's *Ars Amatoria*: 'If you want to be loved, be lovable.' Mauriac, he continued, wrote in the vein of Greek Tragedy rather than in that of the Greek Comedy of Manners. Tribute was also paid to his friendship for Great Britain in times of peace and war. Graham Greene, then a director of Eyre & Spottiswoode, was now arranging for a Collected Edition of his novels in a translation by Gerard Hopkins; and this brought him a wider public among English-speaking readers.

It is easy to understand the mutual admiration and affinity between Mauriac and Graham Greene. Each was a specialist in sin, and the possibility of salvation between losing the stirrup and falling to the ground. Before leaving Oxford, Mauriac was eager to see Newman's old rooms in Oriel, and he was shown them by one of the College tutors. 'Et le petit oratoire?' he enquired anxiously. The tutor then opened a cupboard which contained nothing but a collection of golf clubs. Horrified at the sacrilege, Mauriac clasped his hands to his forehead, and exclaimed: 'Mon Dieu! le golf!'

3

When General de Gaulle withdrew from power, though not from politics, in February 1946, Mauriac endorsed the opinion of Léon Blum that the French had not known how to incorporate 'this great, haughty, and solitary spirit' in a democratic institution. Nevertheless he could sympathise with another observer to whom it seemed that the General 'did not want one to like him.' He had received a similar impression himself when he had gone to plead for the life of Brasillach. De Gaulle had been extremely courteous, but it was the courtesy of an officer and an aristocrat. He was stiff with the consciousness of a superiority which Mauriac did not deny. He was the man that Mauriac was waiting for, though not quite the man he had imagined. But then no one had imagined de Gaulle. 'I had the feeling' said Mauriac afterwards 'of spending half an hour with a cormorant'[1] – a comparison to which the General's appearance lent a certain plausibility. Whatever the motives of his withdrawal, Mauriac could only look back on a great dream that was dead:

> All the Resistance tightly gathered round its leader; the C.N.R.[2] as the nucleus of the new Assembly; prompt punishment for traitors and assassins by regular courts martial, whose impartiality was beyond suspicion – a punishment followed, after a few months, and in despite of all the complaints, by a total amnesty for those whom the legality of Vichy . . . had led astray; the prisons reserved for crime, and adolescents rescued from their corruption; and finally reforms, at once bold and proportionate to the needs of a country which has been drained of its blood, and is covered with graves and ruins . . .[3]

[1] *Un autre de Gaulle*, 98.

[2] Comité National de la Résistance.

[3] *Journal IV*, 217.

France, for a few weeks and months after the Liberation, had seemed like 'a woman who had been unable to walk for five years, miraculously cured, and running, stark naked, across the city weeping tears of joy.' Now, another image came to mind – that of old Paul Bourget, on November 11, 1918, leaning out of his window and looking down on the frenzied rejoicing of the crowd as he exclaimed: 'Voilà les bêtises qui recommencent?' They had been going on for a good long time, since August 1944, before Charles de Gaulle retired to a pavilion in the woods of Marly-le-Roi. When Mauriac was taken to see him there, he explained that there had been two kinds of Resistance – and he might have added that there had been two kinds of war; that since the Liberation no understanding was possible between them. 'There was my Resistance – and yours – which was resistance to the enemy; and then there was the political resistance, anti-fascist, anti-nazi, but in no way national.' With the Resistance as it had now developed it was impossible to come to terms, because it was infected from within. The Communist party was the strongest party in the Assembly, and it took its orders from the Kremlin.

Mauriac was well aware of this, and henceforward he devoted his polemic to exposing the true face of communist propaganda – a kind of secular clericalism which 'used the revolutionary faith of the people to satisfy an imperialist will to power.'[1] Even a young Catholic poet like Loys Masson had not only accepted the 'out-stretched hand'; he had positively clutched it. Pierre Hervé, writing for *L'Humanité*, described Mauriac as an 'elegiac old jackdaw'; Mauriac retorted by taxing him with ingratitude, since he had given him a 'certificate of existence' which otherwise he would never have had. 'Who is this M. Pierre Hervé?' people were asking; Mauriac replied that he was the most subtle spokesman at the disposal of the Communist party, and that if he were reduced to describing Mauriac as an 'elegiac old jackdaw', it was because there was no valid answer to Mauriac's arguments. Otherwise he would certainly have found it.

In asking for a man, Mauriac – perhaps unconsciously – had been asking for a monarch. The Maurrasian formation of de Gaulle was clear to him at one of their early meetings. Maurras had been right, the General had said – 'and that is why he has landed up where we see him today' – and the irony of the observation was not 'essentially malevolent'.[2] But although the monarch had abdicated, he had no intention of quitting the stage. His reply to the parliamentarians, busy at the party game, was the *Rassemblement du Peuple Français* to which he hoped that all

[1] Ibid., 206.

[2] *Un autre de Gaulle*, 99.

patriotic Frenchmen would rally. Mauriac did not share these expectations or agree with this policy. The R.P.F., he maintained, would only rally the conservative elements of public opinion, and among them a good number of quasi-repentant Pétinistes. These fears were shared by Claude Mauriac, who was still working for the General, and by André Malraux who was eager for Mauriac's adhesion. Mauriac was reticent in his opposition, but he still placed his faith in the M.R.P. He was unwilling for the cause of Christian democracy to go by default. Parliaments, he admitted, had been France's undoing, and he was not encouraged by the return of their discredited performers. A chance remained, however, that Parliamentary government might be 'reinvented'. The new men of the M.R.P. were not tainted with the follies, and worse, of their predecessors. If Mauriac's fears for the R.P.F. were to be confirmed, his hopes for the M.R.P. were to be equally disappointed.

On the 4th July, in this year of disillusion, Claire Mauriac was married to Ivan Wiazemski, a young Russian of patrician birth, in the church of Notre-Dame d'Auteuil. The Mass was celebrated to an accompaniment of Mozart, and a reception followed in the offices of the *Figaro*. Claire, with her husband, left immediately for the occupied zone of Germany.

The verve and occasional ferocity of Mauriac's polemic recapture the climate of the cold war between 1946 and 1952. His articles were written at a time when a Soviet invasion of liberated Europe, or at least a communist take-over of government in France, was regarded as as imminent possibility by responsible opinion. Mauriac fought against the temptation to exclaim with Lamartine on the morrow of Louis-Napoleon's *coup d'état*: 'I have become a political atheist'; or — which came to much the same thing — to add his voice to the neutralism then fashionable among intellectuals speculating on the sidelines. 'If the worst happens' the editor of *Esprit* had written 'we shall at least have our Barrès.' Mauriac would normally have been flattered by the comparison, but he was exasperated by the air of moral superiority behind it. What he denounced in the neutralists was not the 'apostles of peace' but the 'benevolent auxiliaries of death'. To be described as a 'cannibal' by a Soviet newspaper made him smile, but to find himself in opposition to Claude Bourdet — a friend and former ally — made him sad. The alternatives were clear; 'the right for M. Claude Bourdet to put down on paper whatever comes into his light head; or the obligation for M. Claude Bourdet to return to the camps where his heroic resistance has led him once already.'[1] Bourdet held that neutrality was 'the only political terrain which would not divide the French'; Mauriac made no bones

[1] *Mémoires Politiques*, 401.

about what united them:

> A certain idea they have of the human being, and his dignity; and also the instinct for the modest happiness an individual has the right to enjoy in this world, with his family and in his own house – no matter how humble – behind a door which he can lock in order to think, write, pray, and dream at his leisure, with no fear of its shaking at dawn under the fists of the prison warders of the State.[1]

Recent history had taught that peace was not procured by unilateral disarmament. To put the United States and the Soviet Union in the same category was as much as to say that a 'free democracy was worth no more than a totalitarian state'. When the editor of *L'Humanité* was arrested for encouraging the violent demonstrations which greeted the arrival of General Ridgeway as Commander-in-Chief of N.A.T.O., Mauriac was not moved to protest. The visit was linked to the foreign policy of the country, and sanctioned by the National Assembly. The life of the nation was at stake, and the government was bound to protect it.

Mauriac recalled the great voice of Jaurès as he had once heard it in Bordeaux; Jaurès whom Barrès had compared to a 'huge locomotive puffing in a cloud of soot'. But there was no Jaurès in the French Socialist party to speak for Stepinac in Yugoslavia or Beran in Prague, or for such leaders of Balkan resistance as had incurred the displeasure of the Kremlin. Marx had won a final victory over the French humanitarians of 1848; 'he had emptied socialism of its Christian substance'. Mauriac was sensitive to the wall which Marx – and not he alone – had erected between the bourgeois liberal like himself and the milieux he was trying to reach. In the spring of 1951 he was visited at Malagar by a young schoolteacher from a village some way off. They sat by the fire, and the young man confessed that he and his friends were interested in everything that Mauriac wrote, but that they could not read and discuss an article of his together without feeling that they were betraying their own class. The feeling was not reciprocal; Mauriac had no fear of betraying the *bourgeoisie*. Yet the wall was insuperable; only the worker-priests – still very much on probation – had some success in overcoming it. What was the solution? Had there ever existed a classless society? 'It is no use for revolutions to massacre the privileged; the privileges remain, and the wall is never broken down.'[2] Even those intellectuals doctrinally detached from the *bourgeoisie*, like Mounier

[1] Ibid.
[2] Ibid., 412.

or Sartre, wrote in a social vacuum. The workers did not understand what they were talking about; the *bourgeoisie* might or might not understand, and would almost certainly not approve. Mauriac did not pretend to a similar detachment. In this respect academicians cannot be choosers, and the Institut de France, despite its periodic vacancies, can hardly be described as a vacuum.

A correspondent compared Mauriac to a 'weathercock' because he was for ever changing his direction according to the wind that blew. He replied that he changed it according to his principles that were constant. One's political stance depended on the position of one's opponents. Immobility was not a political virtue. If he stood on the left during the Spanish Civil War and the German occupation, and on the right when the *épuration* and the Communist danger were matters of debate, it was because his Christian principles dicated his polemic. In each case he knew what he was talking about, and was able to quote chapter and verse for his opinions. The war in Indo-China he could only judge from a distance, seeing this, too, in the light of a Communist bid for power. He was not insensitive to the faults of colonialism, and afterwards reproached himself for not admitting them more candidly. But he was equally aware of what the French had given to Indo-China – spiritual and material benefits which it was their duty to safeguard. If he had talked with General Leclerc on the latter's return from the Far East, the 'weathercock' might well have shifted a little in conformity with the 'wind of change'. He was quick to do so when it blew from another quarter.

4

The *douceur de vivre* lost no time in resuming its rights over a people so long deprived of it. In spite of present fears and hopes deferred, Mauriac was a resilient character. At Aix-en-Provence, in July 1949, the Commendatore held the Don once again in his iron grip; and the warning given to the west by Mao Tse-Tung was here translated into the 'most *supernatural* music ever invented by the genius of the human mind'.[1] The relative failure of *Le Passage du Malin* had not deterred him from the theatre. Although his days in Paris were eaten up by journalism – letters to answer, visitors to see, information to collect – he was able in three weeks of a vacation to complete the first draft of a play. *Le Feu sur la Terre* was produced in Lyon at the Théâtre des Célestins on the 12th October 1950. Before the curtain rose Mauriac explained – a little imprudently perhaps – his purpose in writing it.

[1] Ibid., 351.

The subject was a sister's possessive and self-destructive love for her brother — a passion, he was careful to emphasise, in no way incestuous; and his treatment of it was suggested by a visit to the château of Maurice and Eugénie de Guérin. Deprive Eugénie of her religious faith, and what sort of woman would she have been? Where would she have found the strength to agree to her brother's marriage? How could she have helped hating her sister-in-law? The character of Mauriac's heroine, Laure, was born of this question; and as might have been expected, he gave it a dusty answer.

He wrote *Le Feu sur la Terre* at Malagar in the summer of 1949, overlooking from his terrace the glow of the forest fires, and discovering in these an image of Laure's disruptive passion. The play's sub-title — *Le Pays sans chemin* — signified that there was no way through the jungle of an obsession that fed upon itself. But the *pays sans chemin* was not a *pays sans frontière*, and one only needed the strength to cross it. Or, to change the metaphor —

> No matter how stifling is the cell where passion imprisons a human being, one is never without a key which will open the door, and release one into the service of God, or into the service of mankind — which is another way of reaching God; and the name of the key is charity.'[1]

A hint of this solution was dropped at the close of the first act, but too casually for the audience — or for Laure herself — to pick it up. Jean-Louis Barrault wrote that he found the play even more dispiriting than Kafka — whose *Le Procès* he had just produced at the Marigny — because Kafka's prison did not altogether forbid escape. Mauriac replied that neither did the prison of his heroine; the play would go on, even when the curtain had come down. But an optimistic ending would have falsified his theme, and handed yet another excuse to the critics who were always ready to accuse him of giving way to the fear of scandal.

> The saddest thing is that they were nearly always right. One cannot force one's talent. In life I am not in the least a despairing sort of man, but it is true that as a writer I am not naturally hopeful. We writers have good reason for complaint; no one thinks of reproaching a painter for the way he paints. No one ever criticised Greco for painting Grecos, or Manet for painting Manets. The characters I am presenting to you today could only be my sort of characters . . . I should add that all my protagonists are not so black, and that I have set in opposition to Laure a simple and tender young woman, a wife and lover in whom many

[1] *D'autres et moi*, 288.

women from our part of the country will be able to recognize themselves.'[1]

Plays were quicker, if not easier, to write than novels; and for one so constantly preoccupied with current affairs they were less absorbing. But after the indifferent reception of *Le Feu sur la Terre* Mauriac never again tried his luck in the theatre. The play in performance could never be the same as the play that he had conceived and committed to paper. If it won its place in a permanent repertoire – which was the case with *Asmodée* and *Les Mal Aimés* – characters passed through successive reincarnations at the hands of different actors – each, as often happened, further away from the author's original conception. The novelist was in control of his creation in a way that the dramatist was not. And so, while Mauriac was still at work on *Le Feu sur la Terre*, the novel, to which he thought he had said good-bye, began to exercise its old fascination, although it did so in a roundabout way.

He now headed the editorial committee of *La Table Ronde*, a monthly review of excellent quality, intended to replace the discredited *Nouvelle Revue Française*. Among the contributors were writers from all sides of the political spectrum, including a number of *maurrassiens*, of whom Thierry Maulnier was the most respectable. 'Never' wrote Mauriac of his own collaboration 'had a hen hatched so many ducklings.'[2] When the N.R.F. reappeared the *Table Ronde* was put upon its mettle, and Mauriac was asked to supply a short novel. Having nothing for the moment in his head, he turned up a manuscript left uncompleted during the war. He had dictated some forty pages to his wife, who found them unsatisfactory, and he agreed with her. But he now looked at them again, and was at once possessed by the character of the boy – the *sagouin*, well translated by Gerard Hopkins as 'the little misery' – which had previously lacked definition. He saw how and why the boy would meet his death, and thus the book – short in length but rich in substance – took shape. It was the first time that Mauriac wrote a novel at another's bidding – and he was not far wrong in thinking that of all that he had written this was 'perhaps the most perfectly finished'. The film subsequently made of *Le Sagouin* confirmed his judgment. As a short novel, or long short story, it takes its place beside the best of Conrad or Turgenev or Henry James.

Guillou – or the 'little misery' – is the unloved, and superficially unlovable, child of a *mésalliance* between a woman of modest birth and a decayed aristocrat. Paule Meulière could not resist the title of Baronne de Cernès, but a single night in the arms of Galéas de Cernès

[1] Ibid., 289.

[2] Preface to *Bloc-Notes I*.

proved the limit of her marital capacities. It was enough, however, to land her with a child undeveloped in mind and body. Since he is too backward for a normal education, she conceives the plan of asking the local school-teacher to give him private tuition. Robert Bordas is an honest socialist and anti-clerical for whom Jaurès is the law and the prophets. Guillou spends the afternoon with him and his wife; is shown the room where their brilliant son, Jean-Pierre, sleeps during the holidays; shells the haricot beans for Madame Bordas; and reads aloud to her husband from *Vingt mille lieues sous les mers*. The teacher and the 'little misery' take to one another; but Bordas, persuaded by his wife, is unwilling to involve himself with anyone from the château, although he does not realise that Paule de Cernès, in her fury of sexual frustration, has already cast upon him a lubricious eye. People will talk, as they had talked about Paule and the former curé. Besides, the barriers of class are unbridgeable – as Mauriac had discovered for himself, when another schoolteacher came to visit him.

So Guillou is sent home to the château, and overhears a conversation between his mother, his father, and the old Baronne de Cernès. Paule has received a letter from Bordas, declining to accept Guillou as a pupil. She accuses herself of attempting to compromise the schoolteacher in the eyes of his own class. 'And for whom, I ask you? For a backward little boy, for a little degenerate . . .' Pointing to her husband, she exclaims: 'Look at them both! Isn't one the replica of the other.' This is too much for Galéas de Cernès. Followed by Guillou, he takes his usual walk to the cemetery where his ancestors lie buried. Presently he sees that Guillou has gone ahead of him in the direction of the river. The boy knows that he will never again pass an hour in the bedroom of Jean-Pierre Bordas. It was odd to feel affection for a boy that one had never seen, and would never know. 'And if he had seen me, he would have found me ugly, dirty, and stupid.' That was what his mother never stopped telling him. And there was something else – a word which had struck his father 'like a stone in the chest'. It sounded like 'regenerate'. So Galéas de Cernès foresees for his son a future not unlike his own. Hatred for his wife is mingled with shame that he had been her 'executioner', leaving her with many years still before her 'to howl after the absent male'. If Guillou had no reason to live, neither had he; and although it was generally accepted that the father had thrown himself into the river to save his son, and that the boy clinging to his neck had dragged him down, others were doubtful whether it had happened quite like that.

Such then is *Le Sagouin* – a minor masterpiece of compassion. It was followed in 1952 by *Galigaï*; the success of the one had done much to inspire the other. Mauriac had thought of entitling his new novel 'le désir et le dégoût', and this was a promising theme if the 'désir' and the 'dégoût' had been experienced by the same person. But here the 'désir' is all on one side and the 'dégoût' all on the other, each felt at its maximum intensity. 'Galigaï' is a young schoolteacher, Madame Agathe, so called after Léonora Galigaï who had exercised a dominating influence over Marie de Medicis. Madame Agathe is in the service of the Dubornet family and, for reasons never adequately explained, is determined to frustrate the nascent love-affair between Marie Dubornet and Gilles Salone, the son of the local doctor. At the same time she is consumed with a passion for Nicolas Plassac — Gilles' closest friend, in whom it is possible to recognize certain features of André Lafon. Like Lafon he is an usher in the school, and we catch an echo of Mauriac's friendship with Lafon when we are told that 'Nicolas maintained that one only truly possesses what one loves in withdrawal and solitude.' Mauriac was surely looking back to those troubled, and yet idyllic, years before his marriage, and the first world war, when he writes here of 'the very secret alliance between two young men convinced that they can remain permanently close without the risk of getting tired of each other's company; who have everything in common, books, dreams, and passions; who discover, even in their silences, a mutual accord.' The novel turns on this passionate friendship, the reciprocal love of Marie and Gilles, the 'désir' of Madame Agathe, and the 'dégoût' of Nicolas Plassac.

Gilles is persuaded that if Nicolas will engage himself to marry Galigaï — with the secret purpose of breaking the engagement later on — Galigaï will not frustrate his own marriage to Marie. Nicolas hesitates at first, and then agrees. The story hangs upon this glaring improbability. Nicolas does not conceal his disgust, nor Galigaï her desire. Eventually disgust prevails over altruism, and by then it is too late for Galigaï to take her revenge. Madame Dubornet, equally opposed to her daughter's marriage, has died, and M. Dubornet proposes marriage to Galigaï. Everyone in Dorthe — *alias* Bazas — where the action takes place, predicts that Galigaï will be a very lucky woman. Everyone, that is to say, except Galigaï. 'How good you are!' she had sighed on Nicolas' reluctant shoulder. 'Yes,' comments the author 'he was good. Unfortunately for her, good is what he was.' We leave him sitting on a parapet beside the river 'detached from every creature . . . as if he had given someone a rendezvous.' It is clear, though not explicit, for whom he was waiting; there was no need for Mauriac to tell us in a 'Postface'. In *Galigaï* he was concerned not only with desire and disgust, and two young people likely to live happily ever after, but also with the idolatry of friendship. For Nicolas loses the companion he had loved, as well as the fiancée he had loathed. Galigaï's Amazonian temperament and forbidding aspect are vividly conveyed, but the novel as a whole was a disappointing successor to *Le Sagouin.*

5

In June 1951 Claude Mauriac was engaged to Marie-Claude Mante, the great-niece of Marcel Proust and the daughter of Madame Mante-Rostand. It was nothing if not a literary alliance. A family dinner was held in Madame Rostand's elegant house with its Corots and eighteenth-century panelling. Here, said Mauriac, as they sat listening to Bach and Schumann, was all the 'bonté' of the Second Empire; Claude replied that here was 'the royalty of the triumphant bourgeoisie'.[1] Any prickings of social conscience were stilled by this happy prelude to a remarkably successful marriage. With his studies of Balzac, Malraux, and Cocteau, and his film criticism, Claude had himself acquired a promising reputation. His father regarded it with a 'bewildered, incredulous, and vaguely admiring' eye.[2]

In December of the same year Paris resounded with a controversy from which Mauriac emerged with a certain loss of popular credit. A play by Jean Cocteau — *Bacchus* — was produced by Jean-Louis Barrault at the Marigny. Cocteau described it as a 'play about hard goodness as opposed to soft goodness', illustrating the need 'to render unto God the intelligence that has been paid to the Devil'. The scene was set in a small German town in 1523. A Cardinal arrives from Rome to purify the province of heresy, and his visit coincides with the election of Bacchus, the Carnival King who will reign during the grape harvest. A young man, Hans, in whom it was possible to recognize certain features of the author, having lost his wits during a man hunt, pretends to be the village idiot in order to escape torture. Elected as 'God's fool', he wields his power like a lunatic. The Cardinal offers him refuge in a monastery if he will abjure his opinions, but he refuses and dies with the arrow of one of his own guards through his heart. The play showed the Church of the Renaissance in all the colours of its corruption.

Mauriac was present with 'le tout Paris' at the opening performance, and when 'le tout Paris' sniggered at a blasphemous treatment of the *Paternoster* he ostentatiously left the theatre. He had also been moved to indignation by the description of the Church as 'la femme-tronc'. Cocteau, writing in *France-Soir*, claimed that all the subversive lines were historical, and that 'femme-tronc' was a commonplace of Calvinist invective. He insisted that *Bacchus* was a play which redounded to the

[1] *Le Temps Immobile,* 190.
[2] Ibid., 198.

glory of the Church by showing what it ought to be, but was not; and remarked that he would 'prefer not to go to Paradise for fear of finding myself face to face with Mauriac.' In the *Figaro Littéraire* Mauriac addressed an open letter to Cocteau, written at great length and more in sorrow than in anger. It touched on Cocteau's short-lived conversion, and his personal friendships at the time when they had both talked away the small hours at 'Le Boeuf sur le Toit'. He had been shocked by the play as he had not been shocked by Sartre's *Le Diable et le Bon Dieu*, because Sartre was writing as a professed atheist and Cocteau as a Christian who had turned his back on Christianity. The 'death of God' was a slogan of the hour, and Cocteau had spent his life in 'catching the draughts'. Sartre had been a jubilant spectator of *Bacchus* while Cocteau 'tied his old Mother to the column of the Marigny, and for three hours turned her into a figure of fun.' Mauriac echoed the cry of Clovis when St Rémy told him the story of the Passion: 'If only I had been there with my Franks!' There was sanctity as well as simony in the Church of the sixteenth century. Had Cocteau never heard of St Teresa? And had he forgotten the priest — a follower of Charles de Foucauld — who had absolved him of his sins? The controversy was a nine days sensation of the kind that Paris enjoys with its *petit déjeuner*. Looking back on it, Mauriac claimed that he was perfectly justified in expressing the pain that he had felt at the Marigny, but that he might have been wrong in referring publicly to the author's religious life, his conversion, and his friendships. *Bacchus* was a failure, and Cocteau may have had the breach with Mauriac in mind when he observed that 'no good came to me of it'. It was not long, however, before the breach was healed. Mauriac sent Cocteau a copy of his next novel with the inscription 'from your enemy who loves you'.[1]

The following year (1952) was something of an *annus mirabilis* for François Mauriac. On the 6th November he received a telegram informing him that, after deliberating for three quarters of an hour, the Swedish Academy had awarded him the Nobel Prize for Literature. This was confirmed by the Swedish ambassador who called personally at the apartment in the avenue Théophile Gautier. Mauriac greeted the news with genuine astonishment; it was an honour that he dreamt not of. He had no false modesty about his work; nevertheless he felt, as a writer, that he belonged to a past which enjoyed little present consideration. *Le Sagouin* had shown that, even if he had returned to the novel, the *nouveau roman* held no attraction for him. Moreover there were other writers — Claudel in poetry and drama, Malraux and Jules Romains in

[1] For an account of this episode see *Jean Cocteau, the Man and the Mirror*, Elizabeth Sprigge and Jacques Kihm (1968).

fiction – who created on a larger scale, if not in greater depth. The polemicist in Mauriac was any man's contemporary; the novelist looked back to a period far out of sight. That he was a controversial writer did not matter; but what would his Catholicism say to Scandinavia?

He was awarded the prize for 'the depth of psychological analysis, and the intensity of artistic expression with which, in his novels, he has evoked the drama of human life.' This was a sufficient answer to the surprise of Paul Claudel – not perhaps altogether disinterested – that 'an international prize should have been given to a regional novelist.' The literary pilgrims who now make the journey to Saint-Symphorien and Malagar, and follow the *itinéraire mauriacien*, are moved by the same curiosity that brings others to Egdon Heath and the sombre parsonage of Haworth. A regional novelist is not necessarily provincial; we do not admire Proust because he is Parisian, but because he is profound. Mauriac would have been the last person to compare himself with Proust. Nevertheless they invited admiration for similar reasons – an infallibly selective memory, and the sorcery of their style.

Congratulations poured into the apartment on the avenue Théophile Gautier, including a telegram from President Auriol. Roger Martin du Gard – himself a Nobel Prizewinner – and Colette, looking as Mauriac had once described her like a 'fat bee', were among those who called. It could be said of these two – the one incurably Christian, the other incurably pagan – that 'one touch of nature makes all writers kin'. Like Colette, 'Mauriac had less the sentiment than the sensation of nature; not the vague romantic sympathy for a consoling or decorative solitude, but an aptitude for carnal communion with the earth, the air, and the sky.'[1] Later he held a press conference in the offices of the *Figaro*, with the family beside him. He was ascending the same ladder of fame as Mistral and Maeterlinck, Romain Rolland and Anatole France, Bergson, and André Gide. 'The moralist follows the immoralist' as one journalist put it 'he has clothed a combative humanism with a lofty elegance.' In Stockholm, at the banquet given in his honour, he referred to the place of the child in his fiction. 'Here you will find the loves of children, and the first kisses, and the first loneliness, everything that I have cherished in the music of Mozart. People see the vipers in my books, but not the doves that also make their nests there.' He reminded his audience of the 'O Crux, Ave Spes Unica' that Strindberg had asked to be engraved on his tombstone. But what he took away from his visit – and the crowning moment of his career – was to outlast the plaudits which had greeted him and his pleasure in the prize that he had won. He had been met at the station by a representative of the French

[1] Pierre-Henri Simon: *Le Monde*, 2 Sept. 1970.

ambassador who brought him sinister news of what was then happening in Morocco. Mauriac had drunk his fill of the *douceur de vivre*; this was a call to conscience which he dared not disobey.

THE CRISIS OF
THE FOURTH REPUBLIC

1

On his knees in the chapel of the Dominican Fathers in Stockholm, Mauriac had prayed to be delivered from the fever and futility of journalism. It was a vain petition. He could not help admitting the 'incredible pleasure' of watching the arrow quiver in the target even – and perhaps especially – when the target was a human being. Hardly had he returned to Paris when some young Christians of left-wing sympathies, whom he scarcely knew, begged him to join them in opposition to French policy in Morocco. Under the inspiration of Louis Massignon, the eminent Islamic scholar, they founded *France-Maghreb* of which Mauriac became President. The members of this would meet for a Moroccan *déjeuner* at a house in the vallée de Chevreuse, and enjoy their 'couscous' seated on cushions on the grass. Mass was celebrated at an altar made out of tree trunks on the ground floor of the adjacent barn. Here the races and the religions met in a mutual understanding. The Moroccan students in Paris rallied in great numbers to *France-Maghreb*, and Mauriac was at home with them. The end of Ramadan, June 13, always kept as a day of total fast by pious Moslems, was celebrated this year by a union of prayers and penitence in the presence of the Blessed Sacrament, and beneath the timbers of that same barn in the vallée de Chevreuse.

Prayer and penitence bore fruit in action, and this was little to the liking of the publishers who had now taken over *La Table Ronde*, though it was swallowed readily enough by Mauriac's fellow-contributors. His articles on Morocco, though they drew support from General Catroux, were also beginning to trouble the powerful interests behind the *Figaro*, and they brought him a mail in which sympathy and insult were pretty evenly balanced. In the handwriting of a soi-disant 'worker at the Renault factory', he recognized the script of a certain nobleman, and contrasted this excrement of aristocratic abuse with genuine letters from the working class which were 'nearly always serious, studied, admonitory, and refined in their expression.'[1] He had now lost contact with the British Embassy, but on June 11th he attended an evening party to

[1] *Bloc-Notes 1*, 22.

celebrate the Queen's coronation. There was a ballet under the trees and the artificial moonlight. Society was there in force, and 'if looks could kill', he wrote, 'I should by now be very sound asleep.'

A few days later he resigned from the Council of the Légion d'honneur, and on the 24th June he was handed a copy of the speech that Marshal Juin was to make on the following day to the Académie. None of his *confrères* had thought to warn him of the attack in preparation. It was unimaginable that a recently elected member, even if he were a Marshal of France, should vilify another member with the complicity of his colleagues. 'You don't realise' he was told 'how they hate you.' His crime was to occupy a place in society, and not to play its game. They forgot that when serious matters were at stake, he had always taken his stand, and at some personal risk, on principles which had been the breath of life to him since he was a boy. He replied to Juin in an article — *Un coup de bâton étoilé* — in which he parried the Marshal's blows without insulting his prestige. Marshals of France, he concluded, were 'a luxury that enfeebled states would do well to deny themselves.'[1] After this he rarely went to the Académie except to vote.

In August (1953) he was taking a cure at Vittel in the Vosges, and working on a new novel. On the 12th, at 9 a.m., some young Moroccans, who had driven 700 kilometres all through the night, arrived with the news that the Sultan, Mohammed V, had been deposed. Mauriac authorised a communiqué in the name of *France-Maghreb*. On the following day a voice told him over the telephone that the Sultan had signed his own deposition. 'Yes' replied Mauriac 'like Schuschnigg, like Hacha'. An immense Cadillac drew up before the hotel, and out of it stepped a sun-tanned figure beaming with prosperity and satisfaction. He had just returned from Morocco, and Mauriac caught an injurious reference to the Sultan. Everything, it appeared, was lost. On the 15th he obtained an interview with the Prime Minister, M. Laniel. But M. Laniel was not much interested in Morocco; that was the business of M. Bidault and the Quai d'Orsay — though it was asking too much of the Quai d'Orsay to realise that not only in Morocco, but throughout Islam, the Sultan was 'the incarnation of that spiritual power which at no cost should be disparaged or humiliated.'[2]

Neither the publishers of *La Table Ronde*, nor so fast a friend as Pierre Brisson, director of the *Figaro*, could any longer afford the attacks to which Mauriac's articles exposed them. In November, therefore, he took his *Bloc-Notes* to a new weekly, *L'Express*, edited by Jean-Jacques Servan-Schreiber. They first appeared on the 14th of the

[1] Ibid., 184.
[2] Ibid., 45.

month. After an interval of ten years, the bankruptcy of Christian democracy had replied like an antiphon to the bankruptcy of 'nationalisme intégral'; and over the ruins of both the sovereign voice of General de Gaulle 'made the dictatorship of Lilliput invisible to the eye.'[1] Mauriac was as eager as de Gaulle for a true 'rassemblement' of the French people, but he knew that this would not come about through the R.P.F. Meanwhile he was happier with the democrats of *L'Express,* and particularly with Pierre Mendès-France, who made no parade of Christian principles, but whose policies were a good deal more Christian than the practice of many people who did. On the 29th May the issue of *L'Express* was seized by the police, and on the evening of the 11th June a service of intercession for an amnesty was held in Notre-Dame. The Mysteries of the Rosary were first the subject of meditation in *malgache,* then in the dialect of the Ivory Coast; afterwards they were chanted by the Vietnamese, and finally in Arabic. This demonstration may have had some effect. A tract was circulating in Morocco, which declared that 'the ministers are looking at Morocco through the spectacles of a Mauriac'; on the 20th June Pierre Mendès-France became Prime Minister; and on the 21st July, when Mauriac was on holiday at Belle-Ile, off the coast of Britanny, the voice of a woman whispered to him at Mass that an armistice had been signed that night.

'My vocation is to irritate' – this admission of Mendès in an interview with Mauriac published in *L'Express* might well have been reciprocated, and it was to be justified by events. The authority of a Prime Minister under the Fourth Republic was not such that he could irritate with impunity. Mauriac shared Mendès' distrust of the project for a European army; he was hostile to the plan for so long as he could maintain his belief in France as a great nation, and resigned to it when he could not. But he relied upon Mendès as the man who, 'without reversing its alliances, could give back to the nation the power to follow, in foreign policy, the directives of General de Gaulle'.[2] In November Mauriac dined with some Moroccans who had spent five years in prison without being brought to trial, and remembered how they had laughed like children; but hardly had peace been restored to Morocco than war broke out in Algeria. 'I conformed to the customs of my profession' boasted the Commissioner Brieussel; and these included torture and arbitrary arrest. Forty-five Algerian prisoners had been kept for twenty hours in a cell, three metres square; fourteen had died; and the survivors had not yet been found guilty. For his campaign against the erosion of justice,

[1] Ibid., 72.
[2] Ibid., 149.

Malraux allowed Mauriac a place beside Chateaubriand and Bernanos.

On the 4th February, 1955, Mauriac was insulted in the Chambre des Députés, and Mendès-France rose in his defence. In replying to Mauriac's letter of thanks, the Prime Minister wrote: 'I have owed you this homage for a long time, and to tell the truth, I have been slow in paying it.' He was just in time, for the next evening he was voted out of office. Mauriac described the scene in the Chambre as 'horrible'. Mendès had shown what one man of courage and integrity could do off his own bat, but Mauriac was not surprised at his downfall. 'We nourish a particular hatred for the superior mind';[1] and the floods of rancour the Assembly had secreted for as long as they were obliged to put up with it had finally swept Mendès from power.

2

It was no sin, as Falstaff reminded Prince Hal, 'for a man to labour in his vocation', and Mauriac would certainly have thought it sinful not to labour in his. How then did he regard it, now that he was turning the corner at seventy?

> As my life draws to a close, I have the right to be imprudent. That is all that matters — the direction that one's life is taking. I consider myself as the servant of those men and women in France who are spewing up the lies of the politicians. My role is to upset the official interpretation of events.[2]

The avoidance of *cliché* — for Mauriac was resolved that the journalist should remain a writer — implied the formulation of a political philosophy for oneself. But was he altogether disinterested? Yes, but 'with too much passion, and often with too much pleasure'[3] for him not to be mistrustful of his expertise. The *Bloc-Notes* occupied most of his time and thought, yet he could not quite forget that he was a novelist. A character or a situation would nag at him until it was translated into fiction. But now, for the first time, he wondered if fiction were not a frivolity.

> At my age, the conflict between the Christian and the novelist has moved on to another plane. It's much less a question of the Jansenist scruples that used to trouble me in describing the passions than a kind of disenchantment with everything to do with art in general, and with my own art in particular. A feeling that

[1] Ibid., 141.
[2] Ibid., 213.
[3] Ibid., 264.

art is literally an idol, that it has its martyrs and its prophets, and that for many people it is a substitute for God. And not art alone, but the word — the word that has not been made flesh.[1]

But Mauriac could change his moods, even if he did not change his mind. On the same day that he wrote this in his diary — the 29th July 1953 — he notes that he has resumed work on a new novel, *L'Agneau,* determined not to put it aside 'until I have found the balance that I'm looking for, and the young saint, my hero, is burning at the heart of the furnace.'[2] He had written the first chapter at Malagar a year or two after the Liberation, but had then put it aside, afraid that the meeting of the two protagonists in the train from Bordeaux to Paris would scandalise the reader. This evidently contained overtones of a potential homosexual relationship. After the Nobel Prize it was naturally expected that Mauriac would continue to exercise the art for which he had been awarded it, and again it was a literary review — perhaps the *Table Ronde,* since he describes it as 'bourgeoise et bien pensante'[3] — that asked him for a novel. As in the case of *Le Sagouin,* he was not impelled by an 'inner necessity', but he was quickly obsessed by the characters he had originally conceived. He began the story in the first person, as he often did, to get it going more easily and, working with his usual rapidity, took the completed manuscript to the review in question.

The editor was dismayed; the public, he said, would be as shocked as he was himself. Mauriac then showed the manuscript to Pierre Brisson who reacted even more strongly. Mauriac had set out 'to write the life of a saint, but another character, Luciferian and more than disturbing, had pushed himself into the limelight. My principal task has been to regulate the lighting. Why does the state of grace (if that is where I stand, God willing) profit so little from certain of my characters?'[4] Mauriac shared the panic of his censors, but the manuscript was not easily forgotten. Like a child in its mother's womb, it would not keep still. He therefore rewrote the book from start to finish, with no part in the first person, 'polishing, repolishing, and licking it all over',[5] until he brought it to his publisher on the 10th April 1954. He was justified in feeling that it was a work at once 'organised and inspired'.[6]

Xavier Dartigelongue, aged 22, is on his way to Paris, where he intends to try his vocation for the priesthood. On the platform at

[1] Ibid., 40.
[2] Ibid., 40.
[3] *D'autres et moi,* 291.
[4] *Bloc-Notes I,* 65.
[5] Ibid., 72.
[6] *D'autres et moi,* 302.

Bordeaux he sees a couple saying good-bye to each other, evidently not on the best of terms. The young man, who gets into his compartment, is Jean de Mirbel, the adolescent *maudit* of *La Pharisienne.* The two fall into conversation. They have both been to the same school, and their families are acquainted. It is a mark of Xavier's vocation to concern himself with whomever he meets, and he is already preoccupied by the sad figure of Michèle, Jean's wife, as she disappears from the platform. By the time they reach Paris, Jean has done his best to dissuade Xavier from his intention to enter a seminary; and Xavier, feeling that Providence has put Jean in his path, agrees to return with him the next day to his home in the *Landes.* Here he finds Michèle, and her mother Brigitte Pian, with a young girl, Dominique, who is a victim of Brigitte's indefatigable charity, and an orphaned little boy, Roland, whom Dominique does her best to rescue from Michèle's indifference. Michèle has been unable to produce a child, and the hint is dropped that Jean cannot easily procure her one. Roland has been accepted into the household as a possible candidate for adoption, but since he inspires affection in neither of them their only thought is to return him to his orphanage.

The story turns on Xavier's devotion to Roland — which is not reciprocated; on the child's attachment to Dominique; on the nascent love affair between Xavier and Dominique; on Michèle's attraction to Xavier; on Jean's determination to keep Xavier in the house, and to destroy his faith; and on Brigitte Pian's interference in other people's lives for the greater glory of God. Dominique and Roland are sent away, but not before Xavier has made financial provision for the boy's future, and agreed to return to his family. Dominique looks forward to meetings in Bordeaux, although they will not 'faire le mal'. What Xavier looks forward to is Xavier's secret. He confides Roland to her care, and bids her good-bye in the presbytery at Baluzac, where a modernist priest, disenchanted with his own vacation, has succeeded the abbé Calou. Jean de Mirbel, realising that Xavier has left with the others, although his room shows no sign of imminent departure, sets out in pursuit of him. Xavier has, in fact, every intention of returning, at least for the time being, and borrows the curé's bicycle for the purpose. But the night is dark; he crashes into Jean's car on the outskirts of the village; and is killed.

Such is the skeleton of the story, and it is told with brilliant economy. But it cannot be judged without taking into account the aura of 'indetermination' which surrounds so many of Mauriac's characters. If we are kept guessing, it is because he too is guessing. He does not pretend to know more about people than we know about them in real life, or than they know about themselves. What was the nature of Jean's obsession with Xavier? No doubt the first version of the novel made this uncomfortably clear; nevertheless it is all the more 'Luciférien' for being left in the dark. Did Xavier deliberately crash into Jean de Mirbel's car, or did it happen, deliberately, the other way about? If it were an accident, was the accident unconsciously motivated, on one side or the other? Jean de Mirbel explains to Michèle what the curé had told him, that 'someone else' had propelled Xavier to his death. Who was the 'someone else'? Was Xavier suddenly demoralised by the curé's denigration of Christianity as a 'myth'? The curé had known cases when a 'saint could be abandoned, for the fraction of a second, to the one who awaits everything from our despair. But it can happen that despair leaves hope intact.'

Certain aspects of the characterization are disconcerting for a reader of *La Pharisienne*. Brigitte Pian, at seventy-eight, is the Brigitte whom we met at the beginning of the previous novel, not whom we left at its close. She is very far from having learnt her lesson. Jean de Mirbel has belied the abbé Calou's prediction that only Michèle can save him – a prediction that *La Pharisienne* seemed to confirm. The novel was read by many, but understood by few; and Mauriac would have feared that its meaning was incommunicable if the letters from readers sharing his own beliefs had not shown that to them, at least, it was clear. What he had tried to show was 'the doubtful struggle that goes on, right up to the end, in a human being, no matter how saintly they may be. But in life you do not see the struggle, it does not leap to the eye. Even more than in my other novels, *L'Agneau* brings it to light, and with less artifice . . . The Christian life is indeed this struggle, where the victor is only sure of his victory at the last second, because he assumes not his own destiny alone but, like his Master, that of the souls committed to his charge.'[1] This is strikingly illustrated in the passage, among the most moving that Mauriac ever wrote, where Xavier drags a heavy ladder to the open window of Roland's room, and is left with bleeding feet and shoulder. For the author, *L'Agneau* was the most essentially 'truthful' of his novels. It is a sombre book, but it leaves 'hope intact'. 'Why are we shedding tears for him?' Jean de Mirbel asks Michèle, as he joins her in bed for the first time after a long absence. 'He possesses at last the One he loved.' Assassination or involuntary suicide, Xavier's sacrifice had not been in vain, either for himself or for his adversary.

Mauriac had a particular attachment to his '*agneau*'. Xavier was not a portrait from life, although certain features of his character could be deduced from people the novelist had known. A few years later, a friend – and no doubt an admirer of the novel – gave him the picture

---

[1] *D'autres et moi*, 303.

of a lamb by Bernard Buffet. Its front paws were folded over a long, thin cross, and behind it in the semi-darkness were stakes and an up-right ladder. The picture hung over his bed, and 'at any hour of the day or night, I look at the lamb and ask nothing more of anybody.'[1]

Shortly after the publication of *L'Agneau*, he was saddened by the death of Colette; never again would he receive a letter signed 'votre grosse abeille'. Hers was a sane sensuality, but when he was asked whe-ther he were not 'disgusted with all this politics', he replied that it was the exhibitionism of current literature that made him sick. People should say to their children, as they did in the Jardin des Plantes, 'don't look at the monkeys'; and he called down a blessing on anyone who talked to him about beetroots instead of talking to him about Proust.

3

The death of Colette was followed, in February 1955, by that of Paul Claudel, and Mauriac attended the state funeral in Notre-Dame. In June he was in Florence, at the invitation of Mayor de la Pira, to speak at the Congress for Peace and Christian civilisation in the Signoria. In the autumn he had not the heart to attend the reception of Jean Cocteau at the Académie. There was too much in common between what was happening behind the scenes in Paris and Algeria, and 'the drawing-room comedy that we are playing for our mutual benefit on the aca-demic stage.' But he wrote to Cocteau, through the *Bloc-Notes,* that 'I shall be with you, and I shall re-read your verse; not perhaps the best of them, but those you used to recite to me in 1910.'[2]

The Sultan of Morocco had been restored to his throne, but the Algerian tragi-comedy was moving to its climax. Edgar Faure was now Prime Minister, and 'of all the stones which pave the way to the hell that we are in, the good intentions of M. Edgar Faure will have been the worst.'[3] Yet a single one of Mauriac's articles had been enough to suspend, for two or three months, the methods of the police in Algiers. The day of indecision arrived on the 6th February 1956 when Guy Mollet, who had succeeded Edgar Faure, was pelted with tomatoes by infuriated *colons,* and reversed the policy of *rapprochement* with which he had set out. Catroux was replaced as Resident-General by the social-ist, René Lacoste, who was to define his policy in an 'immortal perora-tion'. 'I am there, still there, very much there, and I shall do everything in my power to stay there.' Mauriac warned the parties of the extreme right:

[1] *Bloc-Notes II,* 16.
[2] *Bloc-Notes I,* 203.
[3] Ibid., 198.

Take care lest the Popular Front, which is the object of your terror, is not born in the street and does not rise up from the pavement. And you will have been responsible for its birth. It is you that have joined the members of the family at the bedside of the invalid to prevent the great doctor from approaching it.'[1]

Charles de Gaulle had become the 'irreplaceable protagonist' in the drama that was tearing the French apart.

On the 3rd March, *L'Express*, now appearing daily, was forced to revert to weekly publication. In April Claude Bourdet was arrested, stripped, and confined with criminals of the Common Law at the Sûreté. October of the same year saw the Suez fiasco which could be better judged, according to Guy Mollet, after a certain lapse of time. The retrospect cannot have encouraged him. In the spring of 1957, Mauriac testified before the Parliamentary enquiry into the allegation of torture in Oran, disconcerted by the 'closed faces, pursed lips, and shifty gaze' of the Commissioners.[2] Not even an Easter at Malagar could exorcise the *malaise* that gripped him. 'The sediments of a long life which have enveloped everything here, and created a miracle out of the meanest object, cannot resist the acid of politics.'[3] Mauriac confessed that he was more at home with 'certain Gentiles and certain libertines than with many of my brothers in the faith.' Why, he asked, 'do our spiritual leaders practice the virtue of prudence with a perfection that so disheartens us?'[4] He was not to forget the radiant greeting of Monseigneur Grente, the Bishop of Le Mans and one of the more inexplicable members of the Académie française, when they met *sous la coupole*. 'You should write novels, my dear Mauriac, and plays.' At moments like these one had 'to bolt the doors on the inside, fasten the chains, and return one smile with another.'[5]

On the 25th May, 1957, Guy Mollet — his reputation still stained with tomatoes — was overthrown by conservative votes in the National Assembly. His duplicity, wrote Mauriac, had been 'open to the sky; he wears heavy boots, and you can always hear him coming.'[6] Mollet had weathered, with remarkable tenacity, the storms of 'every Trafalgar, diplomatic or otherwise.'[7] Later that summer a peaceful manifestation in the avenue de l'Opéra against the Government's Algerian policy was

[1] Ibid., 212.
[2] Ibid., 310.
[3] Ibid., 309.
[4] Ibid., 346.
[5] *Bloc-Notes II*, 35.
[6] Ibid., 326.
[7] Ibid., 305.

dispersed by the police, and the paratroopers ran amok in the North African quarter of Marseilles, leaving 18 wounded and one dead. Mauriac was staying near by, and giving an interview for the *Observer* to Philip Toynbee. In August he was listening to Chopin, with Arthur Rubinstein, at the Festival of Lucerne.

The paratroopers had given an example of what they were capable; and in January (1958) a more measured warning came from a young officer. 'If the Parliament does not bring about a quick solution, you can fear the worst in the spring.' Félix Gaillard had succeeded Mollet as Prime Minister, but the question – as de Gaulle had put it – was 'not to know whether M. Félix Gaillard will put an end to the war in Algeria, but whether the war in Algeria will put an end to the ministry of M. Félix Gaillard.' An army of 500,000 men was in Algeria – the largest that had ever crossed the sea – and in five years had failed to decide the issue. Yet the Government was calling for 60,000 more. What was needed, Mauriac suggested, was not fresh soldiers, but a single fresh idea.

He had once obtained an interview with President Coty, who spoke of 'exemplary' punishment. It was a great honour, he said, for people to be shot with full military ceremonial, who in strict justice should have their heads cut off. In some respects these first months of 1958, when France was trembling under the threat of a military dictatorship, were the climax of Mauriac's career. Hated by some and admired by others, he was the most eloquent spokesman of an *avant-garde* who felt that both the ethics and the common sense of politics were on its side. Yet in Paris the surface of life was unruffled, with *Le Misanthrope* at the Comédie-Française – the Molière to whom Mauriac felt closer as the iron of experience entered into him, although Jacques Dumesnil's performance was something of a 'voyage au bout de la voix'. At Vémars the note of the woodpecker was heard – for Mauriac it was always the 'oiseau de Pâques' – and the first daffodils smiled in the salon. The most beautiful lime tree in the grounds had fallen on the day when he was awarded the Nobel Prize. In compensation he had planted a number of chestnuts, birches, and pines. But not far off the 'choreography' of a new Presidential election reminded him of 'a quadrille danced by the bourgeois of Labiche.'[1] Time and hope were running out, and when, in May, the Fourth Republic crumpled on the doorstep of La Boisserie,[2] he turned to *Coriolanus* for a comparison.

> *I had rather be their servant in my way*
> *Than sway with them in theirs.*

[1] *Bloc-Notes II,* 50.
[2] General de Gaulle's house at Colombey-les-Deux-Eglises.

MAURIAC AND DE GAULLE

1

It was said that the followers of Charles de Gaulle were divided into three sects — *Combat, Carrefour,* and François Mauriac; and that there were enough of Mauriac to fill an entire place of worship. These categories excluded those forces on the right who hoped that de Gaulle would bring to fruition the benighted policy which it was his vocation to annul. Like other annulments in the matrimonial courts of the Sacred Rota, this one took a long time, and its issue remained in doubt. But the genius of de Gaulle had already given its proof of patience; it was not for nothing that he had waited for seven years at Colombey-les-Deux Eglises, writing his Memoirs and reading the *Cahiers* of Maurice Barrès. Mauriac, too, had waited for de Gaulle; but when the appeal came, he would have preferred it to come from the united forces of the left, rather than from General Massu. Left and right, however, were alike the Bourbons of the hour. De Gaulle was feared by the socialists, and the M.R.P. detested him hardly less than they detested Mendès-France. All that the left could do was to march in silence to a Bastille that de Gaulle had already taken.

The relationship between Mauriac and de Gaulle was exceptional in the history of France. If others were irritated or maddened by Mauriac's fidelity, the General was himself surprised by it. But he shrewdly understood the motives or, more exactly, the temperament by which it was inspired.

'Two reasons' he wrote after Mauriac's death 'drew Mauriac towards me, and to the work we had in hand. An ardent patriotism, with which he never compromised, and which may seem surprising in a man so many-sided, so compact of subtlety, finesse, and acute sensibility; a man responsive to life in all its forms, who shuddered at the slightest appeal and had an eye for all the dramas of mankind. He had understood, from the beginning, everything I was bringing to France, and his support never failed me. For what has been extraordinary in the help he had given us, was its constancy — and for me this had considerable weight. But he also had the sense of greatness, and this was the second reason

200

for his support. In choosing to stand beside me, and to fight there up to the end, his aestheticism played an important part. He had understood all the beauty of what we were doing, and in politics, as in art, quality strikes the eye at once. His intuition told him that we were operating on no ordinary plane. The artist in him discovered, through his certainty of judgement, the same path that his patriotism signalled out to him ... What brought him to me was the sense of History, the impression that he was watching, through me, the pursuit of a task that went back to the origins of France. For him, I was carrying on a great tradition.'[1]

Mauriac understood de Gaulle just as shrewdly. Whether he was justified in the imprimatur he gave to policies always controversial is another matter. But it is worthwhile recalling Mauriac's diagnosis of himself as an 'esprit mystique et raisonnable'. He was sensitive to the charge of uncritical adulation in his support of the General; he replied that this was not unconditional, but that in every case it was governed by lucid analysis. For the first time in his life, he repeated, he found himself governed 'raisonnablement'. He measured the enormity of the task that de Gaulle was confronted with, faced as he was by the opposition of a left and a right, both of which required to be 'reinvented'. He expected the minimum, and was well satisfied with what he got, recalling the General's own warning on the 11th November, 1945: 'We must realise that the salvation of our country will always remain precarious.' It was still precarious in the autumn of 1958. What Jean Guitton had written of St Augustine was exactly applicable to de Gaulle: 'the solitary man, builder or reformer, who takes up whatever is living in the past, and creates from it the substance of the future.' As Mauriac put it, de Gaulle was at once 'Shakespearian and contemporary'.[2]

Mauriac found himself immediately at odds with those who had been his allies; 'the violins of *L'Express*', he noted 'no longer always played in unison.' Although he was no royalist, Mauriac, on his own confession, did not have republicanism 'in his guts'. He rallied easily enough to the Consular régime that de Gaulle was adumbrating, returning in September from Malagar to vote 'Oui' in the referendum where Mendès-France had voted 'Non'. Nearly all the young Christians of his acquaintance had voted 'Non', and quite a number of well-known Communists had voted 'Oui'. 'In politics' he wrote 'the reasons of the heart should be on speaking terms with the reasons of the head. My head and my heart were never

1 *Mort du Général de Gaulle*, Jean Mauriac (1972), 134-6. Conversations with Léon Noël and Wladimir d'Ormesson.

2 *De Gaulle*, 18.

in closer agreement than on the day when I said "Oui" to General de Gaulle.'[1]

Looking back into the history of France, with mingled horror and fascination, he picked out 1789 — the Revolution before Robespierre — and the Consulate of 1799 as the two moments in which he could take most pride. 'The colonial system is finished for us' Bonaparte had declared at St Helena 'and it is finished for Europe. We should give it up.' De Gaulle had come to the same conclusion, but he had to reckon with the constitutional fiction that Algeria was a part of France as well as its possession. Mauriac was not alone in seeing him as the legatee both of the Sillon and the *Action Française*. From the second he had taken the principle of monarchy, minus the fleurs-de-lys; from the second that of popular election and personal liberty. In this dual inheritance, and reconciliation, lay the secret alike of his solitude and his strength.

Meanwhile the Algerian agony dragged on, and politics more than ever seemed like 'a heavy stone that we push, but which falls back and incessantly repels us to where we started from.'[2] Mauriac was again subject to threats against his life; had the parachutists descended on Paris, he knew on certain evidence that he would have been shot. At the anniversary Mass for Charles Du Bos in November, 1959, a figure stepped out from the shadows and whispered to him that the ill treatment of prisoners, suspended for several months, had been resumed. 'Tell them so, I beg you, tell them so'.[3] Training in torture, according to *Le Monde*, was being given in a camp placed under the patronage of Jeanne d'Arc; and Mauriac's comment on an indiscretion of General Massu was very much to the point: 'The Ligue is still with us, and the King of France is still alone.'[4] For de Gaulle was equally opposed to the ideology of the left and the thinly camouflaged interests of the right. Of the politicians, 'locked away in the rat-traps of their parties', Mauriac wrote that 'St Francis of Assisi wasted less of his time preaching to the birds.'[5] Elsewhere in Africa, however, the liberation of an empire, and the consolidation of a partnership, proceeded smoothly. Jean Mauriac was standing beside the General when Léopold Senghor, the President of Senegal, and the poet and philosopher of *négritude*, said to him, as one Christian to another: 'Stay with us, for it is late, and the day is nearly over.'[6]

Recent history had shown the peril of dragging Christianity into politics; the thought of General Franco on his knees made Mauriac

[1] *Bloc-Notes II*, 65.
[2] Ibid., 228.
[3] Ibid., 272.
[4] Ibid., 293.
[5] Ibid., 323.
[6] Ibid., 277.

squirm. 'All things considered, and because I am a Catholic, I prefer Stalin to the man who pinned the image of the Sacred Heart on to the burnous of his Moorish guards.'[1] When de Gaulle came to London in 1940, he was asked by Denis Saurat, director of the French Institute, if he were a Catholic. 'Yes' replied the General. 'A liberal Catholic?' enquired Saurat hopefully. 'A Catholic' came the terse rejoinder. It was enough for Mauriac – and he certainly did not ask for more – that de Gaulle attended Mass in Moscow as well as at Colombey-les-Deux-Eglises. Nevertheless it was a sense of Christian responsibility which had brought Mauriac into the arena and governed his political options. Whether the responsibility weighed as heavily on de Gaulle was the business of de Gaulle, and of no one else.

In February 1960, Mauriac was in Rome lecturing to the Société Africaine de Culture. Having been kissed on both cheeks by John XXIII, he was presently to be kissed on both cheeks by General de Gaulle. On Saturday, the 19th March, the General invested him with the insignia of the Grand-Croix de la Légion d'honneur. The weather, so to speak, was chilly. De Gaulle had disappointed many of his liberal adherents by his speeches to the army in Algeria without winning the support of its intransigent leaders; and the projected cease-fire had not materialised. If the General knew where he was going, the direction was anything but common knowledge. He had compared himself to 'an old and watchful cat, seated on the extreme right of the stove, that surveys what is simmering in the various casseroles.' This vigilance, however, did nothing to cloud the occasion. Mauriac, with his wife and family, arrived at the Elysée in three motor cars. Alain Le Ray, recently promoted to General, was with them, and Claude Mauriac's little boy, Gérard, only eight years old. The ceremony took place before luncheon in front of the glass door which opened on to the garden. After the customary formula of investiture the General added in an undertone: 'This is an honour that France pays to herself.'[2]

Mauriac had increasingly found his friends outside his own social milieu, and among them Emmanuel Mounier, the philosopher of 'personalism', director of *Esprit,* and a Catholic totally committed to the causes of the left, had a particular importance. They had met, shortly after the Liberation, in the company of an American diplomat who had suggested the preventive use of the atom bomb. Their mutual horror at this proposal had brought them close. Mounier's disappointment at Mauriac's silence during the war in Indo-China had counted for much in persuading him to hold his tongue no longer. Mounier was later to write

[1] *Bloc-Notes I,* 244.
[2] *Un autre de Gaulle,* 401.

that 'Mauriac is often wrong, because of his friendship for certain men, but when the decisive moment arrives he is always to be found on the side of truth and justice.' In the case of Indo-China Mauriac admitted that the struggle was between 'the bourgeois writer, busy with his work and his career, and the Christian reduced to silence and tied to the chariot of a prize-winning novelist.'[1] Now he confessed that the singularity of de Gaulle, his inimitable style, which irritated so many others, appealed to his novelist's sense of character. For much the same reason, no doubt, it appealed to Malraux. They were both exceptions to the manifesto against the General issued by 121 writers and artists in the autumn of 1960. The manifesto left the General as unperturbed as the exceptions made him proud. He drew his strength from the concierge who declared that whatever was said against him on the left or on the right, he would have her vote — and there were still a good many of them.

Mauriac's position on *L'Express* was now becoming difficult. Although he did not write exclusively about politics, his articles, when he did so, were in direct conflict with the policy of the review. He disliked the tone of certain contributions, and sought the advice of two priests — the one a conseiller d'Etat and student of history, the other an eminent member of a religious order. The first condemned the review for its eroticism, and asked Mauriac whether he were sure of redressing the balance? The second begged him to remain as the leaven in a pie not very attractive to a healthy appetite. Mauriac inclined at first to the latter point of view, but in the spring of 1961 he decided that he could no longer write for *L'Express,* and from now onward his *Bloc-Notes* appeared in the *Figaro Littéraire.*

In the autumn of that year certain elements of the army revolted in Algiers. It was not the moment for *L'Express* to describe de Gaulle as a 'roi fainéant'. Mauriac returned the accusation with a vitriolic verve:

> The *roi fainéant* is in reality a *reine fainéante*; it is the left, of which you are the last petty Merovingian; it is the bald-headed queen at the end of her tether, and even a little ga-ga, that the old parties, cuckolded and castrated, continue to drag across their ancient quagmires.'[2]

A Berber friend prophesied that de Gaulle would end up like Christ insulted by the soldiery. Mauriac replied that the 'spittle of the left' was more injurious than the expectoration of the right — for Georges Bidault, at the Mutualité, was summoning the Europeans in Algeria to revolt. At the same time a manifestation against the Algerian *ultras* was

[1] Ibid., 385.
[2] *Bloc-Notes III,* 49.

forbidden by the police, and de Gaulle was the sufferer. It lost him much credit with the young. He was to remain the living simulacrum of a unity which only existed among the French at certain moments of their history. He could say 'Je suis la France', and other nations would take him at his word; but his own people would not. This was the secret of his solitude.

On the 19th February, 1962, an Algerian settlement was agreed at Evian-les-bains, and in April a referendum decisively confirmed it. But the hour of the O.A.S. had sounded. At El Biar six officials of a social centre — three Europeans and three Moslems — were murdered by one of their committees. A lieutenant wrote to Mauriac that he would like to see the signatories of the manifesto in support of insubordination beheaded, and their heads exhibited on the palings of the Tuileries. Salan, who had led the military revolt, was discovered in hiding, arrested, and brought to trial. Mauriac confessed himself scandalised by the extenuating circumstances allowed to a man whom he had wished to see condemned to death and subsequently reprieved. In June the O.A.S. ordered its commandos to resume operations; the Library at Algiers was burnt; and Georges Bidault formed a dissident committee in Vienna. This inspired Mauriac to an article whose bitterness he later regretted. He pictured the former Minister for Foreign Affairs and prophet of Christian democracy standing on the pavement outside the Quai d'Orsay, and imagining the panoply of power which he had once enjoyed — 'a power for which no alcohol can console us, once we have lost it'[1] — and a gendarme gently tapping him on the shoulder, and telling him to get a move on. The extremists of the right with whom Bidault had joined forces were succinctly described as 'Vichy tout entier à sa proie attaché'.[2] It was an ironical alliance for a leader of the French Resistance.

At the end of 1963 Mauriac agreed to the suggestion of his publisher that he should write a book on de Gaulle. It might have ranked among the best of his books; in fact it was one of the least satisfactory. The essential had already been said — and was to be said again — in the *Bloc-Notes*. During the six months he was at work on it, he read all the historical plays of Shakespeare until the General appeared to him like the protagonist of a Shakespearian drama. Comedy, certainly not; tragedy, perhaps. Just as life in Shakespeare goes on when the hero is killed, has died, or committed suicide, so the speculation began as to whether the General would present himself for re-election, and if he did not who would succeed him. Perhaps some tyro of the M.R.P. would enter the lists; 'but how' asked Mauriac 'should a tadpole resign himself to die a

[1] Ibid., 163.
[2] Ibid., 264.

tadpole, and willingly renounce the system which turned him into a
frog?'[1] Whoever it might be, Mauriac prophesied that he would follow
where de Gaulle had pointed the way; and in this he was not far wrong.
He thought it a great advantage for Georges Pompidou not to have
been previously mixed up in politics; and he foresaw, without much
personal sympathy, the future career of Giscard d'Estaing: 'still young,
able, rich, powerful, intelligent, well balanced, quick to pick up a clue,
who always wins his game. A type fixed by the American films, and an
ideal T.V. personality.'[2] On the 5th June (1964) he finished his book on
de Gaulle with the feeling that he had 'repaired an injustice and not
succumbed to an idolatry'.[3] It must be admitted that the feeling was not
generally shared; irreconcilables on either side could only see the censer
in full swing.

The whirligig of time had brought its revenges when the young King
of Morocco was received at the Elysée. 'You were right' murmured de
Gaulle to Mauriac; and Mauriac returned the compliment in everything
he wrote about the General prior to the Presidential election. François
Mitterand, one of the two challengers, he had known for many years,
and was grateful to him for a review of Les Chemins de la Mer. The
other, Jean Lecanuet, stood for a 'Europeanism' that Mauriac compared
to a 'beheaded duck'. A Europe in which the nations beyond the Iron
Curtain or the Pyrenees had no place was arrogating to itself a title to
which it had no right. He looked forward to a 'federation where each
people will keep its own character, and its particular, irreplaceable
vocation.' But the advocates of the E.E.C. could not have defined their
aims more succinctly, and it is strange that so good a European as
Mauriac should not have seen that half a continent was better than no
continent at all. The weakness of Mitterand was to proclaim his solidarity with a past which still scorched the memory. Whatever might be
said against the consular republic, it had 'replaced the woman without
a head who had presided over so many massacres, disasters, and shames,
by a republic which had the head of a man, and was possessed both of a
brain and a heart.'[4]

In December, 1966, Mauriac was invited, with Sartre, to sit on a
tribunal set up to pass judgement on war crimes committed by the
Americans in Vietnam. He declined on the ground that American crimes,
like Americans themselves, were 'indecipherable'. He had lunched, a few
years before, with Cardinal Spellman and felt that he might as well have

[1] Ibid., 390.
[2] Ibid., 393.
[3] Ibid., 415.
[4] Bloc-Notes IV, 316.

been lunching with the Dalai Lama. The General's re-election had not ratified his mysterious contract with the French people, and the future was obscure. When the students of Nanterre and the Sorbonne revolted in May 1968, Mauriac was 'passionately on the side of the State. The greatest misfortune for a people is no longer to have a State. Every other calamity flows from this.' Here was de Gaulle's philosophy of politics read, learnt, and inwardly digested, not from books but from experience. In fact the General had judged the barricades more leniently, consoling himself with the thought that 'la France est toujours exemplaire!' Of course the intellectuals of the left sided with the students because they 'fortify themselves with blinkers to be sure of not seeing what they have no wish to see.'[1] Mauriac knew a lycée in Paris where boys of sixteen were taught the Marxist catechism; he had observed the ravages of a materialist education among the younger of his own relations. He did not believe that a revolt which nearly brought the government to its knees was spontaneous; it was the result of long and insidious preparation, from which the Church itself was not immune. When at a Mass celebrated by the Dominicans a voice was raised asking prayers for General de Gaulle, the reply came from the altar: 'How brave you are!' Nor was it true to describe the Gaullist manifestation in the Champs-Elysées as the reaction of 'domestics in the service of good families and old ladies of the 16th arrondisement'.[2] Nevertheless the Gaullist success at the polls in June proved to be a Pyrrhic victory.

The actions of de Gaulle during what remained of his political life have never been satisfactorily explained; and Mauriac did not proffer an explanation. Why did the General dismiss a Prime Minister whose sagacity had saved the State when its head was out of the country? Why did he risk his future on a quite unnecessary referendum? Were these merely mistakes, or were they, as some have suggested, a form of masochism? Did he wish to punish himself for misjudging a youth with which he had lost all vital contact? Had such contact ever really existed? As he asked the question, Mauriac regretfully shook his head. This was a signal failure of the consular republic, and the consul himself must be held responsible for it. Charles de Gaulle was still Shakespearian — never more so than now, perhaps, as the shadows were closing in — but he was no longer quite contemporary. If he had addressed himself to the youth of France, the appeal would have echoed hollowly. He might be still the 'man of the day after tomorrow', but the march of time had accelerated since those august footsteps had first trod the parquet floors of the Elysée — 'more Valois than Bourbon', as Mauriac put it —

---

[1] *Bloc-Notes V*, 74.
[2] Ibid., 75.

and today would not wait upon tomorrow. Had de Gaulle, in the depths of his sub-conscious, willed his own rejection, bitterly as he took it when it came? Certainly his disassociation from Israel during the six day war had cost him dear. Mauriac noted how many of his Jewish friends, ardent supporters of the General, had then turned against him. For himself, he had joined the committee for the 'defence of Israel', and confessed that he had never felt more intensely 'a son of Abraham'. If the Soviet Union sent arms to Egypt, why should not France send *Mirages* to Israel? His reason went some way to meet de Gaulle, but his heart did not. The General's resignation was the end of a chapter, not only in French history but in French literature; not only in the life of Charles de Gaulle but in the life of François Mauriac. This attachment of the writer to the statesman, so passionate and yet in a way so impersonal, had no parallel in the interaction of politics and the printed word. Each, a master of his own art, was also a survivor; and the one did not long survive the other.

ACCOUNTS RENDERED

1

It is a mistake to confuse survival with sclerosis. A man or woman may survive because they have lived, and are still living, more intensely than other people. Mauriac, in Joubert's definition, was a temperament 'with wings that enabled him to fly and also to go astray'. He dreamt much, now that he was over seventy, and always that he was young. More conscious than most of the eventuality, and perhaps the imminence, of death, and more pessimistic about the world he lived in, he had looked back too constantly to his youth, and was presently to look back on it again, not to enjoy the society and sympathise with the problems of the young. Visiting a group of adolescents in the 19th arrondissement, he established an immediate contact, He answered freely all their questions, and none of them was stupid. When some Communist students came to see him, he found them not very different from many of the younger clergy. With both he was careful neither to shock nor disturb. In a country of Catholic tradition, Communism was no more than the latest heresy, and like all the other heresies it secreted a grain of truth. What troubled him more was the wave of eroticism against which the young had no defence but a formation which many of them had outgrown, if indeed they had ever received it. There were ugly stories of sadism in the schools.

In a family as tightly knit as Mauriac's, with grandchildren growing up all round him, there was no need for the younger generation to come knocking at the door, because the door was always open. With Claude the bond was particularly close. He rejoiced at his literary success, and the more so for his fear lest his own prestige should have embarrassed his son's development. 'With a woman' he confided to Claude 'even with one's wife, and however much one loves her, one is never quite on the same level, one is not part of the same story. Hence those inevitable clashes. Your mother and Jean are part of the same story; they have the same interests, and the same subjects of conversation. You and I are also part of the same story.'[1] It was not quite the same story, because Claude did not share his father's unswerving religious faith. Yet here,

[1] *Le Temps Immobile*, 530.

again, Mauriac placed little value on a 'foi de famille'. Nothing was more secret and individual than a man's relationship with God, and it was not for a father to interfere with it. The affection was as mutual as it was generally unspoken. 'After all' said Marie-Claude Mauriac to her husband 'he was your great love.'[1] They were both to remember him, sitting up in bed in the morning, and explaining to little Gérard the pictures from *The Swiss Family Robinson.*

On the 4 June 1963 François and Jeanne Mauriac celebrated their golden wedding; but in the following January the death of Claire's husband, Ivan Wiazemski, leaving her with three children, brought a sudden grief to the family. The funeral took place in the Russian church in the rue Daru, and afterwards in the cemetery of Sainte-Geneviève-des-Bois. The dead man was given all his titles of nobility, and emphasis was laid on his family's role in Russian history. Mauriac was deeply moved by the beauty of the Orthodox rites. 'In my sorrow I felt an obscure happiness in what once would have seemed a separation. Now it made me draw upon all the riches of the primitive Church which others, maybe, have kept more carefully than we have.'[2]

Three years later, on the 9th October 1967, Jean Mauriac was married, and a new daughter-in-law did something to fill the gap which the son-in-law had left.

The rhythm of life for Mauriac changed very little despite the daily preoccupation with politics. Paris had lost much of its charm since the days when a *fiacre* of the Compagnie Urbaine would take you from one end of the city to another in three quarters of an hour. But his study looked out on to the adjacent roofs, and all he asked for was a divan, a fountain pen, books, and the Benedictine abbey in the rue de la Source only a few steps away. Next door was the salon with a score of Mozart open on the grand piano, or the 10th Dance of Granados which Jeanne was so fond of playing,[3] and the bronze bust by Zadkin. Some good pictures hung on the walls — a Dufy, a Villon, and a drawing by Matisse. Except for correspondence, for which he employed a secretary, Mauriac was incapable of dictating what he had not already written in long hand — rapidly and with many corrections. The *Bloc-Notes* were composed daily at first, but afterwards as a weekly exercise.

He now resumed his attendance at the Académie, and in his capacity of Directeur introduced the newly elected members to President de Gaulle. Some of these like Pierre Emmanuel, Pierre-Henri Simon, Jean Paulhan, and Thierry Maulnier had stood at his side against either

[1] Ibid., 500.
[2] Ibid., 464.
[3] Ibid., 297.

collaboration with the enemy, the excesses of the *épuration*, or the follies of the Fourth Republic. The latter, in his *discours de réception*, had done justice to Maurras, and even Mauriac acknowledged that, up to a certain point, Maurras had always been right. It was beyond that point that 'une certaine idée de la France' had taken shape in the mind of Charles de Gaulle, and of those who followed him. With Henri Massis, another *maurrassien* of less flexible intelligence, Mauriac had stood in opposition, though not at enmity. They professed the same religion, but professed it differently. Montherlant was elected with Massis, and behind the classical façade of his style and the pomp of an affected *hispanidad* he too had maintained those standards of literary rectitude which it was the duty of the Académie to preserve. But the 'Immortals' were extending their notions of immortality; a right-wing academician had proposed the candidature of Aragon. A particularly happy occasion was the tribute paid to René Clair by all the members of the Institut in the theatre at Versailles.

Mauriac still went occasionally to other theatres, but here sleep was the principal enemy of pleasure. If he were to turn again to playwriting, it would be in the direction of Chekhov where the poetry was always present but nowhere explicit, inseparable from the stuff of humanity. He delighted in the transposition of his novels to the screen. Diego Fabri, who was at work on a theatrical adaptation of *Thérèse Desquey-roux*, brought Fellini to see him; 'the first time' he wrote 'that a celebrity of the cinema has left me dumb with emotion and respect' — for Fellini had shown himself capable of 'revealing the human soul which today is denied over and over again, and driven out from so many films and novels.'[1] The film of *Thérèse Desqueyroux* was made by Georges Franju, and shown in Venice at the Biennale in September 1962. The ending of the book had been changed, however, not to its advantage. 'Thérèse dies of thirst beside the spring, and I make it very clear. The curé of Saint-Clair is only there, however discreetly, in order that people shall understand this.'[2] *Thérèse Desqueyroux* was not a Christian novel, but only a Christian could have written it. Albert Riera's trans-position of *La Fin de la Nuit* justified Mauriac against the damaging criticism of Sartre; he realised, when he saw it, how intensely Thérèse and Georges Filhot came alive. In *Destins*, adapted for television, one could see Alice Sapricht as Elisabeth Gornac 'suffering from one moment to another'.[3]

Mauriac's resistance to non-figurative art was due to its absence of

[1] *Bloc-Notes II*, 142.
[2] *Bloc-Notes III*, 182.
[3] *Bloc-Notes IV*, 69.

human and natural content. An art which turned its back on the face and figure of mankind was, essentially, a denial of the Incarnation; and where Picasso had passed by 'the grass would not grow any longer'.[1] But where Mauriac could only see the ruins of an immense destruction – inspired, it was true, by genius – a Dominican father, writing in *Art Sacré*, wistfully wondered if eventually 'the Christian faith would illuminate this image of mankind'. Mauriac opined that if the men and women on exhibition at the Grand-Palais should leave its walls with their features intact, it 'would be as great a miracle as when Lazarus stood at the entrance of his tomb with all the grave clothes at his feet.'[2] But man survived his creations in art and literature. It was not because painting had become abstract that the world, too, had become faceless; not because the novel was interested only in objects that man himself had become uninteresting, and sanctity, where it existed, was no longer held in honour. In future we should not read the novels or regard the pictures, since they told us nothing essential about ourselves.

Sedentary by nature and occupation (though he enjoyed a walk in the mountains near Mégève), Mauriac was happiest listening to music either in the concert hall or in his arm-chair. When *Don Giovanni* was being broadcast from Aix-en-Provence, he would not go to bed until the Commendatore had made his fearful entrance, and he imagined his own staircase echoing to that stony tread. 'He comes to all of us at every moment of our lives, and we are always one or other of them; the Don Juan of Molière and Mozart who dares to defy his God, or the one who kneels and begs for grace, and has time, at the last minute, to become a saint.'[3] At the Lucerne Festival in 1958 von Karajan was conducting the Ninth Symphony of Beethoven, more perfect than Furtwängler two or three years after the Liberation, but less pathetic. For the first time Mauriac had then felt pity for a prostrate Germany, as the Ode to Joy went up from a 'crowd risen from the charnel house'.[4] By contrast, in the *Stabat Mater* in the Jesuitenkirche, Rossini's smile showed how easily it could turn to tears. Schubert's Fifth Quintet on the radio gave him the conviction that nothing else mattered except what was secreted in the music he was listening to at that moment; and Mozart's Clarinet Concerto seemed like 'a reproach to God, at once desperate and tender'.[5] In both these works he felt that a 'living soul was suffering before his eyes'.[6] But he also loved to hear Edith Piaf singing 'Je ne

---

[1] Ibid.,279.
[2] Ibid., 311.
[3] *Bloc-Notes II*, 80.
[4] Ibid., 99.
[5] *Bloc-Notes III*, 381.
[6] *Bloc-Notes V*, 98.

regrette rien', which – ironically enough – had been a favourite song of the 'paras'.

Most of July he liked to spend at Vémars. Here he had his study on the top floor, and part of the money which had come to him with the Nobel Prize – 11,500,000 francs – had gone to embellishing the bathroom. But the avenue of pear trees in the plain had been cut down, and by 1966 the bulldozers were hard at work on the autoroute between Paris and Lille, disagreeably within sight and hearing. Vémars had become like a village besieged. But the house was well protected by its trees – poplars and wellingtonias, magnolias and cedars – and every year, as the spring came round, Mauriac waited for the first notes of the oriole and the nightingale, the wood-pigeon and the turtle-dove. The oriole never sang when the grandchildren were playing in the garden. These became so numerous that at Mass on Sunday they overflowed the two benches normally reserved for the family.

In 1963 Madame Lafont, who had remained the gently presiding genius of Vémars, celebrated her 100th birthday. She died a few months later. The springs of history tasted very fresh when she told how her mother had danced at the Tuileries, and dined once a week with Gounod. After her death Mauriac moved his study into what had been her bedroom under the great tulip tree which she had planted. In earlier days he had been fond of playing croquet, but he now contented himself with a regular walk in the afternoon, though he now walked more slowly. The only other effect of age he admitted to feeling in his seventy-eighth year was a certain difficulty in getting up from his knees after receiving Holy Communion. In the evening he would move about the house in his patent-leather dancing slippers; they were only the second pair he had worn since the days when he came home in the small hours from an evening in Montmartre, and they showed no sign of coming to the end of their leather.[1] He had the television by his bed, and he never tired of doing crossword puzzles.

Nevertheless the years were milestones of mortality as they took from him those who had played a part in his public or his private life. His brother, Pierre Mauriac, who died on November 1, 1963; Pierre Brisson, director of the *Figaro* from 1934 to 1965, who would always call to see him on Sunday morning, who had never sided with his enemies, even when the enemy was himself, a man of the right, who was prepared to fight tenaciously on the left. They had only disagreed over Pierre Mendès-France. His funeral at Saint-Philippe-du-Roule was accompanied by Fauré's Requiem, one of the rare compositions of French music with which Mauriac felt at home. André Maurois, of all his

---

[1] *Le Temps Immobile*, 231.

contemporaries 'the least easily understood by our juniors, and the most likely to last so long as a society endures similar to that reflected in the novel from Stendhal and Balzac to Proust and Henry James.'[1] Jean Cocteau, who had sent Mauriac his poems in 1910 inscribed 'Aux mains jointes, les mains ouvertes'. Claude had written a book on Cocteau — *Une amitié contrariée* — and Mauriac was touched that it had counted for so much to Cocteau that 'Claude should be the son of François'.[2] Francis Poulenc — 'a son of Mozart' — recalling the brilliant and frivolous innovations of 'Les Six', buried from Saint-Sulpice which was Mauriac's favourite church in Paris. José Antonio Aguirre, his face worn with despair visible to the last below an opening in the coffin. Henri Massis — they had lived 'like cat and dog' for fifty years; Massis had wanted a *rapprochement*, and Mauriac was sad not to have brought it about. First of them all to go, and in a way the most sharply missed, was André Gide.

> So long as he was alive, there was still a literary life in France, a life of exchanges, an argument still open between writers who were not professional philosophers, who spoke the language of honest men. The stone sealed over the tomb of Gide has also been sealed over the most exciting period for the life of the mind that France has known.[3]

Mauriac shed no crocodile tears over the loss of an adversary, who had also been a friend. Gide had blinded too many others before turning his own face against the light to merit a facile epitaph. But had he definitively turned it? Mauriac, to the annoyance of Gide's sectarian allies, clutched at a straw to raise the question.

At Easter, and again in September, he was always at Malagar, staying over, very often, until his birthday on October 11th when the *vignerons*, their task completed, would leave a bouquet of flowers in the kitchen. Many souvenirs of his childhood were buried in the garden, but there was still the statue of the Blessed Virgin which had stood in his mother's bedroom, although the Child's hand had been broken. In his study, on the ground floor facing north, were the heavy Venetian mirror and barometer which she had in her salon, and the folding table at which his grandfather used to sit for his meals beside the fire at Langon, and the portrait of Barrès by Jacques-Emile Blanche above the console. He showed to some American visitors one of the last oxen to plough the fields of the Gironde. Now that the tractor had taken over, the old plum

---

[1] *Bloc-Notes III*, 15.
[2] *Bloc-Notes V*, 337.
[3] *Bloc-Notes V*, 222.

trees beyond the ranks of vines had been felled, but he had dug up some young pines in the *Landes* and replanted them at Malagar; and the two great beams which supported the ceiling of the salon had kept the shape of the oak or the elm from which they had been hewn so roughly. In the courtyard the grandchildren had made a miniature golf-course, and overhead the aeroplanes did their best to break the sound barrier. But each return to Malagar was a rediscovery, as the Parisian *malgré lui* caught the whiff of beeswax in the salon, and the scent of the first hyacinths.

2

The primacy of religious belief in Mauriac's life and work has already been sufficiently emphasised. The theme recurs in two important essays, *La Pierre d'Achoppement* (1951), and *Ce que je crois* (1962). The first of these justified its title; certain aspects of the Church had always been a stumbling block. But when Mauriac looked back on the *bien-pensants* of the bourgeoisie, reserving their seats for Heaven in a first class sleeper, and the enthusiastic converts looking down their noses at the superstitions of the faithful, he still found his faith intact. That life should have developed from its primal sources until it took the shape of a particular expression on the face of a particular child, or in a larghetto of Mozart, seemed to him a mystery that asked for recognition even if it could not be explained. The 'fact of Christ', so lightly dismissed or ignored, stood the test of history and experience alike. For Mauriac the experience was contained in Newman's 'myself and my Creator', and its confirmation in the priest's 'This is my Body' and 'I absolve you from all your sins.' Sometimes, it is true, he was tempted to wish that in a life so privileged, he had spent as much effort in disguising his convictions as he had in making them known. But the urge to bear witness (though never to proselytise) always proved too strong.

He measured how far his sensibility had affected his judgement, and his intermittent reactions against it. How far was his delight in those Gregorian Masses in the rue Monsieur an aesthetic self-indulgence? After all, it was there that he had found the model for *la Pharisienne*. Now, as he grew older, the visible forms, and incidental deformations, of Catholicism left him relatively undisturbed. All that mattered was how Catholics behaved in the light of the faith which they professed. They had not always behaved very well. He remembered the anti-Semitic tracts of his boyhood; a father showing his little boy pictures illustrating the kiss of Judas, and Dreyfus receiving a purse of gold from a Prussian officer. The destruction of the Albigensians — a crime without parallel in the history of the Church — had been attributed to the intercession of the Blessed Virgin. Mauriac was convinced that if he had lived in that century he would himself have been burnt alive.

The question of André Gide – 'why do Catholics not love the truth?' – insistently craved an answer. It was not enough to reply that the Gidian 'sincerity' amounted to a pretence that good was evil, and evil good. The vice of clericalism was the utilisation of the truth for institutional ends; there was a clerical as well as a Marxist imperialism. *La Pierre d'Achoppement* was written before the Second Vatican Council came to meet many of its criticisms, and John XXIII to appear the greatest of the Popes that Mauriac had known. *Ce que je crois* was written just as the Council was opening. 'For the first time since I was a young man, the Spirit is visibly manifest, at least to me.' The barriers between those who professed the name of Christian, even if they belonged to different communions, were crumbling; and he did not mind if the décor was crumbling with them, and if many devotional frills were being swept away. If the Church was a mystery and a paradox and something of a stumbling block, it was because the mantle of Constantine had for too long covered the naked body of its Founder. No one rejoiced more heartily in the death of triumphalism than Mauriac. Even St Peter's had been built with money from the sale of indulgences – and this was to purchase architectural beauty at altogether too high a price.

Albert Béguin, as penetrating a critic as any in his time, used to say to the present writer that *La Pierre d'Achoppement* was 'du meilleur Mauriac'. For Julien Green its successor, *Ce que je crois*, was the favourite among all his writings. It is a deeper, more personal, and more essential book. It looks at the Church, and also well beyond it. It tries to answer the three questions that Gauguin inscribed below a famous triptych: 'Who are we? Where do we come from? Where are we going?' Mauriac faced, and accepted, the existence of two temperaments within the Church. 'The same baptism and the same Eucharist do nothing to narrow by a millimetre the abyss which separates a Maurrasian positivist and a progressive worker-priest.' There were those primarily concerned to protect the deposit of faith, and those eager to extend its message. Mauriac felt closer to a believing Jew or Moslem than to a 'frère ennemi' of his own Church, because he was here under no constraint to regard as a brother one who treated him as an enemy, and whom he regarded in the same way. There was no solution except to kneel side by side with such a man, and take no account of what seemed to one idolatry, whether of the nation or the race.

He measured the gulf that now yawned between himself and the public he was addressing indirectly – for each of these books is a meditation, not a homily. He did not burke the problem of chastity, even though for the present generation it had ceased to be problematical. He offered no comfort to those who counted erotic satisfaction among the basic human rights. Chastity — no one knew it better than he — was difficult; but it was also reasonable. He distinguished, as ever, between 'amour-passion' and 'amour-tendresse'. The second, even when illicitly indulged, could lead to the love of God; the first created a cataract over the spiritual vision. When the encyclical, *Humanae Vitae*, split the Catholic world in two, he did not add his voice to a pretty general protest. Nor was the problem peculiar to youth, when the clamour of the senses was supposed to be loudest. He noted that the conversation of his own contemporaries was often more salacious than that of the young he met. If old age was not holy, it was obsessed. Mauriac was well aware of the damage he had suffered from his upbringing; 'I live in a world that no longer believes in evil, and I have been obsessed by it to the point of absurdity. The truth lies somewhere in between.'[1] But he never quite established the liaison between 'amour-passion' and 'amour-tendresse'. For him, the one was simply a gift, and the other simply a grab. Mauriac was always more conservative than the liberals would have liked, and more liberal than the conservatives would have approved.

In these years the influence of Teilhard de Chardin was at its height. Here Mauriac compared himself to the old peasant who was alone in not weeping at a sermon on the Passion, and excused himself by saying: 'I don't belong to the parish.' He was not drawn to Teilhard's 'dionysiac evolution'; this was too reminiscent of Renan's 'immense stream of oblivion dragging us towards a nameless abyss'. He had met Teilhard at luncheon, at the Ritz, in 1946, and been somewhat put off by his bitterness: but he recognized that his thought satisfied the needs of the modern world, meeting the Marxists, as it did, rather more than half-way. A young Communist had confirmed how strong was his influence among them. To Teilhard's cosmic Christ, Mauriac opposed the personal Christ of Newman and Pascal, though his attitude softened when he learnt of Teilhard's admiration for Newman. It would have softened still further if he had known of Teilhard's comparison of God to 'a note of music'. As for the cosmos, man contained it within himself — for, as Pascal had written, 'all the bodies, and the firmament, and the stars, and the earth and its kingdoms, are not worth the smallest mind; for the mind knows all that, and it knows itself; and the bodies know nothing.'

The promise of the Vatican Council was fulfilled in some directions, frustrated in others. When a priest, finding a young man on his knees

[1] *Bloc-Notes V*, 317.

before the Blessed Sacrament, asked him: 'Haven't you got beyond all that?', it seemed as if a pastor of the flock had become a wolf in shepherd's clothing. Nor indeed were the shepherds clothed as they used to be. Mauriac signed the letter of loyalty to Paul VI in opposition to the 600 *prêtres contestataires*, for he was no Gallican in his views on the Papacy. 'It is not those who leave the Church, however many they may be, who will make it explode from within, but those who remain inside, and who no longer believe in the power given to Peter to bind and unloose. On this essential point they have lost the Faith. Today, and for the clergy in particular, everything comes back to a crisis of faith, and a conversion to the world.'[1] He raised an eyebrow, but not in disapproval, when Jean-Louis Barrault helped an eminent Dominican to preach the Lenten retreat at Toulouse; and he was not opposed to the ordination of married priests. He accepted a vernacular liturgy because he realised its pastoral necessity, but he missed the Latin which, through long usage, had acquired the resonance of eternity. Interior prayer was not encouraged by an 'elementary pedagogy and the terror of being outdone by Marxism in the quest for happiness on earth'[2] – and by a discreet silence over the way of the Cross. He drank in with approbation every word of Maritain's *Paysan de la Garonne*. In 1961 he addressed the Semaine des Intellectuels Catholiques at a time when the Algerian crisis was still unresolved – 'indiscreet, imprudent, and uselessly rash'.[3] But the time came when the Dominicans, to whom he had been so close, accused him of a 'senile change of mind'. If this was meant as a reference to the hardening of his arteries – and by now they had the right to harden a little – it was no less a tribute to his independence. Even before the Vatican Council had opened, the Church in France appeared to him the '*sole* exception to a regression in every other domain'; and before it had closed he could write of his fidelity to the Catholic religion that it was founded 'on an instinct of conservation, because this alone remains human in an inhuman world.'[4] When the rock of Peter seemed to be trembling on its axis, Mauriac trembled with it; but he was secure in his conviction that 'the whole Christian mystery was comprised in the relationship of one man, isolated from all other men, and the living God.'[5]

[1] *Bloc-Notes V*, 143.
[2] *Bloc-Notes IV*, 352.
[3] *Bloc-Notes III*, 64.
[4] *Bloc-Notes III*, 431.
[5] *Bloc-Notes V*, 97.

3

Whatever may have been his private feelings, Mauriac never fell from the literary state of grace. It was style that gave permanence to a writer, provided that it met Buffon's definition, and was 'the man himself'. This was as true of the *Bloc-Notes* as it was of more formal or imaginative composition. It was supremely true of the two volumes, *Mémoires Intérieurs* and *Nouveaux Mémoires Intérieurs*, published respectively in 1959 and 1965. A critic in *Le Monde* wrote of their 'divine musique'; and indeed '*Musique* Intérieure' would have been an appropriate title for either of them, if Charles Maurras had not already captured it, so closely, easily, and elegantly were thought and expression at one. They furnish an indispensable source for any study of the author, the first devoted to the books he had read, and the second to life as he had known it.

On the 11th October 1965 he celebrated his eightieth birthday. None of his forebears had lived to be so old. In a special number of the *Figaro Littéraire* homage was paid to him by Jacques de Lacretelle and others, while José Bergamin spoke for the Christian adversaries of General Franco. His publishers, Grasset, gave a dinner for 200 guests at the Ritz, with the British Ambassador, Sir Patrick Reilly, and Lady Reilly among them. A week later, in the Grand Théâtre at Bordeaux — which is the most beautiful theatre in France — he was welcomed by the *maire*, Jacques Chaban-Delmas, and a large audience of his fellow-citizens. Thinking of Jeanne, who was naturally at his side, he wrote that it was a day 'scanned to the beating of two hearts'. If he had ever suggested ill of Bordeaux — and what he meant was of course the Bordelais — he now made graceful amends. He was especially moved by a letter from the chaplain of the Hôpital des Enfants de Bordeaux. 'While you were speaking my prayer went up to Heaven, to the Lord by whom all your work has been inspired . . . . The wounded pines of Saint-Symphorien proclaim his glory, like the cedars of Lebanon'; evoking also the picture the novelist had drawn in the last sentence of *Le Mystère Frontenac* of 'the group for ever gathered round the mother and her five children.'[1]

Mauriac had not forgotten them either. Shortly after entering his eightieth year, he was dreaming of a last novel. He would give to it all the strength that remained to him, for he now talked much about his death, and 'the incomprehensible scandal'[2] of dying. Touching the grass, he would say how much he was still in love with life. 'Ah! my

---

[1] *Bloc-Notes IV*, 118.
[2] *Le Temps Immobile*, 514.

children, how short it is, how short!'[1] His sight was troubling him, and he would sit for a long time together under the fig tree on the terrace at Malagar, or at Vémars on a stone bench looking at the alley of flowers and the sunset. Here, too, he had planted pines in what had once been the kitchen-garden, calling it his 'other Saint-Symphorien'. In the evening he told stories to the grandchildren; and of the story he had in mind to write, he predicted that it would be different from any that his readers might expect of him, or from any that he had hitherto transposed. But he had not yet completed *Nouveaux Mémoires Intérieurs*; when he had done so, in August 1965, the voices came to him, insistent and familiar, from the creatures of his imagination: 'Nothing anyone has been able to say against the novel as you have conceived and practised it can resist the reality of our presence. Nothing permanent can be hoped for from an art that has forsworn its features. A novel that endures has a name, and a Christian name. It is called Emma, or Adolphe, or Dominique, or Anna.'[2] He would approach his subject 'like an island, very secret and unexplored, where people asleep from all eternity are waiting for us to give them a destiny.'[3] In the old days he would come back to Paris from the seclusion of the Trianon-Palace at Versailles with 50 or 100 essential pages already sketched out. Now he saw the development of the story in a flash, even if its climax remained uncertain. The character of the young woman evolved very differently from the way he had imagined it, and was the more alive for doing so. He decided to call the book *Un Adolescent d'autrefois*. A young friend advised him to drop the 'autrefois'; but Mauriac had never been afraid of 'autrefois'. The further away he grew from it in time, the closer it became to him.

The story is told throughout in the first person, and the narrator, Alain Gazac, is ostensibly Mauriac himself. The setting is undisguised. Alain lives with his mother in the rue Chéverus – the last address in Bordeaux to which Madame Jean-Paul Mauriac moved house – and Maltaverne is the chalet at Saint-Symphorien. Donzac, Alain's contemporary, to whom he confides his story, is just as clearly André Lacaze who had died shortly before Mauriac started work on the novel. But the other characters are invented, and so are the relationships between them. *Un Adolescent d'autrefois* may not unfairly be described as a novel within an autobiography. Here, as we find them elsewhere, are the Brunschvicg edition of Pascal; the Druidic oak in the forest, and the time-honoured trickle of the Hure; the challenge and, as it were,

[1] Ibid., 484.
[2] *Bloc-Notes IV*, 91.
[3] Ibid., 293.

the necessity of modernism; the neighbours whom 'on ne voit pas'; the maternal reproaches — 'You're talking nonsense' and 'You think everyone else so stupid'; the inhibitions of a pious adolescence — 'Je suis né dégoûté'; Lacaze's 'You are not quite as intelligent as I am, but very nearly'; the prize for composition; the impact of Gide's *L'Immoraliste* and Barrès' *Sous l'oeil des barbares*; the presentiment of a literary career; and the intoxication of Paris during those first months in the rue de Vaugirard. 'Nothing in France has changed since Balzac' says the narrator; nothing had changed for Mauriac since he had written *L'Enfant chargé de chaînes* except what life had taught him — and this was everything that mattered for the novelist, and much of what mattered for the man.

Alain had never known his father, and he loses his elder brother at an early point in the story, which covers a period of five years. His only confidant is Simon Dubercq, the son of Madame Gajac's bailiff, and a student at the Petit Séminaire. Against Alain's advice, he interrupts the studies which should normally have led him to the priesthood, and pursues them in Paris with the encouragement of the free-thinking *maire* of the commune. Later he returns to a modest teaching job at Talence, his *landais* accent now considerably modified. Meanwhile Alain has made the acquaintance of a young woman, Marie, some years older than himself, who is the principal assistant in a bookshop. They become attached to one another, and it is only later that she tells Alain of the scandal which has clouded her name. Of another, involving a priest, he learns afterwards, although in this case the 'mauvaises langues' had lied. Circumstances had forced her into a liaison with a man much older than herself. Alain is bent, at all costs, to escape eventual marriage with a rich girl of the district, Jeannette Séris — to whom he gives the disobliging nickname of 'Le Pou'. His mother is set on this alliance because, as it appears, it would enrich the Gajac properties — for like so many other characters in Mauriac, she has the pines in her blood, and not least when she has prayers on her lips. Alain holds 'Le Pou' in abhorrence, although at the outset of the story she is only twelve years old. Marie is anxious, not to marry Alain but to wean him from his mother's despotism, his Christian scruples, and the territorial obsession of which he, too, has his share. To frustrate the threat of marriage to 'Le Pou', Alain, in conspiracy with Marie and Simon, writes to his mother, when she is absent at Lourdes, that he is engaged to be married to Marie. The three of them spend the night at Maltaverne, Alain and Marie in each other's arms. Mauriac's description of the scene shows how far he had shaken off the Jansenism of his own adolescence.

Perhaps that night was the moment of our lives when we

came closest to the truth of which we both had the presentiment
. . . that human love is the prefiguration of the love that created
us, – but that sometimes, as on that night for both of us, and
however sinful it may have been, it resembles the love of the
creator for his creature, and of the creature for the creator, and
that the happiness that filled us to overflowing was like a
forgiveness granted to us in advance.

Marie and Alain are for a moment lulled into the belief that a false
engagement will prove to be the foundation of a true marriage. But
Madame Gajac foils their plan by insisting on a delay of four months
before its public announcement. This gives time for the ecstasy of a
summer night to dissolve – at least on Alain's part – into the disgust of
a furtive liaison. He learns from Simon Dubercq that Marie had agreed
to a *mariage blanc* with the elderly proprietor of the bookshop, which
she would inherit; and that her assurances that she would manage the
properties of Maltaverne better than he would himself were dust thrown
in his eyes. When she tells him of her interview with Madame Gajac, who
comes to see her in the shop, he takes, angrily, his mother's side. He
cannot free himself from the authority which holds him in thrall.

At this oint the story takes an unexpected turn. Alain goes back
to Maltaverne, and walking in the forest sees a girl bathing in the Hure.
His gaze is riveted, with admiration but not immodesty. He watches her
dress and walk away, following her at a respectful distance. Suddenly
she takes fright at the sound of the bracken crackling under his foot;
turns round and recognizes him; and flees into the wood. Recalled to
Bordeaux by an urgent telegram from Simon Dubercq, he is shown a
newspaper cutting with the photograph of a girl who had been raped
and then murdered in the woods near Maltaverne. It is the girl he had
seen bathing, and he recognizes her as 'Le Pou', now grown to an age
and comeliness when she might have inspired his love. The assassin
is caught, and Alain gives evidence of what he had seen of her last moments alive. It then transpires that a deep affection for 'Le Pou', of which
Alain had no suspicion, and not a desire to unite their properties, had
been his mother's principal motive in trying to bring about their
marriage. If the mother has discovered much about the son, the son
had discovered much about the mother. There is no reason to see more
than superficial resemblances between Madame Gajac and Madame Jean-
Paul Mauriac; but in each case too close, and yet too difficult, a
relationship was preserved by separation. For Alain, as for François,
there was a world elsewhere; and neither was afraid to explore it.

Un Adolescent d'autrefois was published on the 11th March, 1969,
and was received with practically unanimous praise. Even one of the few

hostile reviews admitted that the characters had rediscovered the liberty of which Sartre had accused the author of defrauding the characters in *La Fin de la Nuit*. It was not the novel of an old man: Mauriac never felt his age before a blank sheet of paper. Another critic described him as a 'limited genius'. This was true enough, but it was a property of his genius to recognize those limits so precisely. For economy of phrase and narrative technique, the evocation of landscape and the correlation of this with the mood of his characters, in the penetration of a social milieu which he knew and could describe better than anyone else, an assessment of his art could be based on *Un Adolescent d'autrefois* alone. He gave a copy of the book to his friend, Père Massabki, a Benedictine monk of Lebanese extraction, and a close neighbour in the rue de la Source, with apologies for what was not, in all respects, an edifying story. 'Just as edifying' replied Massabki 'as *Destins* which decided my vocation.'[1]

At eighty-four Mauriac signed a contract with Flammarion for three more novels. He was thinking of a sequel to the *Adolescent* but found it hard to place it in Paris because this would 'remove Alain, each day, further away from his sources, to which I must always return for inspiration.'[2] On the 20th April (1969) he went into hospital for treatment of an infection, and on the same day de Gaulle announced that his future would depend on the result of the referendum. The news came to Mauriac as a severe shock, but he was encouraged by the deluge of admiring letters that reached his bedside. A week later, the day of the referendum, he fell down on his way to Mass and to the voting booth, fracturing his right shoulder in three places, and was taken to hospital in an ambulance. For some time he was unable to use his right hand, and since he was incapable of dictating a novel, he could only turn over in his mind what he would do with Alain Gajac. The character would have the same age as himself, and would die unmarried and alone, 'watched over by the last surviving pines' at Maltaverne. Mauriac found it hard to resist the crowd of memories that besieged him; readers would say that he had 'forced his own destiny not to be Alain Gajac.'[3]

While he was still convalescent, Père Massabki brought him Holy Communion to the apartment on Sunday mornings. He received the Sacrament with quiet ceremony, two lighted candles on the table beside his bed. Later in the summer he went to Vémars, and towards the end of July he was painfully climbing the stairs to his work room, now once again at the top of the house. Any day now, he might 'start again

---

[1] *Bloc-Notes V*, 162.
[2] Ibid.
[3] Ibid., 305.

to live in a character which will be myself, and yet not myself.'[1] He stayed at Vémars all through that very hot summer; with its big rooms and high ceilings, it was a house where an old man did not feel too confined. Slowly he got to work, writing four or five pages a day for as long as his strength allowed.

Maltaverne is the name of the single novel that Alain Gajac wrote shortly after he came to Paris. It won him, as *Les Mains jointes* had won for Mauriac, a precocious celebrity. He frequented the literary salons, and considered himself 'on leave of absence from God'. Donzac is studying for the priesthood in a seminary opposite the Hôtel de l'Espérance, but Alain does not see him. The first part of the book is addressed to an unknown correspondent and admirer, curious to discover why, after all these years, Alain has never published another novel, although he has contributed regular articles to the *Echo de Paris* and the *Figaro*. Suddenly Alain is recalled, not to Maltaverne, but to Noaillan — *alias* Malagar — where his mother is living alone, still haunted by the rape and murder of 'Le Pou'. She is dangerously ill, and before she dies Alain realises that it was through this atrocious sacrifice that he had come at last to understand her.

After the funeral the guests gather for the canonical *gigot* and a 'very honourable Médoc' at Maltaverne; and then Alain decides to travel, with no very clear idea of what he will do with his life. 'The rest I will tell you one day, if you would like me to — a sequence of human contacts, brief or long, where it was, more and more often, my turn to suffer.' He then resumes the story, which is now addressed to no one in particular. A fortnight after his mother's death an unexpected visitor is announced at Maltaverne. This is his correspondent, Jean de Cernès, who has brought along his girl friend, Isabelle. They have made a collection of Alain's articles, and obtain his permission to publish them. Alain, childless and alone, with cruel memories and considerable properties around him, adopts Jean as his son — and at this point the story is left in suspense. 'If I do not die before I finish it' he had written 'I shall be able to sleep quietly in the Lord, and this is what I ask of Him every day.' But Mauriac's strength was failing; 'My father is weaker' Claude noted on New Year's Eve 'and there is nothing we can do for him.'[2] The last two paragraphs of *Maltaverne* were dictated to Jeanne on the 15th August 1970, and the rest was silence. He had given only scanty indications of how the book would have developed, except that Jean de Cernès was to be killed in a car accident. As so often happened, he was waiting for his characters to tell him what to do with them.

---

[1] *Bloc-Notes V*, 201.
[2] *Le Temps Immobile*, 264.

On July 27th his last *Bloc-Notes* had been published in the *Figaro Littéraire*, and on August 23rd he was admitted into the hospital of the Institut Pasteur, having fallen, it seemed, into a profound sleep. But before completely losing consciousness, he received the Apostolic blessing from Pope Pius VI, conveyed to him by Cardinal Villot, the Secretary of State. In the late afternoon of August 31st, he was brought home, now in a deep coma, to his own apartment. Here, with all his family beside him, he died at 2.40 a.m. on the morning of Tuesday, September 1. His body, dressed in a grey suit with the button of the Légion d'honneur on the lapel of his coat, and his hands clasping a rosary and a bunch of wild carnations, lay in the salon, where a stream of visitors filed past in sympathy until late in the afternoon.

During his long lifetime honours had come to Mauriac, unsolicited though not unwelcome, and in death they did not fail him. On the evening of Friday, September 5, his body lay in state before the Institut de France. The uniform and sword of an Academician, with the insignia of the Légion d'honneur, had been placed on the coffin. The *garde républicaine* presented arms, and the tricolour was dipped in homage. His colleagues of the Académie, all controversy now put aside, stood by, with members of the Government; and it was not inappropriate that while Pierre Gaxotte was speaking for literature and Edmond Michelet for the Government, their orations should have been punctuated by the distant rumble of thunder — for the storms had not been lacking to the universe of Mauriac's imagination, nor to the world of his polemic. As darkness fell the scene was picked out by searchlights, and six cavalry officers mounted guard over the catafalque until midnight as Paris — and not only 'le tout Paris' — paid their last respects to the man who had tried to reconcile their divisions, for his very successful appearances on television had brought him close to a wide public. A casual passer-by was overheard to remark: 'Il doit s'agir d'un grand bonhomme.'

On the following morning a Requiem Mass was celebrated in Notre-Dame by Cardinal Marty, attended by President Pompidou; and François Mauriac was afterwards buried in the cemetery at Vémars. He had never cared for cemeteries. He said they were the last place where the living should look for the dead, and it is not there that we shall find him.

SOURCES AND BIBLIOGRAPHY

This book has been written mainly from François Mauriac's own writings. All of these, with the exception of the *Bloc-Notes* and his last two novels (one of them unfinished), are included in the twelve volumes of his *Oeuvres Complètes*, although several are available in other editions. The references given in the text are, wherever possible, to the *Oeuvres Complètes*. The following works by Mauriac have appeared in English, published by Eyre & Spottiswoode (Eyre Methuen). They were all translated by Gerard Hopkins, except *That which was lost,* for which the late Sir John McEwen was responsible.

FLESH AND BLOOD (La Chair et Le Sang), 1954
THE STUFF OF YOUTH (La Robe prétexte), 1960
THE RIVER OF FIRE (Le Fleuve du Feu), 1954
YOUNG MAN IN CHAINS (L'Enfant chargé de chaînes), 1961
QUESTIONS OF PRECEDENCE (Préséances), 1958
THERESE (Thérèse Desqueyroux: with two stories from *Plongées* – Thérèse chez le docteur, Thérèse à l'hôtel – in one volume with *The End of the Night*), 1947
SOUFFRANCES, 1944
THAT WHICH WAS LOST (Ce qui était perdu: with *The Dark Angels*), 1951
THE END OF THE NIGHT (La Fin de la Nuit: with Thérèse), 1947
THE UNKNOWN SEA (Les Chemins de la Mer), 1948
THE DESERT OF LOVE (Le Désert de l'Amour), 1949
THE DARK ANGELS (Les Anges Noirs), 1951
THE ENEMY (Le Mal: with *The Desert of Love*), 1949
A KISS FOR THE LEPER (Le Baiser au Lépreux: with Génitrix), 1950
THE KNOT OF VIPERS (Le Noeud de Vipères), 1951
LINES OF LIFE (Destins), 1951
MEMOIRES INTERIEURS, 1960
THE FRONTENAC MYSTERY (Le Mystère Frontenac), 1952
THE LITTLE MISERY (Le Sagouin), 1952
THE LOVED AND THE UNLOVED (Galigaï), 1953
A WOMAN OF THE PHARISEES (La Pharisienne), 1946

GENITRIX, 1950
GOD & MAMMON (1936) was published by Sheed & Ward.

The reader's attention is drawn to the interesting essay on Mauriac in Donat O'Donnell's *Maria Cross* (Chatto & Windus, 1953); to the longer study by K.R. Srinivasa Iyengar (Asia Publishing House, 1963); and in French to Pierre-Henri Simon's *Mauriac par lui-même* (Editions du Seuil).

*

With one exception as indicated, all quotations are given in my own translation. My thanks are due to Editions Bernard Grasset for permission to quote and translate from *D'autres et moi* and *Mémoires Politiques.*

INDEX

229